Architecture, Actor and Audience

This is the first book to chart the evolution of a philosophy of European and American theatre architecture through the centuries. Iain Mackintosh is a practitioner directly involved in designing new theatres, restoring old ones and adapting found space, and has lectured and written widely on the subject. He provides an invaluable overview of the subject, informed by a practical understanding of the complex nature of our cultural relation to our environment.

Iain Mackintosh is design director of Theatre Projects Consultants. He is also a theatre historian, and was co-founder and producer of the drama touring company Prospect.

Theatre Concepts
Edited by John Russell Brown
University of Michigan

Theatre Concepts is a new series designed to encourage a precise understanding of each aspect of theatre practice. Most books on the theatre promote a particular personal or theoretical point of view. Theatre Concepts are written by experienced practitioners in direct and accessible language in order to open up debates and experience of theatre.

Acting
John Harrop

Architecture, Actor and Audience
Iain Mackintosh

Theatre Criticism
Irving Wardle

Architecture, Actor and Audience

Iain Mackintosh

London and New York

First published 1993
by Routledge
11 New Fetter Lane, London EC4P 4EE

Simultaneously published in the USA and Canada
by Routledge
29 West 35th Street, New York, NY 10001

© 1993 Iain Mackintosh

Phototypeset in Linotron 300 10/12 point Baskerville by
Intype, London
Printed in Great Britain by
Butler & Tanner Ltd, Frome and London
∞ Printed on paper manufactured in accordance with the proposed
ANSI/NISO Z 39.48–199X and ANSI Z 39.48–1984

British Library Cataloguing in Publication Data
Mackintosh, Iain
   Architecture, Actor and Audience. –
   (Theatre Concepts Series)
   I. Title   II. Series
   725

Library of Congress Cataloging in Publication Data
Mackintosh, Iain.
   Architecture, actor and audience / Iain Mackintosh.
      p.   cm. — (Theatre concepts series)
   Includes bibliographical references and index.
   1. Theater architecture — Psychological aspects.   2. Theater
   audiences.   I. Title.   II. Series.
   NA6821.M25   1993
   725′.822′019 — dc20   92–18625

ISBN 0–415–03182–6   ISBN 0–415–03183–4 (pbk)

Contents

Illustrations

Introduction

Theatre architecture is more than the frame to a picture. Theatre people understand this instinctively though rarely speak out except when opening a new theatre. On these occasions the actor often inveighs against modern theatres which, lacking the character of the old, fail to support his or her art. The commercial producer may not often talk about theatre architecture but nevertheless makes shrewd judgements when carefully choosing the particular West End or Broadway theatre in which to present his or her show. The audience is generally less aware of the contribution of theatre architecture to the theatre experience. Many mistake decoration for architecture. Others put the architecture, along with the ease of getting a drink at the bar, of parking or of buying a ticket, as a necessary adjunct to the evening, not central to the event.

Those who ought to be analytic of all the elements in the theatrical experience, theatre critics, generally ignore the part played by theatre architecture. Couple this with the fact that in few countries are students of theatre and literature taught to assess the contribution of architecture to art and to society, and you will understand how unbalanced has been most people's appreciation of the role of 'place' in theatre making and theatre going.

This is hardly the case with religion. For most churchgoers the architectural atmosphere is as essential to the experience as the words with which the mystery is invoked. Only the most fervent believer of any faith can hold communion with God in an aircraft hangar or a shed. Few brides and grooms prefer the registry office to church, synagogue, temple or mosque. You may talk to God anywhere yet all but the hermit require to return to the holy place to rediscover the intensity of faith in the supportive presence of the faithful.

Or, to move from the sacred to what some call the profane, just imagine seduction without the low lights or the romantic sunset. The shift is deliberate as a sense of 'place' is not a solemn idea. Sir Anthony Quayle, one of Britain's theatrical knights, was entrapped in a campaign for yet another summer festival and defined a successful theatre as being half a church and half a brothel. His audience in conservative Californian Visalia woke up to the dangers of theatre and decided an art gallery might be safer.

The act of theatre is more complex than either holy communion or physical congress. For a start more than two are involved. Theatre is a three-dimensional and three-way event, actor or actors communicating, not simply with you, the spectator, but with you and he, or she, over here and that group over there. All interact one with the other. The event is also unique, not just another performance of a particular production. The production represents a set of artistic aims and attitudes while it is the performance itself which is the unique event. Performances vary greatly from night to night as both the performer and the dedicated theatregoer will confirm.

This is because the audience's role is an active, not a passive, one. In cinema, which is a passive art form, you and your reactions are pre-programmed by the director, crew, cast and writer. The air conditioning must break down, the seats collapse or the man in the row in front snore before you are made as aware of your surroundings as of the film. And even if they do, your reaction and loss of interest has no effect on the actors who, once recorded on film, cannot alter their performance. They are not physically present in the cinema auditorium and hence are unaware of your declining attention should you find your companion or your pop-corn more interesting than the film. The cinema goer's communication with that ghostly image on the screen is one way: all he or she can do is listen or watch.

Theatre is different. Despite the production having been precisely prepared by the director, both audience and actor find themselves in a situation which is essentially anarchic. Anything might happen. If all goes well the event will 'take off', as the saying goes.

The sense of danger, of community and of shared experience felt at a successful theatrical occasion is what distinguishes live theatre from cinema. And yet, paradoxically, for much of the twentieth century cinemas and theatres have borne a superficial resemblance one to the other, the screen having evolved as the canvas which was thought of as filling the picture frame of the theatre proscenium. Indeed ever since the establishment of moving pictures three-quarters of a century ago the failure by architects to discern the difference between cinema and theatre, evidenced by their rating sightlines to the stage picture (= film screen) above all other criteria, has been a principal cause of so much dreary theatre architecture which fails to provide the opportunity for the spark of performance to ignite the conflagration of communication.

The central thesis of this book is that theatre architecture is one of the most vital ingredients of the theatrical experience and one of the least understood. The aim here is to explore the contribution of the sense of place to the theatrical event. The function of the architecture of theatre space, both in the physical and metaphysical senses, is examined. Whenever possible, the sayings and writings of actors and audiences as well as those of the few philosophers of theatre space have been plundered to illustrate a variety of viewpoints. Anecdote illustrates.

The book is in three parts. The three chapters of Part I provide an account of the evolution of the English-speaking theatre space from the time of Shakespeare on Bankside to the creation by Tyrone Guthrie between 1948 and 1953 of the full thrust stage, here seen as being the final and the most enduring dramatic success of the purifiers of the new movement of which the first flowering had been Wagner's Festspielhaus at Bayreuth in 1876. The eight chapters of Part II approach theatre architecture today in all its diversity from a number of different professional and public viewpoints. Part III proposes a rationale for the successes of the past plus a proposal for the future.

Finally, in this short introduction, some definitions and explanations are needed. First, 'actor' is used in the widest sense to include actresses on the one hand and singers and dancers on the other, except where a distinction is needed between the performers of the drama and the performers of the opera or dance. It is important for the student of drama to understand that innovations in opera house architecture, for example Bayreuth in 1876, can be deeply significant to the often parallel development of the playhouse.

Second, there is little in this book about façades, entrances, foyers, lobbies or even backstage areas, the focus being on auditorium and stage where the mystery takes place. (There are plenty of handbooks for the architect or technician who wants to know how to plan those vitally important but essentially secondary spaces.) Third, the argument does not extend to the attitudes the audience adopts before arriving at the theatre – 'what shall I wear? is it grand?' – or to the semiotics that trigger those attitudes. The latter are rarely studied but would suggest that the sidewalk of 45th Street in New York or the lawns at Glyndebourne have as great or possibly greater effect on the attitudes these audiences bring to the theatrical event as does the architecture of facades or lobbies.

Fourth, the most experimental of performances such as non-textual 'happenings' are not covered. Scholars of performance studies will be able to trace for themselves the origins in the avant-garde of recent manifestations of actor/audience relationships in mainstream theatre. This author's standpoint remains that of the curious theatregoer through the ages rather than that of the specialist. Thus the concept of ritual as central to the active involvement of the audience has been avoided although it is the vogue in academic American theatre studies of the early 1990s.

Fifth, measurements are generally given in feet and inches with the metrical equivalent in brackets. This is because most of the theatres referred to were designed in feet and inches. However, some were designed in metres, in English rods or in Mantuan *brazza*. This results in a lot of measurements. But the physical dimensions of a theatre are worth studying as they are of greater significance than many innumerate commentators think and certainly more reliable an indication of all important than oft-quoted but misleading seating capacities. Costs are generally those of 1992.

Lastly, the author's own prejudices will inevitably surface for, while this is his first book, he has conceived the designs of many theatres and assisted architects on more. His prejudice is for the sort of theatre which involves the audience to the extent of becoming active participators in the theatrical event, of experiencing the catharsis which is variously attained at great tragedy, opera or epic theatre and of enjoying the orgasmic release of uncontrollable laughter (if you've never fallen off your seat laughing live theatre may not be for you).

The 1990s follow on a decade in which most 'modern architecture', i.e. that dating from the middle decades of the twentieth century, has been questioned. It also seems likely that in the 1990s green or environmental issues will engage millions to an extent hitherto undreamt of. The result may be to encourage an examination of the 'where' of theatre as well as the 'what'.

This book aims to reopen the debate on the part played by theatre architecture in the prickle on the back of the head, the chill in the stomach, the tears of laughter and the community of celebration. It is dedicated to all those who suspect that the place is almost as much the thing as is the play. Most readers of this book would regard as plain damn silly the piece of copy heading an advertisement for performing art videos in a recent *New York Times*: 'Why sit in a crowded theatre when you can have first class entertainment at home?' Harder is a reasoned response to twentieth-century American drama critic Brooks Atkinson who, in a piece entitled 'The theatre is not the thing' in the *New York Times* of 31 October 1974, wrote 'Nothing is really important except the performances on stage. The sole function of a theatre is to provide a place where people can assemble and enjoy the show.' There is no suggestion of community of celebration either in the advertiser's promotion of a home video for private pleasure or in the drama critic's requirement of a machine for passive enjoyment. This book combines a search for those theatres in which the community is celebrated with an examination of how the architecture of auditorium and stage interact with actor and audience.

Part I

History

Chapter 1

Continuity of character?

Most guides to theatre architecture take the reader back to the Greeks or even to the forest clearing, if the author seeks to suggest that theatre in the round is the most 'natural' of theatre forms. But if we are to understand the continuing evolution of western theatre, then not only is there no need to go back beyond the theatre of Shakespeare, but to start with ancient theatre may be confusing for all but the specialist. Of course, the ancient theatre, the medieval theatre and the oriental theatre are relevant, but these forms of theatre did not shape our theatre directly. Rather have theatre people in the last couple of hundred years become enthusiastic for the introduction of this foreign style or for the revival of that past practice. Often the motives and prejudices of those who advocate foreign or archaic forms of theatre are of greater interest than the forms themselves.

Shakespeare and his contemporaries in Europe and, most significantly, in Italy are the primary influences on western theatre. They are our theatrical forebears. Our present theatre has evolved directly and continuously from theirs.

However, so incomplete has our knowledge of Shakespeare's theatre been over the last two or three hundred years that until recently all 'reconstructions' were conjectural and subconsciously clothed in the fashionable style of the day. The innovatory bare stages and 'contemporary' Elizabethan costume of William Poel at the end of the nineteenth century, ideas taken up by Granville Barker in London, Nugent Monck in Norwich and Folger in Washington, appear today curiously dated. Nevertheless each generation of the last hundred years has found some architectural inspiration in Elizabethan theatre. Within a single generation different groups have provided different interpretations. Compare, for example, the thrust stage conceived by Tyrone Guthrie at Stratford, Ontario (1953 and 1965), which is enfolded through more than 180 degrees by the audience, and the open-air 'Globe Theatres' of the American west, where fan-shaped auditoriums confront Elizabethan 'tiring houses' with no encirclement but a lot of period architectural detail behind the acting area, such as might have been conceived by a movie art director of the 1930s. Yet both satisfy audiences and provide for them a sense of Shakespearian occasion.

The cauldron of theatre architectural history bubbles with many unusual ingredients. It is equally tedious to extract one element and examine it to the exclusion of the others as it is to examine all the influences as if all were equally important. The purpose in devoting the first three chapters of this book to theatre history has been to take a rapid walk down the main street of British and American theatre architecture over 400 years and see whether its development is marked by sea changes which transform the nature of theatre or whether there exists a continuity in the character of the playhouse. Inevitably one starts with Shakespeare's 'unworthy scaffold' or 'the great Globe itself', looked at not as an end in itself but as an ancestor to a family of theatres which have recurring family characteristics.

There are a number of theories on the origins of those multi-tiered open-air public theatres of Elizabethan London which are so familiar from this or that artist's impression. The evidence is incomplete because the primary evidence will always be confined to foundations rather than structure and the secondary evidence to precious few reports or illustrations. But we do know that the first such open-air theatre, The Theatre, was built in 1576 in Shoreditch, north London, by James Burbage, and that the last ones were built only thirty-eight years later in 1614. Every new archaeological discovery refines our knowledge of the high noon of these theatres that spans the openings of the first of the Bankside theatres, the recently rediscovered Rose of 1587, and of the last, the second Globe of 1614. But whatever the archaeologists and other scholars have still to tell us there is no doubt they had a common ancestry and a common purpose.

Some see the latter as having been the need for pragmatic managements to increase the size of their companies' summer audience which hitherto had been accommodated in innyards. Carpenters such as Peter Street, or engineers as we would call them today, provided for managers such as Henslowe as tall a structure as timber technology would easily allow. The management would decide how broad and how long these structures were to be from their knowledge of how far an actor could project. On occasions the size of the site was a factor. No time for architecture: 'get it up and pack them in' is the prosaic picture proposed by some pundits of how and why it was done.

Other scholars are more philosophical, and none more so than Frances Yates in *Theatre of the World* (London, 1969). She sees the Globe not just as an 'original adaptation of ancient theatre in the tradition of the renaissance revival of Vitruvius', but also as a theatre of magic, an actor's microcosm in the image of the cosmic macrocosm which gave real meaning to Shakespeare's words 'all the world's a stage'. The neo-Platonic theory revived by renaissance philosophers was that there were spatial harmonies which were as measurable and as significant as musical harmonies. A theatre which was to work successfully for actor and audience had to have proportions specified by the ancients. These proportions were simple to calculate and could be easily followed by any craftsman who understood a few simple techniques of 'setting out' involving a rope divided by 12 knots into 13 sections (by which a 3,4,5 triangle with a right angle, a 4,4,4 equilateral triangle or a 5,4,4 isosceles triangle, which is a seventh part of a circle, can be produced) and a measuring system made up of 'rods' and their subdivisions. A rod is five and a half yards or 16 feet 6 inches (5m). The whole system was easier to apply than the modern method of starting at one end of the plot and marking out the measures from a scaled plan. Thus the philosophical mystery also provided a pragmatic method.

Both views are probably correct despite being often overstated. Immense scholarship is still needed to unravel precisely what Shakespeare's theatre was like, because until the Rose and the Globe were excavated in 1989 there had been no first-hand evidence and only the one source of reliable secondary evidence, 'the de Witt drawing', which is in fact a copy by Arend van Buchel of Utrecht of what a traveller friend had sketched on a trip to London. De Witt added a commentary, concluding with the information that the Swan which he had sketched was 'supported by wooden columns, painted in such excellent imitation of marble that it might deceive even the most prying . . . its form seems to approach that of a Roman structure'. Add original sources to today's archaeology and it appears that the open-air Elizabethan theatres had six fundamental features.

These were first that they were conventional constructions by craftsmen rather than innovative designs by architects. Second, their scale corresponded with the 'found spaces' previously used as theatres such as courtyards of the inns of London and of principal towns to which the actors toured. Third, their form was recognisably classical. Fourth, the finish of the theatres was itself an illusion, i.e. the marble was painted, not real. Fifth, they packed as many people as possible in a given site or ground plan. Sixth, the focus that is all-important in a theatre was given by a pure geometry which was not only a technical tool but also had then and still has a mystical significance which cannot easily be explained.

No single feature would seem today to be unusual except possibly the sixth. That these theatres had all the other features might be expected from intelligent business-like managements commissioning confident craftsmen. What is truly remarkable is that all these elements were in balance one with another. The Elizabethan theatre managements and their craftsmen got it right and the buildings were not only huge public successes, but also helped inspire the greatest flowering of dramatic literature.

The need for further research and for conjectural reconstruction is no longer in question. Scholars are being constantly surprised at fresh discoveries, for example in late 1989 that the second Globe may have been fourteen-sided. This may not fit the geometrical rationale of Frances Yates but does relate to the thirteen sections of the medieval measuring rope (the 5,4,4 triangle which is one-seventh of a circle) and is, incidentally, the geometric basis of the Royal Exchange, Manchester, built in 1976 where the internal diameter of the fourteen-sided space relates to the outer perimeter through the square root of 2, the key to the *ad quadratum* geometry of so many successful theatre spaces.

But although we are still some way from unravelling the more esoteric mysteries of Elizabethan theatre architecture, it is clearer now that these essentially simple structures were highly efficient at maximising the box office. Their builders succeeded in getting as many people as close as possible to the actor without jeopardising the actors' primary task of communicating with every spectator, however distant.

The Rose excavation in summer 1989 illustrated perfectly the practicalities of pragmatic Elizabethan theatre architecture. What was immediately apparent was that there were two stages and two lines to the inner wall of the encircling tiers. The first theatre of 1587 was a regular twelve-sided doughnut with the central area occupied by the standing groundlings around three sides of a stage. This projected far out into the yard but not quite to the middle. But in 1592, only five years after it had opened, Philip Henslowe enlarged the theatre. The stage was pushed back 8 feet, and the encircling tiers extended on each side of the stage with the result that the form became far from regular.

In addition, a well-documented altercation with the authorities meant that Henslowe had at the same time to realign the audience end of the structure to remove the foundations which were interrupting the flow of the open drainage ditch to the south. C. Walter Hodges in a paper entitled *The Rose: A Reconstruction in Progress* given to the Society for Theatre Research at the Art Workers' Guild on 16 October 1990 suggested that the changes to the stage were occasioned by the real need for increased room for properties and dressing which had been badly provided for in the original harmoniously shaped Rose. However, Professor Andrew Gurr suggests the consequential 25 per cent increase in capacity would have had to have been sustained for over twenty-five years for Henslowe to recover his expenses in remodelling the Rose – not the last time that the cost of theatrical improvements has exceeded estimates. The second enlarged Rose may have staged the first performance of *Henry VI* by the young William Shakespeare but it seems to have lost the purity of the original form and presented a lopsided appearance. Was the second as good a theatre as the first?

The second enlarged Rose had a life of less than ten years. In 1600 Philip Henslowe replaced the Rose with the Fortune, which we know from the original building contract to have had the most regular form possible:

a square. At the Fortune the demands of the box office and backstage needs were satisfied within a totally harmonious form. The regular square of the Fortune is less attractive to us than the polygonal Rose, Swan and Globes but the Fortune flourished for over forty years until all the theatres were closed by the Puritans.

The tension between the demands for spatial harmony and for increased box office are complex and universal. In 1989, irrespective of whether one focused on the footprint of the first or second Rose, what was marvellously simple about the exposed foundations was the sense of scale it gave to the visitor. This was the theatre of Marlowe's 'mighty line'. Here, in the first Rose, Alleyn played Tamburlaine. Yet that summer, standing at the side looking down on the excavation, exactly where one would have been in 1587 in the front row of the middle tier slightly to one side and facing the stage, one felt one could reach out and touch the actor. The original stage line was less than 30 feet (9.1m) away and the internal yard about 49 feet 6 inches (14.8m) – 3 rods in old English measure – wide. How many did the Rose hold? Some commentators, including those as distinguished as Anthony Burgess, were confused. Writing in the *New York Times* of 11 June 1989 he concluded: 'It now appears that only a couple of hundred could get into the Rose. This seems commensurate with the size of the area the excavators have exposed, but one wonders how, with such a limitation, the Rose made any money.' This is quite wrong. Anthony Burgess miscalculated because he thought that density was a constant through the ages. A different attitude to density is needed. Thomas Middleton (1570–1672) described 'the groundlings', standing in the central area surrounded by the rising tiers of boxes, most vividly in *The Roaring Girl* which played at the Fortune in 1611:

Within one square a thousand heads are laid,
So close that of heads the room seems made;
As many faces there, filled with blithe looks,
Show like the promising titles of new books
Writ merrily, the readers being their own eyes,
Which seem to move and to give plaudites;
The very floor, as t'were, waves to and fro,
And, like a floating island, seems to move,
Upon a sea bound in with shores above.

The first Rose was two-thirds the size of the later and larger houses, such as the Globe. There is enough secondary evidence that the Swan and the Globe held 3,000. Ergo, the first Rose held 2,000, the second probably 2,500, in a space which today, for a number of reasons, would hold not more than 400 or 500. First, the twentieth-century body is larger in height and width than the average Elizabethan body. Second, few today would stand for an entire show as all the audience did in the central yard of an

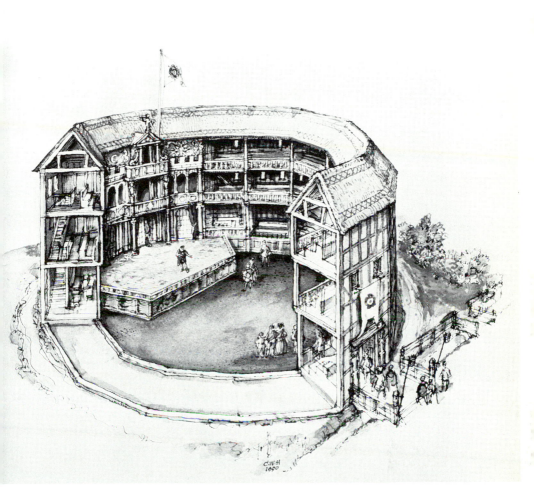

1 *(left)*   The Rose revealed in a photograph taken by the archaeological unit of the Museum of London in May 1989 before the controversial office block was built above. Two-thirds of the theatre is revealed and the lines of the two stages, of 1587 and 1592, are clear, as are the piles for a 1957 office block which miraculously missed the then undiscovered foundations.

2 *(above)*   Reconstruction by C. Walter Hodges of the original Rose of 1587 into which 2,000 people must have been crammed.

Elizabethan theatre, although a modern pop concert audience stands and will sway in the way Middleton suggested. Third, the seated audience today demands comfort as well as space for its longer legs. Fourth, the fire officer of the twentieth century demands gangways, aisles, staircases and a limit on capacity at each level so that the audience is controllable in an emergency. All these are measurable, and the sum effect is that the Elizabethan theatre would have held three or four times as many people as a modern theatre of the same size.

The intimate scale of the excavated Rose was for many a surprise. It appeared to be more like the Cottesloe or the Criterion in London or a West 42nd Street off-Broadway theatre in New York than to possess the size which a capacity of 2,000 conjures in the mind. This will be but the first of assertions that seating capacity is an unreliable measure for the size of a theatre. The Rose excavation provides early evidence that great theatres which nurture creative drama are usually very small.

The Elizabethan public theatres were closed in 1642 as a result of the rise of Puritanism. Theatre activity in the eighteen years of the Commonwealth which followed was restricted to private houses, and the public theatres that reopened on the restoration of the monarchy in 1660 appeared to be very different. However, many textbooks have over emphasised the difference between the post-Restoration indoor theatres, created by Davenant at Lincoln's Inn Fields (1661) and at Dorset Garden (1671) and by Killigrew at Drury Lane (1662), and the pre-Commonwealth public theatres of Bankside. By stressing that Restoration theatres had proscenium arches while the earlier ones apparently did not, many historians have given too little weight to the continuity of theatre architecture. This continuity becomes apparent when comparison is made between the relatively well-documented Restoration theatres and not only the little we know of London's 'winter' or private theatres, such as the indoor Blackfriars as used by Richard Burbage and hence Shakespeare's company, but also the great deal we know about an indoor theatre designed by Inigo Jones in the mid-1630s, probably as a reconstruction of the 1616 Phoenix in Drury Lane, for which plans survive.

The Inigo Jones design shows an adaptable theatre capable of being used either as a single-space theatre with a platform surrounded by audience on three sides, not unlike the pre-Commonwealth public theatres, or as an end-stage scenic theatre, not unlike the post-Restoration theatres. The possibility of placing within a pre-Commonwealth indoor private theatre the sort of scenic spectacle which hitherto had been thought to be confined to the Royal Masking houses of Charles I and not to have made its appearance in the public theatres until 1660 was first proposed by this author in *Tabs* Vol. 31 No. 3, September 1973 and later endorsed by Professor John Orrell in *Shakespeare Survey* 30. Two scene designs exist which would fit the Cockpit in court perfectly. One is a drawing by Inigo

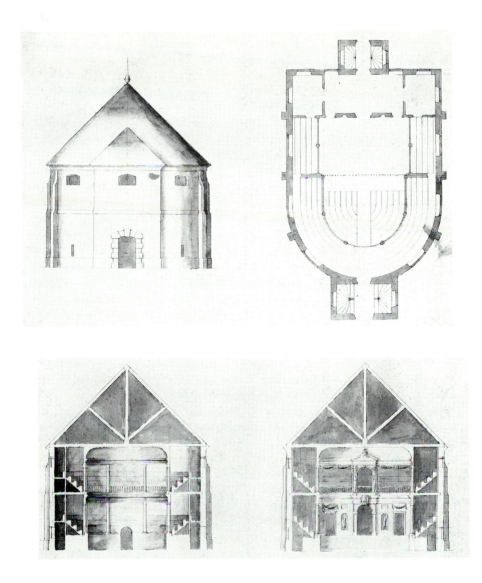

3 and 4   The drawings by Inigo Jones now in Worcester College, Oxford, which
may be for a rebuilding in 1636 of the Phoenix, Drury Lane first opened in 1617.
Whether executed or not they are the oldest extant drawings of any theatre in the
English-speaking world. That this may have been an adaptable theatre is suggested
by the wall either side of the front of the stage which is unnecessary for any
structural purpose. It is possible that on occasions the audience was banished
from the sides and the rear of the platform stage which then served as a proscenium
stage. The latter is precisely sized for Davenant's *The Siege of Rhodes*, ground
plans of which are in the British Museum. The drawing by Inigo Jones, dated
1639, of a perspective setting behind a round arched proscenium would also fit
precisely between the walls each side of the front of the stage.

Jones himself inscribed 'For ye Cokpit to my lo Chambralin, 1639' and the other a stage plan for *The Siege of Rhodes* in the Lansdowne Collection at the British Museum which was designed by John Webb in 1656 for William Davenant and which after the Restoration in 1660 was revived at the aforesaid Phoenix (or Cockpit).

This is evidence of a continuity of character in theatre architecture which connects the Restoration back to the time of Shakespeare. It is also possible to demonstrate that this continuity of character stretched on even further to the end of the eighteenth century through the nineteenth century to the present day. Evidence includes the building today of theatres of a scale and capability such as the Tricycle Theatre, Kilburn, London (1980, and rebuilt after fire 1989), similar to the still extant Georgian Theatre, Richmond, Yorkshire (1788). Such mainstream playhouses hold between 150 and 450 at modern densities, have an acting area at one end which is between 16 feet 6 inches (15m) and 33 feet wide (10.1m), dimensions which are, precisely and respectively, one and two rods. They generally have galleries either at one end or on three sides of a central space. The gallery facing the main acting area is generally between 16 feet 6 inches (5m) and 33 feet (10.1m) from the edge of the stage. There is usually either a proscenium arch or a point at which the architectural treatment of the side wall changes. This break is at right angles to the longitudinal axis. The existence of the proscenium, or break in the architecture, did not necessarily mean that the audience's territory stopped at this point: in many such theatres, old and new, the audience sat at the sides of the acting area upstage of any proscenium arch if there was one and, on some occasions, behind the actor.

Of such a basic form were the indoor theatres of Elizabethan London, the aforementioned Inigo Jones theatre and the theatres at Lincoln's Inn Fields which flourished intermittently between 1661 and 1733. Most theatres of that period both here and in France were no bigger than a royal tennis court – not surprisingly since many were conversions of royal tennis courts, which means that the internal dimensions of the whole structure into which backstage, stage, auditorium and entrance would be fitted was 110 feet (33.5m) long by 31 feet 8 inches (9.6m) wide. Garrick's Theatre Royal, Drury Lane, up to 1775, and some 300 playhouses recorded by James Winston (author of *The Theatric Tourist* published in 1805) in the first decade of the nineteenth century were of the same size or only slightly bigger. Theatres of this scale reappear as 'minor' theatres in London in the nineteenth century, and elsewhere in Britain as 'number two' or 'number three' dates in the early twentieth century. Their scale was shared by the 'little' or 'art' theatres of the repertory movement in England between the wars, by the early off-Broadway theatres of the 1950s, by many of the later off-off-Broadway and the smaller not-for-profit theatres of America of the 1960s and 1970s. Also similar in scale and form is the

Royal Court Theatre in London which has been the home of much of the best new writing in Britain since the middle 1950s. A second group of even smaller spaces, usually dedicated to new writing, include the end-stage Hampstead Theatre Club in London, various loft theatres in New York and the second stages or studios of most of the larger civic, regional or national producing theatres of the English-speaking world built in the 1970s and 1980s. The latter may be more flexible but tend to get used most of the time as open end stages with the audience overlapping the edges of the acting area as in older theatres.

The view that the theatre architecture of mainstream English-speaking playhouses changed little over nearly 400 years is at variance with most accounts which punctuate a more linear theory of theatre history with the introduction of this or that innovation, such as the proscenium arch, which for a long time was erroneously thought to have been imported from Europe at the Restoration of 1660. But most of the innovations were not in practice as radical as proponents have suggested, and generally failed to influence the mainstream of playhouse practice as much as their supporters hoped.

The linear theory that the form of theatre was improving age by age, older theatres being somehow inferior, was unchallenged until the end of the nineteenth century. However, scholars were and often still are confused in their understanding of the nature of older theatres by a number of highly misleading paintings, engravings or 'artist's impressions'. These have too often been taken to be evidence of 'what it was like' but on examination turn out to be a puff for something quite different. Two examples, both from the eighteenth century, will suffice.

The first arises from the well-known image of Act III Scene ix on the first night of *The Beggar's Opera* at Lincoln's Inn Fields on 29 January 1728. Two almost indistinguishable versions of the finished picture by William Hogarth exist, one at the Center for British Art at Yale University, painted for the show's producer John Rich and dated 1729, and the other a replica of this at the Tate Gallery in London. Both have been endlessly reproduced in books of theatre history as authentic illustrations of eighteenth-century theatre by an artist who was an acknowledged master of social realism. They are, however, nothing of the sort. They show not the scene as it was but the scene as producer Rich would, with hindsight, have liked it to have been, having made so much money from this, the most commercially successful dramatic piece of the entire eighteenth century. The proceeds from *The Beggar's Opera* were the main source of capital for the building of the first Theatre Royal, Covent Garden, in 1732.

Hogarth painted six versions. Two are illustrated on page 18, the final 'finished' picture and the original study. The other four consist of another near-identical version of the final picture and three intervening paintings executed over one or two years. The differences are striking. In the earlier

5 *(above)* The original sketch by Hogarth for *The Beggar's Opera*, probably done in February 1728 after the opening on 29 January. This is in the collection of Her Majesty the Queen at Windsor Castle.

6 *(below)* The final version of a sequence of six images exists in almost identical paintings at the Center for British Art at Yale University and at the Tate Gallery, of which this is a reproduction.

The poses of the central figures are constant except that of Mr Peachum, stage left. It is the positions of the audience and the scale and character of the mise-en-scène which differs strikingly not only between sketch and final version but also progressively among the four intervening paintings, one of which is now at the National Gallery, Washington DC. In comparison with the final version all the others indicate a much smaller theatre and a simpler dressed audience. They are more reliable evidence than the familiar final fantasy which has given so many people the wrong impression of the scale and character of early eighteenth-century theatre in Britain.

versions the onstage audience on each side are fewer and in more plausible costumes than in the final 'finished' picture. This is because so famous was that first night in 1728 that within a year it became fashionable to have been a member of that first-night audience and preferably to have sat in elegantly contrived stage boxes. In earlier versions the stage is smaller and the scenery simpler. In one the upstage crowd of beggars in the finished picture turns out to have been the orchestra; we know there was no pit at the tiny Lincoln's Inn Fields and that John Gay, the author of *The Beggar's Opera*, did not add the orchestra until a few days before the opening. In another the same upstage group are shown as audience behind a makeshift draped box front which matched those at the side. This suggests that the first production of *The Beggar's Opera* was performed almost in the round, an assessment supported by the sketch reproduced here, which has all the immediacy of having been drawn in the theatre itself. In this image the audience appears to fill the entire stage, leaving a narrow entrance to a door upstage centre. One can only presume that Hogarth sketched not the first night itself but, having been commissioned by Rich, attended a later but typical performance of this hit show and that he added the portraits of the famous first nighters as the picture progressed and as agreement developed on who would like to be recorded as having been there.

There is ample evidence elsewhere for an onstage audience in the early eighteenth century. Thomas Davies, biographer of David Garrick and one-time member of the Drury Lane Company in the middle of the eighteenth century, reported that the playbill often stated 'for the better accommodation of the ladies the stage will be formed into an amphitheatre'. The result, says Davies, was 'two audiences, one on the stage and the other before the curtain; more specially at the actors' benefits when a large amphitheatre covered the whole stage and the Battle of Bosworth Field can be fought in less space than that which is commonly allotted to a cock match'. On their annual benefit nights the chosen leading actor would receive all the box office less only the manager's 'expenses of the night'. Actors, who have never been great lovers of scenography in that or any other age, were prepared to fill the stage with an overflow of paying audience. The small eighteenth-century acting area could be reduced to something tiny, as was the Elizabethan stage which we know to have been often invaded by the fashionable bringing their own stools. This practice had the advantage that on a small and tightly focused playing area an army could be suggested by a handful of men:

> Oh pardon! Since a crooked figure may
> Attest in little place a million.

The 'crooked figure' of Shakespeare's Prologue in *Henry V* is a figure under ten.

The permanent stage boxes, positioned at the side of the Georgian acting stage, were regarded by the manager, the monarch and others as providing the best seats in the house for viewing the players, hence the tradition in Britain of placing the 'royal box' at the side. The low level of oil and candle lighting at English eighteenth-century theatres was such that a close-up position was desirable and even the English monarch sat at the side not to be seen but to see the actor better, the English theatre being unable to afford the sort of more brightly lit spectacle for which European monarchs sat dead centre in both court and public theatre. An audience of the privileged, sitting in stage boxes hard by the actor, were a regular feature of the English playhouse for over 200 years.

This practice of audience flanking or even invading the actors' area was not confined to Britain. Gordon Craig noted in his journal *The Mask* of October 1925 an engraving by the architect Blondel of the old Comédie Française of 1689 as it was in 1752 when five rows of benches were placed in front of the stage boxes. These benches extend 12 feet (3.7m) into the first three portals of the 'scène à l'italienne'. The resulting acting area was 15 feet (4.6m) wide at the front, 11 feet (3.4m) at the rear, and embraced on three of its four sides by the audience.

Such an encroachment was soon to be in conflict with the mid to late eighteenth-century introduction into the English playhouse of perspective scenery or 'scène à l'italienne'. David Garrick, Britain's greatest actor-manager and controller of London's most famous playhouse, the Theatre Royal, Drury Lane, from 1747 to 1776, managed finally to banish the audience from the stage itself. But although Garrick long resisted pressures to rebuild what had remained since 1674 a perfectly proportioned medium-size theatre, no bigger in volume than the Rose, he finally had Drury Lane 'done over' by Robert Adam in 1775, cynics say to increase the value of his real estate which he was shortly to sell on his retirement. Pastorini, who provided an engraving of the interior of the 'new' theatre, used real estate rhetoric to give a false sense of scale by drawing the few men and women strolling around the new theatre only 4 feet (1.2m) high. This is a regular practice of architects who, along with salesmen of sleeping bags and compact cars, have fooled their customers by peopling their products with midgets. This misrepresentation of Drury Lane is the second example.

But the true scale of Adam's remodelling of Drury Lane is accurately depicted in the engraving of the screen scene from Sheridan's *The School for Scandal*, which Garrick directed in 1777 after his retirement. Here the audience is focused on a space bordered by a 'proscenium arch' which is no more than 28 feet (8.6m) wide. Acting area and auditorium seem to occupy the same space: the entrance to the library is through the pro-scenium arch doors which were part of the permanent fabric of the theatre, blending on this occasion with a set which was in the same style as Adam's new auditorium decor. Add the fact that the acting area and the auditorium were equally well lit and the picture is complete of the relatively small scale and immediacy of what in 1777 was nevertheless the grandest of Britain's 200 or so theatres.

These two images of *The Beggar's Opera* and *The School for Scandal* span the fifty golden years of British theatre. The years were golden not because great plays were then being regularly written (they were not) but because this was the age when for the first time theatre captured not only the imagination of a people, as it had in Shakespeare's day, but also a central role in the fine arts of a major civilised nation. 'In the days of Garrick [actor-manager at Drury Lane from 1747 to 1776] the theatre engross'd the minds of men to such a degree', wrote playwright Arthur Murphy in an early biography of Garrick, 'that it may now be said that there existed in England a fourth estate: King, Lords, Commons and Drury Lane Playhouse.' Garrick had made the theatre both respectable and popular. In 1714 there had been one legitimate theatre in all Britain. By 1777 there were between 150 and 200 and by 1814 over 300. By the late eighteenth century the theatre was revered by both polite society and the intellectual, and, at the same time, had become a popular art form as it had been only once before in the smaller society of Elizabethan England. This transformation of the public's perception of theatre happened in buildings which, with one or two exceptions, were no bigger than royal tennis courts.

However, waiting in the wings so to speak were the scenic demands of the Romantic age which would transform the nature of theatre. The English actor was soon to relinquish his place out on that rectangular acting stage which had long had audience on three sides.

The forces that led to the retreat of the actor behind the picture frame of illusion at the end of the eighteenth century in the Covent Garden and Drury Lane playhouses and in other theatres in Britain and America some forty or fifty years later are dealt with in the next chapter. For the present the argument is that in the public theatres the triumph of spectacle, whether illusionistic or formalised, took place later than many imagine and had less effect. Generally the eighteenth-century English playgoer, when attending the theatre for performances other than the more absurd spectacles created for the celebration of Hanoverian coronations or some of the pantomimes produced by Christopher Rich (son of John Rich) at Covent Garden, would have found no greater emphasis on scenery in the playhouses of the day than in Shakespeare's playhouses, whether open air or indoor.

Whether the actor-oriented architectural character of the modestly scaled and equipped mainstream playhouse is the result of theatre never being as rich as it pretends and therefore relying on cheap human talent rather than on expensive spectacle, or whether it is that the public prefers human-scale performance once it has wearied of spectacle, will be endlessly debated. But before these arguments are set forth it is necessary to examine another often neglected strand in the taste and needs of audiences which bears directly on theatre architecture. This is the factor of audience density, already alluded to in connection with the Rose. Density derives from the audience's requirement for comfort or more often from the reverse, which is the preparedness of any audience to accept discomfort from managers anxious to 'pack 'em in'. Comfort is not the only factor in determining density. Not only was an Elizabethan theatregoer on average 9 per cent smaller than his London counterpart today, but also an affluent North American opera goer today is probably 3 per cent to 5 per cent taller than the average European opera goer. It is obvious that it is possible to get more smaller people than larger people into a given space and still provide the same level of comfort.

Almost as great an influence on density as personal comfort are the regulations that govern safety by setting down the width of aisles, number of seats in a row, width between rows of seats and the number of people allowed for each exit. The earliest safety code was the one created in London by the Metropolitan Board of Works, which was a precursor of the London County Council (and hence of its successor, the Greater London Council, which was abolished in 1986). The Metropolitan Board of Works was created by an Act of Parliament of 1878 as the first co-ordinating body for building in London. It laid down a system of control which was soon imitated in New York and other major cities of North America and also in Europe. Safety became a great concern after the 'Ring' fire in Vienna of 1881 when 450 lost their lives and the 'Iroquois' fire in Chicago of 1903 when over 600 died.

As a result of all these factors the differences in density and hence seating capacity between a conventional modern theatre and an Elizabethan playhouse of the same area is 1:3 or even 1:4, as has already been suggested with the Rose, and an eighteenth-century theatre 1:2 or 1:3, and a turn of the century West End or Broadway theatre 1:1.5 or 1:2.5 depending on whether standing capacity is taken into account.

As an illustration, take the Old Vic, the theatre of Lilian Baylis between the wars and of Britain's National Theatre Company between 1963 and 1976. The first theatre was built in 1819. Manager Davidge once boasted that it could hold 4,000 and at the same time exhorted London theatregoers when he booked Edmund Kean in 1831: 'those of the theatrical public who have hitherto only witnessed the efforts of this great tragedian in vast spaces of the Patent Theatres [i.e. the theatres Royal and Drury Lane and Covent Garden after their enlargement at the end of the eighteenth century] will find their admiration and delight at his splendid powers tenfold increased by embracing the present opportunity of seeing them exerted in a theatre of moderate dimension allowing every Master look and fine tone of the artist to be distinctly seen and heard.'

Whether or not 4,000 is a manager's boast or a numerical hyperbole, like today's 'zillions', 3,000 would have been a better estimate for this 'theatre of modest dimensions'. It is certainly a much larger capacity than the present auditorium holds. This was designed by J. T. Robinson in 1871 and has been continuously altered ever since although the site area of the auditorium has not been increased since 1819. *The Stage Guide* of 1912 reports a capacity of 2,000. *Who Is Who in the Theatre* of 1952 reports 1,454 compared with a capacity of 878 before its refurbishment in 1983. Another example is the Theatre Royal, Nottingham, whose present four-level auditorium was built in 1897 and remodelled in 1978 in a way that did not enlarge or reduce the seating areas. Reference once again to *The Stage Guide* of 1912 allows comparisons level by level. The first figure is that of 1900, the second 1978: stalls (originally divided by a timber rail into a few rows of comfortable orchestra stalls in front and pit benches behind, thus forming two distinct zones where now all seats are of an equal comfort and density) 806 (479); dress circle 241 (243); upper circle 345 (227); gallery 600 (189); standing at all levels 1,003 (nil). In 1912 the total capacity of the Nottingham Theatre Royal was 3,000 including standing. In 1978, when no standing was allowed but the same area was occupied by seats, the capacity was 1,138. The comparison shows that the density of the best seats in the dress circle is virtually unchanged but that elsewhere in the theatre the density has decreased by a factor of up to three.

In more egalitarian America at the turn of the century, the differences in density within a single house was less marked. Few two-gallery houses, or two-mezzanine houses as they are now called, were built after 1910. Nonetheless modern American theatres have at least 25 per cent more space allotted in the auditorium per person than theatres had ninety years ago despite an enduring box office imperative.

It is tempting to take the view that it is a good thing that poorer people are being better treated in modern theatre auditoriums, being given the comfort and space that in Edwardian times was enjoyed only by the middle-class theatregoer in the dress circle. But the pricing policy of today suggests that such levelling up limits rather than extends the audience. In the 1900 Theatre Royal, Nottingham, the dress circle cost four shillings, the pit (rear of the orchestra) one shilling, and the gallery sixpence, which is a ratio of most expensive to cheapest of 8:1. This 8:1 ratio was a standard price differential in the late nineteenth- and early twentieth-century theatres which now have differentials of scarcely 3:1. On Broadway today, the top rate of $40 for a straight play applies to all but the last row or two of the orchestra (= stalls). These producers complain that in the older houses they cannot sell a second mezzanine at $20. But such managements have chosen a 2:1 ratio in a house which when built probably had a 6:1 or 5:1 ratio, New York at the beginning of the twentieth century being only slightly more egalitarian than Britain.

The consequence of a narrow price differential in old or new theatres is a middle-brow, more middle-aged and homogeneous audience whose theatrical expectation and taste are all too predictable. A less densely packed house seated in ever greater comfort becomes ever more passive, ever more comatose. The productions inevitably respond to the need to please the comfortably somnolent theatregoers who are now seated in infinitely extended orchestra stalls where they are no longer disturbed by the less affluent, less respectful and hence more demanding audience once packed tightly close by in the pit of old English theatres. The latter has now been renamed the rear stalls and looks exactly the same as the front stalls.

What does this then mean for the actor? It means that in a space loosely packed with expensive seats a full house gives the response received from a half house at the old densities. Comparison between old and new provides vivid illustrations: at the Olivier Theatre at the National in London, where the total acoustic volume is $11m^3$ per person, three times greater than that required for a playhouse, the actor on the stage has to project into a larger volume, in which only 1,160 playgoers are sitting, than that of today's Theatre Royal, Drury Lane (the 1922 auditorium by Walker, Jones and Cromie), which currently holds 2,237. Comparisons of form as related to volume may also be relevant. The volume of the 90-degree fan-shaped auditorium facing the open-stage Olivier is larger than that of the 210-degree fan encircling the Stratford Ontario thrust which holds nearly 1,000 more spectators.

From the 1960s there has been an 'underground' reaction against the sparsely populated wide open spaces of the new theatres of the preceding generation. A few fringe theatres and off-off-Broadway theatres pack each member of the audience into a friendly and undefined 14-inch or 15-inch (356 or 381mm) wide space on benches where thigh touches thigh. At the Edinburgh Festival the audiences at the austere Assembly Hall of the Church of Scotland, which Tyrone Guthrie rediscovered in 1948 and which the Festival has used for major offerings of classical theatre every year since except 1989, have always sat tightly packed on the original benches. At Wagner's Bayreuth Festspielhaus of 1876 seat rows today are still only 27½ inches (700mm) apart, back to back, in contrast to the 39 inches (1,000mm) for such long unbroken rows demanded by today's theatregoers seeking comfort and today's fire marshals seeking safety. Benches have recently reappeared in Peter Brook's recycled theatres such as Les Bouffes du Nord in Paris or The Majestic in Brooklyn, in the Tricycle Theatre, Kilburn, London of 1980 and 1987 (where director Nicolas Kent claims absence of arms leads strangers to talk and in six cases to marry), in Sam Walters' new Orange Tree Theatre, Richmond, London, opened in 1991 and in the RSC's Swan of 1986.

For promenade productions such as Ronconi's *Orlando Furioso*, presented all over Europe at the end of the 1960s, and the Bryden/Dudley *Mysteries* seen at the Cottesloe, at the Assembly Hall, Edinburgh, and at the Lyceum in London in the 1980s, half the audience stood as at a pop concert. However, these standing audiences were never as tightly packed as Middleton's groundlings of *The Roaring Girl* or those in the parterre (or pit) of the early eighteenth century at the Comédie Française where it was reported that 'the parterre gods of the day, called "Knights of the Chandelier" because of the huge cluster of wax candles that dropped grease into the pit, were so tightly fitted into their pen it made it impossible to faint with decency when the air became as it often did overheated'. The degree of comfort of France's National Theatre at the end of the seventeenth century could hardly have been more different from the effect envisaged at Britain's National Theatre by an advertising agency which, in 1976, unwisely touted the efficacy of the Dunlop foam on the seats of the Lyttelton Theatre with a dinner-jacketed and patent shod young theatregoer asleep in an emptied auditorium, discarded theatre programme beside him.

Peter Brook wrote in *The Shifting Point*, published in 1988, that 'the least important thing in the theatre is comfort'. This would not be good news for the tired executive sitting down to a musical after a large dinner, but is instantly understandable to young theatre makers anxious to involve the audience directly in the creative act of theatre. The evidence is that those theatres which have become the centre of artistic and intellectual life over the last 400 years have rarely offered great comfort or perfect sightlines but have rather been small, uncomfortable and densely packed. In such playhouses, which have generally retained a continuity of character if not of density, the actors are generally placed at one end of the space on a modestly equipped stage. The audience is placed on three sides of the acting area, with the greater proportion to the front.

But such a simple architectural specification of the actors' and audience's requirements has rarely satisfied those architectural or scenic innovators who have always wanted to tidy up the theatre, provide greater illusion, more space for spectacle, a greater capacity for a more comfortably seated public or, latterly, a new shape altogether. The philosophy of the innovators and of the purifiers and their success or otherwise in influencing the mainstream of theatre are the subjects of the next two chapters.

Chapter 2

The innovation of scenic illusion

At certain times in history neither the architectural nor the theatrical character of theatres is debated to any great extent by those who demand or design them. Usually such periods of consensus tend to coincide with a building boom. The first of the great theatre-building booms took place in Britain in the second half of the eighteenth century and the second in the period from the coming of the railways in the 1860s up to the beginning of the First World War in 1914. This boom lasted longer in the United States because of its later entry into the war.

Ironically, these boom-time theatres do not often find their way into the history books unless they are very big and very grand. Most, especially the smaller ones, are taken for granted. What are widely illustrated and argued about at the time, and hence recorded and studied subsequently, are unbuilt projects which their proponents believe are better suited to 'modern times' and to the future as they see it. Often these innovators are promoting their ideas at the very same time as hundreds of theatres to which they are so deeply opposed are in regular use and are still being copied by other architects and their theatrical clients.

The principal innovators can be represented under four headings: first, a solitary seventeenth-century instructor in the science of theatre architecture; second, the eighteenth-century theoreticians who strove to force the actor back behind the proscenium arch to create a picture frame of illusion appropriate to Romantic sensibilities and to the staging of spectacle; third, the Art Theatre Movement who campaigned to purify the theatre from the 1890s to the 1930s and who are dealt with in the next chapter; and fourth the innovators of today and yesterday whose enthusiasms, successes and failures are attended to in the second part of this book.

The seventeenth-century instructor is the little-known Fabrizio Carini Motta who published his *Trattato sopra la struttura de' theatri e scene* as early as 1676. This work has been largely forgotten and indeed was not translated and published in English until 1987 in a well-edited edition by Orville K. Larson (Southern Illinois). In 1972 Edward Craig, son of Gordon Craig, had republished an Italian text justified with the words 'who wants to study Vasari in translation?' (This author does because he can't read Italian.)

Motta was a practical man of the theatre. He was in charge of the theatres of the Gonzagos and thus would have been familiar with the Teatro Olimpico at Sabbioneta which survives to this day. He would have also been familiar with the works of Serlio and Sabbatini who had dealt with auditoriums as part of broader subjects. However, it was Motta who wrote the first book wholly dedicated to the design of the theatre auditorium. It was therefore a prototype in the genre of books on theatre architecture.

After an introduction stressing the necessary difference between contemporary theatre and those of the Greeks and Romans Motta goes straight for the essentials: 'Before beginning the description of the theatre so called because it has an auditorium and a stage upon which to perform, I shall speak first of some things that are generally very familiar and necessary.' He lists good entrances and exits that are safe but quiet, good wardrobes and dressing rooms for the actors, good sightlines, a spacious stage and a division of the audience seating area into three parts: the auditorium floor for the nobility, the tiers on three sides for the lesser nobility and the gallery for the commoners. This is significantly different from the English practice where the best seats were always in the first tier, generally not centre but in the side boxes closest to the stage, until the introduction of three or four rows of orchestra stalls in front of the pit benches in the second half of the nineteenth century.

Motta then goes on to lay out single-tier and triple-tier theatres which are identical in plan area. The form of the tiers is bell-shaped, opening towards the stage. This design concept was imitated in the following century by the Bibiena family and epitomised in the magnificent and still surviving Markgrafliches Opernhaus at Bayreuth of 1748. Motta provides the precise width and height of the proscenium arch on the assumption that an optimum site, 60 feet wide (18.3m), has been chosen. The proscenium arch was to be approximately 33 feet wide (10.1m or 2 rods) at its narrowest, which is at the upstage edge, and have a height seven-ninths of the width (Motta's only measure was the Mantuan *brazza* or *braccio* of just over 19 inches (483mm). He is specific about the height of the auditorium (ideally four-fifths of its length) and about positioning the King or Duke on a dais placed axially in front of the tiers facing the stage. At first glance Motta's plans would suggest that everything is being directed to get the greatest number of people in a position to enjoy the optimum perspective of the deep scenic stage beyond the proscenium. Motta's theatres would therefore appear to be theatres for spectacle set behind a baroque proscenium frame.

However, nestling in Chapter Three is a revealing paragraph about the area under the proscenium arch. This should, he says, 'be not less than 4 feet 9 inches (1.4m, three brazza) and no more than 9 feet 6 inches (2.9m, six brazza) in depth'. This is the area 'in which the players and speakers who walk on stage, that is to say those who do not have to depend on machines, perform. Voices that are usually restricted by this thickness [i.e. muffled by being upstage of a proscenium arch] gain added projection towards the audience because of the cavity of the opening [arising presumably from Motta's instruction that the upstage edge of this thick proscenium be markedly narrower than the downstage]. Others who perform here to the accompaniment of the orchestra are heard just as beautifully as in the orchestra [i.e. the central flat area in the centre of the auditorium which at the time was of equal importance as a performing space as the raised stage beyond] when they are seen and heard in that place [i.e. on the 4 feet 9 inches to 9 feet 6 inches deep forestage which in Motta's theatre is situated within the thickness of the proscenium arch]. This is a most important and necessary point. Some say that performing in the aforementioned space is to come out of the stage picture and consequently not to be part of the scene, but in order to be heard in the auditorium it is best to do this, a lesser evil than to be behind the *scena* [here meaning area under the 4 feet 9 inches to 9 feet 6 inches thick proscenium arch] and not be heard.' Even when Motta's theatre was in scenic mode the performer was to act out in front of the scenic picture if he was to be seen or heard. Only the need to be elevated or lowered by a scenic machine would draw him back inside the scenic picture.

Thus in 1676 the distinction of the acting stage being in front of the separate scenic stage is set down unequivocally by the author of Europe's first treatise on theatre architecture. It was a distinction preserved for at least a hundred years.

The proposition that there should be but a single stage, i.e. that the acting stage should occupy the same space as the scenic stage, was not mooted until well into the second half of the eighteenth century. Its earliest exposition and subsequent development can be studied in the works of a series of theoreticians all of whom gave equal weight to the design of opera houses as to playhouses. These were Count Francesco Algarotti (1712–64) whose work was published in English and Italian; Pierre Patte (1723–1814), a Frenchman who had interesting and sensible things to say about acoustics; and George Saunders (1762–1839) who was a disciple of both Algarotti and Patte and who published his treatise in 1790. In addition there are three further French treatises, by architect Gabriel Pierre Martin Dumont, by André Jacques Rubeau and by Chevalier Jean Noverre, which were published between 1774 and 1783. Of these those by Dumont, Patte and Saunders also provided parallel plans of the major theatres in Italy, France and England so that comparisons could be made between different theatres.

Algarotti dedicated the English edition of his *Essay on the Opera* in 1767 to the Prime Minister William Pitt, averring that opera 'is an object not unworthy of a place in the attention even of those who govern kingdoms'.

The first of two sections of the treatise dealing with the architecture of the opera house which apply equally to the playhouse concerns scale. 'Let us consider that the measure of the length of a parterre or pit and size of a theatre is the performer's reach of voice and none other. For it would be as ridiculous in any person to have a theatre built so large that people could not hear in it as in an engineer to make the works of a fortress in such a manner as they could not be defended.'

This is the language to which Prime Ministers attend. But the advice was not taken. England already had a theatre too big for drama and almost too big for opera: the King's Theatre which Sir John Vanbrugh, playwright and architect, had built in 1703. In 1740 Colley Cibber, actor and playwright, wrote of this theatre in *An Apology for the Life of Mr Colley Cibber written by himself* that 'every proper quality and convenience of a good theatre had been sacrificed or neglected to show the spectator a vast triumphal piece of architecture! And that the best play, for the reasons I am going to offer, could not be under greater disadvantage.' Cibber goes on to criticise the 'immoderately high roof' and the semi-circle of the front seating 'continuing to the bare walls of the house'. Semi-circular or Greek seating on a strict radius is almost unknown in British theatre architecture, the reason being that a true circle or arc thereof placed on the central axis of an auditorium will appear to be a wide ellipse unless compensating architectural devices are used to narrow the circle or arc to make it appear true.

Cibber concluded: 'this extraordinary and superfluous space occasioned such an undulation from the voice of every actor that generally what they said sounded like the gabbling of so many people in the lofty aisles of a cathedral'. By 1740, when Cibber condemned Vanbrugh's attempt to create a playhouse, the King's Theatre had already become an opera house but even then its large size and awkward shape were among the reasons which led Handel in 1734 to transfer allegiance to the smaller and more intensely focused first Covent Garden which moreover was equally effective as a playhouse. Vanbrugh's theatre in the Haymarket meanwhile was constantly tinkered with and, in 1791, ultimately replaced with an even bigger theatre dedicated to opera designed by Michael Novosolieski.

When talking of human scale Algarotti did not indicate a preference for any shape of auditorium but would seem to infer a horseshoe form with seating at the side: 'The architect's principal care should be to leave no article unremedied that might in any way impede the view; and at the same time let no gaping chasm appear by any space remaining unoccupied and lost to every serviceable purpose. Let him also contrive that the audience may appear to form part of the spectacle to each other, ranged as books are in a library.'

However, in a second section on theatre architecture Algarotti changes direction and inveighs against those theatre builders who 'made the stage whereon the actors perform to be advanced into the parterre several feet; by that expedient the actors were brought forward into the middle of the audience and there was no danger of their not being heard. But such a contrivance can only please those who are easily satisfied: who that reflects does not see such a proceeding is subversive to all good order and prudent regulation? The actor, instead of being so brought forward, ought to be thrown back at a certain distance from the spectator's eye and stand within the scenery of the stage in order to make a part of that pleasing illusion for which all dramatic exhibitions are calculated.'

This is the first time that the aim of creating a pleasing illusion within a frame had been so clearly stated. Yet Algarotti was premature. Theatre-goers and actors still sided with Colley Cibber who had deplored the cutting back of Drury Lane's forestage by 10 feet at the beginning of the century. In 1740 Cibber complained about the reduced forestage which Garrick inherited and which Algarotti only twenty-seven years later wished to abolish altogether. Cibber reminisced of the days 'when the actors were in possession of that forwarder space to advance upon, the voice was then more in the centre of the house, so that the most distant ear had scarce the least doubt in difficulty in hearing . . . all objects were thus drawn nearer to the sense . . . every rich or fine coloured habit had a more lively lustre; nor was the minutest motion of a feature . . . ever lost as they frequently must be in the obscurity of too great a distance.'

In 1790, George Saunders published in London his *Treatise on Theatres*. He quoted Algarotti with approval of his attempt to rid the theatre altogether of the forestage. 'The great advance of the floor of some stages into the body of the theatre is too absurd I imagine ever to be again considered. In practice a division is necessary between the theatre and the stage and so characterised as to assist the idea of these being two separate and distinct places.' Saunders did not himself get any of his own theatre designs built although Benjamin Wyatt's Theatre Royal, Drury Lane, of 1812 (the exterior and front of house of which, but not the auditorium, exist today) owed much to Saunders' model drawings. Saunders was influential because he was writing at the time when, after not much theatre building had taken place in London for a quarter of a century, the three major theatres holding a Royal 'Patent' (the Theatres Royal of Drury Lane and of Covent Garden and the Opera House in the Haymarket) were all either totally rebuilt or had their auditoriums gutted and extended. Theatre design had quickly become the topic of the moment.

Henry Holland rebuilt the stage and auditorium of Covent Garden in 1792 and the whole of the Drury Lane Theatre in 1794. As a consequence the two major drama houses presented for the first time prominent and architecturally organised frames to the stage picture. At Drury Lane the architect dared even to abandon the proscenium arch doors, those permanent doors on each side of the forestage that the actors used constantly for entrances and exits and which, together with the stage boxes, were the side boundaries of the acting stage; this, following the principles set down by Motta, had remained in front of the scenic stage. However, despite Holland's attempt to change this ancient theatrical practice the doors were back within three years and the architecture of the house extended upstage into the scenic stage. This had the effect not only of narrowing the scenic frame itself to a more manageable size but also of redefining the acting area in front of the scene and restoring its depth to almost what it had been over the preceding century. The advice of Saunders and of Algarotti, the architectural efforts of Holland to tidy up the downstage zone and the removal both of the proscenium doors and of the deep acting forestage had all been premature.

Again, in 1812, after Holland's Drury Lane burnt and was replaced by Benjamin Wyatt, there was yet another attempt to abolish the proscenium arch doors – Wyatt writing in his *Observations on the Design for the Theatre Royal, Drury Lane*, 1813, that 'nothing being so incongruous than an indiscriminate use of such doors'. Wyatt attempted to confine the performer within the frame of the proscenium as Saunders had suggested. Historian W. J. Lawrence wrote in 1935 of this attempt: 'For the old fashioned proscenium arch was substituted a gilded picture frame, remote from the footlights, over which actors were forbidden to step. Grumblings both loud and deep were heard from among the players over their previous deprivations and finally old Dowton, pluckier than the rest, broke into open rebellion. "Don't tell me of frames and pictures!" he exclaimed with choler. "If I can't be heard by the audience in the frame I'll walk out of it" and out of it he came.' Dowton won. The proscenium doors went back a second time and were only finally banished in 1822 when Samuel Beazley was hired to gut what by then was referred to as 'Britain's National Theatre' and rebuild the auditorium in fifty-eight days to something closer to the needs of the theatre profession than to the theories of a master architect. The *Sunday Times* of 20 October 1822 congratulated Beazley on banishing the ancient proscenium arch doors in the new cause of scenic realism:

Nor blame him from transporting from his floors
The old offenders here, the two stage doors, –
Doors which oft with burnish'd panels stood,
And golden knockers glittering in a wood,
That served for palace, cottage, street or hall,
Used for each place and out of place in all,
So much for visual sense; what follows next
Is chiefly on the histrionic text. . . .

Dowton's problem lay not only in the theories of those architectural cadres

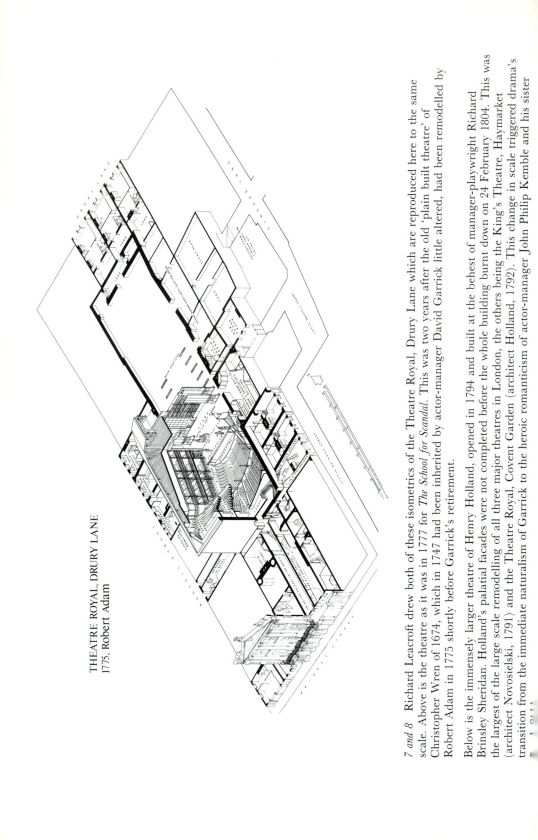

THEATRE ROYAL, DRURY LANE
1775, Robert Adam

7 and 8 Richard Leacroft drew both of these isometrics of the Theatre Royal, Drury Lane which are reproduced here to the same scale. Above is the theatre as it was in 1777 for *The School for Scandal*. This was two years after the old 'plain built theatre' of Christopher Wren of 1674, which in 1747 had been inherited by actor-manager David Garrick little altered, had been remodelled by Robert Adam in 1775 shortly before Garrick's retirement.

Below is the immensely larger theatre of Henry Holland, opened in 1794 and built at the behest of manager-playwright Richard Brinsley Sheridan. Holland's palatial facades were not completed before the whole building burnt down on 24 February 1804. This was the largest of the large scale remodelling of all three major theatres in London, the others being the King's Theatre, Haymarket (architect Novosielski, 1791) and the Theatre Royal, Covent Garden (architect Holland, 1792). This change in scale triggered drama's transition from the immediate naturalism of Garrick to the heroic romanticism of actor-manager John Philip Kemble and his sister

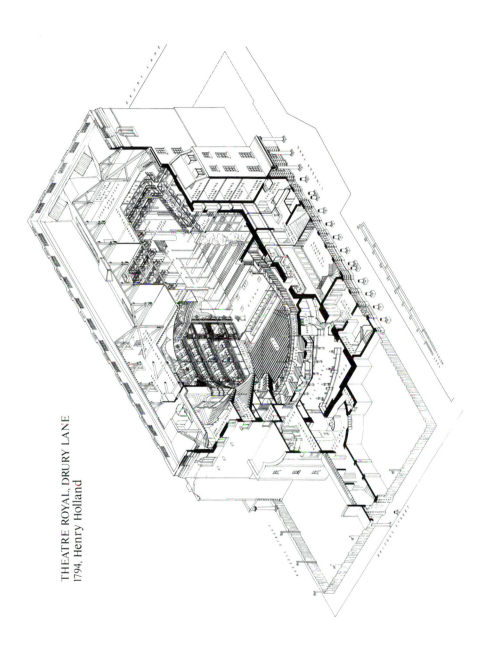

THEATRE ROYAL, DRURY LANE
1794, Henry Holland

of the Romantic movement who would create a realistic stage picture confined behind a picture frame of illusion, but also in the doubling in size of all these theatres. This had not been by choice of the architects but by instruction of the owners. The motive was greed – 'rising costs' as producers always like to say. The architects did what they were told. Stated Wyatt of Drury Lane: 'I was aware of the very popular notion that our theatres ought to be very small; but it appeared to me that if that very popular notion should be suffered to proceed too far it would in every way deteriorate our dramatic performances depriving the proprietors of that revenue which is indispensable to defray the heavy expenses of such a concern.' The architects were able to respond to this request by the owners only because of advances in building technology.

In Holland's Drury Lane of 1794 slender iron columns replaced the thicker timber columns of the old theatre. These were strong enough to support five tiers of audience in what was still supposed to be a playhouse. On the stage huge wooden trusses spanned a scenic area 83 feet (25.3m) wide, 92 feet (28m) long and 108 feet (32.9m) high. The architect himself boasted that this stage was 'on a larger scale than any other theatre in Europe'. It was also on a larger scale than almost all secular buildings in London. Holland's Drury Lane was the first building other than a church that pierced the uniform three- or four-storey domestic building height of London, something all realised when it burnt to the ground in 1809 and members of parliament in Westminster were able to sit on their terrace and watch the fire in Drury Lane.

What the extraordinary increase in scale now made technically possible did to acting styles is illustrated by the accounts of two theatregoers who compared old Drury, where Garrick held sway from 1747 to 1776, to the new, greatly enlarged Drury Lane created by Holland. Reflected playwright Richard Cumberland in his *Memoirs* published in 1806: 'Since the stages of Drury Lane and Covent Garden had been so enlarged in their dimensions as to be henceforward theatres for spectators rather than playhouses for hearers, it is hardly to be wondered at if managers and directors encourage those representations, to which their structure is best adapted. The splendour of the scene, the ingenuity of the machinist and the rich display of dresses, aided by the captivating charms of music, now in a great degree supersede the labours of the poet. There can be nothing very gratifying in watching the movement of an actor's lips when we cannot hear the words that proceed from them, but when the animating march strikes up, and the stage lays open its recesses to the depth of a hundred feet for the procession to advance, even the most distant spectator can enjoy his shilling's worth of show. . . . On the stage of Old Drury in the days of Garrick, the moving brow and penetrating eye of that matchless actor came home to the spectator. As the passions shifted and were by turns reflected from the mirror of his expressive countenance, nothing was lost; upon the scale of modern Drury many of the finest touches of his act would of necessity fall short. The distant audience might chance to catch the text, but would not see the comment.'

A few years earlier John Byng, later Viscount Torrington, recorded in his diary a visit to the newly opened mega-Drury Lane of 1794: '14 May 1794. I adjourned to Drury Lane Playhouse where I enjoyed the highly wrought exhibition of Mrs Siddons's performance as Katherine in *Henry VIII* although lost and sent to waste in this wide wide theatre where close observation cannot be maintained – nor quick applause received! Restore me, ye overruling powers of the drama to the warm close observant seats of Old Drury where I may comfortably criticise and enjoy the flights of fancy. These now are past. The nice discriminations of the actors' feelings are now all lost in the vast void of the new theatre of Drury Lane. Garrick, thou did'st retire at the proper time for were't thou restored to the stage in vain would now thy byplay, thy whisper, thy aside even thine eye assist thee.'

The enormous change at the end of the eighteenth century in the scale of the major theatres was for a long time confined to London. The 300 theatres in the rest of Great Britain retained the scale of 'old Drury' or were even smaller. The surviving Theatres Royal at Bristol (1766, remodelled frequently, principally in 1800) and Bury St Edmunds (1819) show us the relatively small scale of the larger provincial theatres while the Georgian Theatre in Richmond, Yorkshire (1788), indicates quite how tiny were those of the lesser circuits. On the east coast of America the theatres were similar in scale. In New York or Philadelphia nothing approaching the size of contemporary Drury Lane or Covent Garden was built until nearer the middle of the nineteenth century. Nevertheless all these provincial theatres were in turn dependent on the great London houses to set the style of acting. That style changed for the worse with the increase in size of those theatres: out went the naturalism of the eighteenth century and in came the more histrionic style of the age of Romanticism. Theatre was no longer an extension of real life but a different plane of existence, a lofty world dressed with neo-classical images, the greatest of which were those of the tragic heroine Sarah Siddons and her brother, the tragic hero John Philip Kemble themselves. Kemble, the actor-manager of Covent Garden who played the hero demanded by the British public in the Napoleonic wars, provided a panoply of increasingly authentic Shakespearian settings and costumes from Roman antiquity to Tudor England as a proper and spectacular setting for nationalist fervour. Britannia ruled the waves and London had the finest theatres in the world for Romantic spectacle.

At the end of the Napoleonic war a number of factors, including the agricultural problems of England, the decline of interest in matters theatrical, which is so often the aftermath of victory, and the rise of Methodism, contributed to a general theatrical unease. Many provincial theatres closed and few new ones were built. But two further technical innovations came to the rescue and wrought more change in how the theatre organised itself than any treatise or innovative architectural concept. The first of these was the introduction of gas lighting, which altered the character of theatres and theatregoing, and second was the spread of the railway system which, by the second half of the century, was to call into existence a new generation of theatre buildings designed to serve companies able to use the new train wagons to travel special scenes prepared for particular plays rather than rely on the stock 'woodland', 'castle', 'hall' or 'cottage' scenes, which had been kept by the old circuit stock companies in each of their theatres.

In 1817 gas lighting over the stage as well as in the auditorium was introduced, first at the Lyceum and soon after at Drury Lane. In America in 1816 William Warren experimented at the Chestnut Street Theater, Philadelphia, only to burn the place down four years later. By 1829, of ten London theatres described in Horace Foot's *A Companion to the Theatres and Manual of British Drama* only one, the Theatre Royal in the Haymarket, did not use gas. The invention spread into the provinces quite rapidly and was in use in Greenock, Scotland, by 1829. There were pockets of resistance: gas lighting was not installed at Sadler's Wells until 1853 on the occasion of Samuel Phelps' production of *A Midsummer Night's Dream*. In 1837 gas light in major London theatres was first supplemented by the intensity of limelight which, with the addition of a focusing lens, provided a powerful beam from which our follow spot is descended.

By the middle of the nineteenth century the introduction of gas, which after further development turned out to be endlessly controllable unlike the oil lamp, and of limelight had brought about the biggest change in theatre practice both for actors and audience since Burbage and Shakespeare decided to play indoors regularly in the winter. The auditorium could now be dimmed and the audience's attention directed mechanically to this actor or that scene. Theatregoers were able to *see* a show and, due to that well-known phenomenon of the lit actor being more audible than the unlit actor, could at last hear better in the new enormous theatres. The actor was now happier to retreat behind the picture frame because he could be better lit there and therefore could function more effectively. However, he soon became increasingly dependent on the scenic artists and on the 'stage manager', who, within a century, evolved into the director.

The audience also changed out of all recognition. In the eighteenth century in London and until the 1840s in the provinces a theatrical performance had been a major secular social occasion for the whole community. Wrote Sir Robert Talbot in *The Oxford Magazine* of 1771: 'as it was in Athens, the playhouse in London is for all classes of the nation. The peer of the realm, the gentleman, the merchant, the citizen, the clergyman, the tradesmen and their wives equally resort thither to take places and the crowd is great.' Sir Robert Talbot might have added

Elizabethan London to his analogy. Shakespearian critic Alfred Harbage attributed to the undivided audience in the sunlit open-air theatres on Bankside a central role of 'obvious reciprocity' in encouraging Shakespeare to speak to all mankind: 'Mere coincidence will not explain why every Elizabethan play addressed to a sector of the people; high or low; learned or unlearned, is inferior in quality; why neither university nor low school, nor guild hall, nor princely banquet house begat dramatic poetry comparable to what came from the public theatres; or why Blackfriars [indoors and patronised by a narrower more exclusive audience] failed to sustain the level achieved by the Globe. The drama reached its peak when the audience formed a great amalgam, and it began its decline when the amalgam was split in two.'

The gradual darkening of the auditorium at the beginning of Queen Victoria's reign convinced the righteous churchgoer once again that the 'pit' of a theatre was well named. The playhouse became the house of Satan as it had once before at the time of the Commonwealth. At old Drury Lane the ladies of the town had always been evident for what they were and their access to the auditorium controlled rather than prohibited by the management. (Sir John Hawkins, friend of Dr Johnson, had reflected 'Why is it whenever a playhouse is opened in the kingdom it is immediately surrounded by a halo of brothels?') Darken the auditorium and these scouts from the neighbouring brothels might overstep the limits of decency.

A semi-darkened auditorium was therefore a dangerous place. Soon theatres in London developed their own clientele: the upper classes went to the opera or the concert hall rather than the playhouse although Queen Victoria at the outset of her reign was a regular attender at Mr Charles Kean's respectable Princess's Theatre. The middle and professional classes continued to patronise the Theatres Royal of Drury Lane and Covent Garden which remained reputable for a time. The trades people and working classes, while retaining their right to the faraway 'gods' and to the rear of the pit of the major London theatres, started to patronise the 'minor theatres' and south of the river theatres where prices were cheaper throughout the house though still with an 8:1 price differential. Theatres such as the Old Vic, which had been respectable in the 1820s and 1830s, became dangerous and uncouth by the 1860s while the tiny 'penny gaffs' in the East End were even worse. The theatre ceased to be a social catalyst when each class, instead of sharing with others a single place of entertainment aware of each other as well as of the performance, went its own way in its own theatres. It is not an overstatement to say that theatre changed radically at this point, indoor playhouses by reason of their overall illumination having until now retained some of the sunlit oneness of both ancient Greece and Elizabethan Bankside. The dark ages had finally come. By the middle of the century the theatre in London and elsewhere in Britain was in decline, its audience jaded and fragmented, its actors upstaged by scenery and its managers out of pocket trying to fill the vast new stages.

However, from the 1860s onwards the British and American theatres recovered. The technical innovations of the preceding fifty years were digested and a whole new generation of larger theatre buildings, appropriate to the age of gas, opened, many in the new industrial towns. The economics of this boom in the theatre business was fuelled by a third technical innovation which once again was not created for the theatre but was immediately applied to the theatre. This was the steel cantilever.

The small highly focused playhouse, the continuity of which has been proposed from Shakespeare to the present day, depended as much on the vertical emphasis of the column as on the horizontal line of the balconies. Timber post or iron column held up beams. The beam's span was limited if it was to hold tier upon tier of people safely. With iron columns a modest amount of cantilevering was possible. This had the effect of pulling the columns back from the leading edge of the tier, obviously improving sight-lines for the front one or two rows of galleries which continued to be shallow for structural reasons. But the vertical element in such theatres was still very much apparent. Thus the pre-cantilever auditoriums had a human scale which, in its balance between the vertical (column) and the horizontal (closely decorated tier front), recalled the drawings by Leonardo Da Vinci or Alberti of the Man within the Square within the Circle. Man was still the measure of all things, including theatre architecture.

But with the introduction of the steel cantilever, the first major use being in 1891 at D'Oyly Carte's English Opera House, now the Palace, deep shelves of people could be packed one on top of the other. There was an obvious commercial advantage in increased seating capacity for a typical small city-centre site. Not only could bigger capacities be achieved but also the front of the tiers facing the stage could be pulled closer to the performer. At the same time architects such as Frank Matcham in England and J. B. MacElfatrick in the United States solved the problem of the now shorter side walls by retaining only a few boxes and by reducing the density of audience in these areas. For people the late nineteenth-century architects substituted deeply moulded plasterwork, columns, pilasters and canopies which were decorative rather than structural and which retained some sense of enclosure without the management having to sell a lot of seats at the side with bad sightlines now the actors had retreated upstage.

As a result the side boxes now became places for those who wished to be seen with a Duke or a Diamond Lil rather than to see. Hitherto these boxes had provided the best seating positions flanking the forestage on which the actor performed lit only by candle and oil. Now, with the much better gas-lit actor performing further upstage, the sightlines were much less good around the proscenium into the picture frame and thus the whole

9 Gustave Doré (1832–83), the French illustrator, visited London in 1869 and concentrated on low life and the squalor that resulted from rapid industrialisation. The 'penny gaff' or 'blood tub', so called because these theatres generally specialised in melodrama, was the lowest rung in the theatrical ladder of London, below the so called 'minor theatres' which were found in the east end and south of the river. Their equivalent existed in New York and other large American cities in the second half of the nineteenth century, often in the immigrant quarters and generally dedicated to 'burlesque'. The scale of the penny gaffs was roughly equivalent to that of the modern 'fringe' or 'off-off Broadway theatre', although more densely packed.

idea of side boxes took on a mainly decorative significance. The only exceptions were those theatres like Barry's Covent Garden of 1858 or Robinson's interior at the Old Vic of 1871 where the old horseshoe character was retained. But such theatres became rarer and rarer. The theatres which survive from the end of the nineteenth century and from the early twentieth century are not semi-circular or horseshoe in shape but have irregularly curved circles, each usually different in its geometry, with just two or three boxes to connect the ends of the circle with the proscenium arch. In America, because of the different shape of city-centre sites and the earlier abolition of the social divisions in the pit the auditoriums were even wider than in Britain, the facing balconies even closer to the stage and hence the space between the end of the tiers and the proscenium shorter, more splayed and affording even worse sightlines than the British boxes.

Although 85 per cent of such theatres from the turn of the nineteenth century in both Britain and America have long gone, enough survive on both sides of the Atlantic to make it unnecessary to describe further these 'real theatres', the theatres of plush and gilt which many of us associate with early visits to a pantomime in Britain or to *The Nutcracker* or *A Christmas Carol* in America. So successful was this generation of theatre in its heyday that the next group of innovators, those whose aim it was to purify the theatre in the name of art, were going to have to shout very loud to change this 'traditional' theatre of scenic illusion. The traditional theatre thought of itself as immutable and even shaped the past in its own image. It was totally unaware how very different it was in character from the actor-orientated theatre of the centuries that had preceded the Victorian theatre of scenic illusion. The purifiers aimed to destroy this entire edifice of illusion, under which they categorised both the picture-frame Victorian proscenium theatres and earlier post-Shakespeare theatres which, ironically, possessed some of the features they would now seek to introduce. They would replace the traditional theatre with a 'new theatre' housed, if possible, in a new sort of building.

Chapter 3

The purifiers of the modern movement

1875 and 1876 are landmark dates for any study of theatre architecture. In 1875 Charles Garnier's Paris Opera House opened, in 1876 Richard Wagner's Festspielhaus at Bayreuth. The two theatres could not have appeared more different. The Paris Opera House had more magnificent foyers, staircase and auditorium than anything to be found in Vienna, Dresden, Leipzig, Berlin or London although the auditorium was not large. In contrast the Festspielhaus, Bayreuth, was a cut-price building ('we must save, save, save, no decoration', wrote Wagner to his chief collaborator Karl Brandt, a stage engineer). It was a summer festival theatre with no heating and no money, the singers receiving expenses only. It was used for twelve days in 1876 and not again until 1882. It has never since been used for anything other than the works of Richard Wagner and occasional concert performances of Beethoven's Ninth Symphony. Since Wagner's death in 1883 the annual festival, which has taken place every year except for a long gap between 1914 and 1924 and for the American occupation from 1945 to 1950, has been a memorial to him. The Festspielhaus has a fan-shaped auditorium, a single tier plus a few boxes at the rear for the agoraphobic King Ludwig who was Wagner's patron. Subsequently, and especially in North America, this form has been described as being democratic, although in Bayreuth all were equal only as worshippers at the shrine of Wagner's extraordinary genius. In fact the audience was and still is rich. Nowadays it is more of an exclusive club which is so sought after that members have to ballot for a seat.

This has not stopped historians marking 1876 as the start of the modern movement. In this respect the evolution of opera house and playhouse are seen as one. Wagner is venerated as the first to remove all of the distractions inherent in the multi-tier auditorium with the aim of concentrating attention on the stage picture contained within the proscenium arch. The stage pictures which Wagner created behind a heavy black frame were naturalistic in style and were seen in a darkened auditorium as images on a cinema screen were viewed half a century later. Indeed the focus and hence form of Wagner's theatre can be said to be cinematic rather than

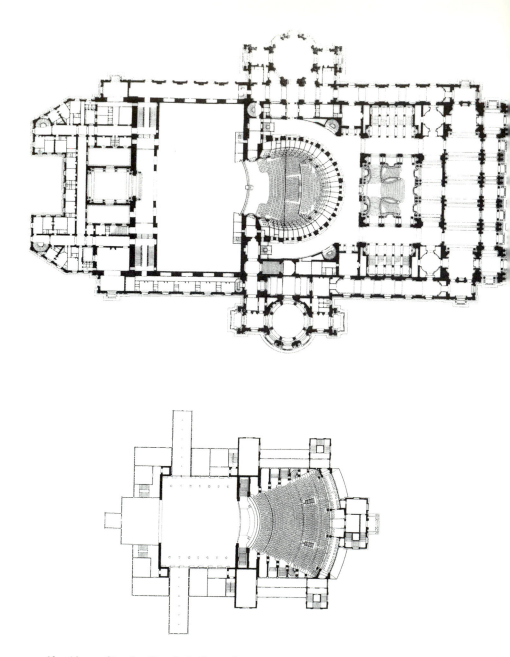

10 Above Charles Garnier's Paris Opera of 1875, below Wagner's Festspielhaus, Bayreuth of 1876 for which the main designer was stage engineer Karl Brandt with Otto Bruckwald responsible for the minimal architectural decoration. The plans, drawn at the same scale, could not appear more different. However, the stage craft in the two theatres was identical resulting in similarly elaborate pictorial presentations. Bayreuth was used for a few weeks only in mid-summer hence the absence of facilities for the audience.

theatrical. His audiences were to forgo any social distractions and, forsaking all others, surrender themselves passively to the music drama of the master.

Wagner was by no means a lone voice. The argument first put forward by Algarotti in 1767 for better sightlines and greater concentration on the stage picture had already been more regularly restated. In 1865, seven years after Barry's Covent Garden Opera had opened and ten years before Bayreuth, *The Builder*, which is the weekly of the building trade in Britain, editorialised in its issue of 23 May that the only virtue of the theatres then in use was their combustibility: 'these venerable archaic theatres must be confessed to have been most bunglingly contrived, or rather not contrived at all, to produce anything like scenic illusion and stage effect. . . . Notwithstanding the perfection to which scenery and spectacle have been brought, the importance attached to, and the expenditure lavished upon them, the arrangement of our theatres, is and is likely to continue to be, such that the stage decorations can be seen – as far as seen at all – only to a very great disadvantage by a very large proportion of the visitors. . . . It is palpable to common sense that everyone should be seated, not only facing the stage, so as to have a clear view of it . . . but likewise, as nearly as possible, on the same level as the stage itself.'

In language not dissimilar to that still being used a century later by proponents of perfect sightlines, *The Builder* proposed removing all side boxes and even the balconies, 'in which visitors are piled up to the very ceiling and consequently have to look down on the heads of the performers'. The logic appeared irresistible: 'In looking down, or even in pretending to look, at a picture no one places himself so as merely to glance at it; but in theatres as hitherto arranged, full more than half of those who are by a sort of legal fiction supposed to be spectators can obtain no more than a mere glimpse of the stage, and that only by squinting or looking quite askance and askew, for they would see only their opposite neighbours across the pit.' Thus did *The Builder* argue against the 'old' theatres, i.e. mid nineteenth-century theatres, as insufficiently satisfying the illusionistic demands of the picture-frame proscenium. Ten years later Wagner followed *The Builder*'s advice at Bayreuth adding perfect acoustics to perfect sightlines for the better enjoyment of his music drama.

Backstage, behind the proscenium arches of Paris and Bayreuth, the one gold and prominent the other dark and vestigial, the stages of the two opera houses were hardly different. Both had raked stages. Both had massive stage machinery. Both theatres opened with gas lighting and both were electrified in 1887/8. Paris had more stage lifts than Bayreuth but this was because it was built for an intensive repertoire of opera and ballet to be staged throughout the year. Wagner would have liked more equipment had he been able to afford it, since his economies were to be felt by the audience, not by the composer and his acolytes whose purpose was to realise the master's vision of epic music drama without compromise. But what Wagner's vision amounted to in scenographic terms is not at all clear.

The staging of Wagner's opera was a consistent failure in the eyes of many radicals who shared his musical taste. The stage settings at Bayreuth were indistinguishable in style from what one would see at the Opera in Paris or any European city. Adolphe Appia (1862–1928), the visionary scenographer and contemporary of Gordon Craig with whom he corresponded, looked back in 1925 in a lecture entitled 'Living Dramatic Art' given in Zurich: 'Today, no one can have any hesitation on this point: the Master set his work into the conventional framework of his period; and if everything in the auditorium at Bayreuth expresses his genius, on the other side of the footlights everything contradicts it.'

Nevertheless Bayreuth does mark the starting point of the modern movement in theatre because this was the first time that the traditions of theatre architecture were successfully challenged by an artist who had radical ideas about the conjunction of actor and audience. Other pioneers would have other artistic aims but the Bayreuth achievement, at least on the audience side of the curtain, showed that change was possible. But if Bayreuth of 1876 marked a beginning in modern theatre architecture, the Paris Opera of 1875 certainly did not mark an end for the older traditions. Even if the latter is an extravagantly celebratory example of the multi-tiered theatres, it must not be regarded as the *ne plus ultra*. The big boom of theatres, variously styled 'bonbonniere', 'peep show' or 'box theatre', was only getting into its stride in 1876. There were technical innovations to come backstage which were to extend the potential for spectacle, just as in front of the curtain the steel cantilever was to increase the commercial value of an auditorium by crowding more of the audience on densely packed shelves in the higher-priced central position. The steel cantilever had not been available to either Garnier or Otto Bruckwald, Wagner's architect – if it had to the latter it is very likely that Bayreuth would have had a large balcony and looked even more like a cinema.

The major technical innovation of the end of the nineteenth century other than the steel cantilever was the electricity and the incandescent lamp, which, it was claimed, did everything gas did only better. Naturally there was a transitional period after the first complete theatrical installation, at the Savoy Theatre, London, in 1881, as in the introduction of any new technology. When in 1891 Ellen Terry, Henry Irving's leading lady, returned after the summer break to the Lyceum, where Irving had previously been Britain's greatest artist in the use of gas stage lighting as well as being the century's greatest actor, she discovered 'the electricity'. Ellen Terry recalled: 'When I saw the effect on the faces of the electric footlights, I entreated Henry to have the gas restored and he did. We used gas footlights there until we left the theatre for good in 1902. The thick softness of gas light with the lovely specks and motes in it, so like natural light, gave illusion to many a scene which is now revealed in all its naked trashiness by electricity.' Ellen Terry won – but only for a season or two. It took some time for electricity to attain the warmth of gas.

Another technical innovation was the first flat stage in a major nineteenth-century theatre, introduced by Charles Witham for tragedian Edwin Booth at the latter's own theatre built in New York in 1869 and emulated by English actor-manager Beerbohm Tree who asked architect C. J. Phipps for a flat stage at Her Majesty's Theatre in London in 1897. Both Booth's and Her Majesty's had the sightlines shaped for a flat rather than a raked stage. The raked stage had long appeared flat by reason of the cunningness of the auditorium architecture. It had survived long after the abandonment of formal perspective settings and found a new purpose in the nineteenth century, which was to give emphasis to the upstage actor when seen from the middle or rear of shallowly raked orchestra stalls or pit, something not easy to achieve on a flat stage. The new flat stage lent itself more easily to the presentation of naturalistic settings which were becoming fashionable towards the end of the century.

In 1896 Munich acquired the first revolving stage which naturally requires a flat stage. With these and other successive inventions, all aimed at increasing the effect of scenic illusion, the conventional theatre, 'the real theatre' with its plush and gilt in front of the great red curtain and lots of artistry and technology behind, reached its apogee during the twenty-five years immediately before the outbreak of the First World War in 1914. Electricity, hydraulic stage lifts and flying systems such as the Asphaleia of Budapest in 1884 and of Chicago in 1886, and other labour-saving devices allowed the spectacle, that had previously been available only for the great state occasion, to be spread ever wider into more and more theatres. These were now able to produce the box office revenue to pay for it all without raising seat prices, thanks to the steel cantilever that produced so many more prime seats at prime prices.

Such was the vitality of the mainstream of theatre that the purifiers of the modern movement were hardly knocking at an open door. Many failed. Students of theatre everywhere are familiar with the rejection of Edward Gordon Craig (1872–1976) and his innovative scenographic ideas by the English theatre establishment. Craig had to travel to Berlin in 1905, Florence in 1906 and Moscow in 1911 to gain the total control he sought as director and designer which he promulgated in his *The Art of the Theatre* published in 1911. However, the notion of a blinkered English theatre establishment ganging up on Craig the poet has become somewhat of a myth and has less foundation than many suppose. Such a view tends to ignore Craig's success as an actor working for Irving between 1889 and 1895 and the influence of his mother Ellen Terry who could have gained him any introduction he wanted. But his personality did not allow collaboration with others and he even rejected the invitation of his most loyal disciple Terence Gray, of whom more anon, to make the innovative and essentially Craigian Festival Theatre, Cambridge, his own in the late 1920s. Account should also be taken of the sheer impracticality of many of Craig's ideas. The poetic images of the woodcuts, which were to inspire the scenographers and stage-lighting designers of subsequent generations, represented scenes and screens that, when built on the stage, tended to fall over or to jam even with the full resources of the workshops of the Moscow Arts Theatre. Gordon Craig was a visionary and a genius of the highest order, but sadly could not cope with either the physical realities of theatre as it then was, or the need in any age to be part of a team in which other members would match their craft to his art. Craig's value to the purifiers and to succeeding generations lies in his ability to express the most profoundly poetic ideas on the nature of theatre, a rare talent in a designer, rather than in the creation of habitable stage pictures which serve the play. The technology which made his ideas practicable evolved too late for Craig.

Craig was not the only designer who was also an articulate philosopher of the modern movement. Adolphe Appia (1862–1928), a French-speaking Swiss, wrote, designed and directed from 1884, when he saw the premiere of *Parsifal* at Bayreuth, right up to his death, shortly before which he completed a set of designs for *Faust*. That Appia should have missed Wagner by a couple of years is a tragedy, much of his life being occupied in criticism of Wagner's works as they were staged in Bayreuth under the direction of his widow for half a century after the composer's death. Appia proposed how they might be staged by a soulmate – and indeed were staged in Bayreuth in the 1950s. He had found the actor and singer at Bayreuth, as in all opera houses, placed awkwardly between orchestra pit and painted scenery which was obviously meant to be illusionary but equally obviously was not. He sensed, but did not state, that such a mid-position was perfectly acceptable when scenery was emblematic, but was no longer tenable after the victory of Romanticism when scenery became as 'realistic' as a salon painting or a chocolate box top. In 1908 in the 1 April issue of *La Vie Musicale*, published in Lausanne, Appia wrote: 'Illusion. What should we think of it? How far should we let it go? How should we define it? Is it the purpose of the set? A tasteless joker might for his part reply that illusion is to dramatic art what Madame Tussaud's wax museum is to the sculpture of Rodin. But pay him no heed. He is no doubt exaggerating. But what of lighting? . . .'

With lighting, and not just the art of lighting but also the new equipment designed by Parisian Mariano Fortuny, Appia advanced illusion to envelop the actor. The audience would see not Siegfried in front of naturalistically painted backcloths but 'a man in the atmosphere of a forest . . . Siegfried bathed in moving shadows instead of strips of cloth jiggled by strings'.

Not only did Appia conceive and carry out his scenographic experiment, he also found his own soulmate in Emile Jacques-Dalcroze with whom he collaborated in the specially constructed Institute at the garden city of Hellerau near Dresden. Together they created the Eurhythmic system of movement prescribed for all actors and singers, not just dancers. Jacques-Dalcroze's Eurhythmics, as well as Appia's light which was directed by a single console operator controlling 'every imaginable combination of intensity, movement and direction' from the back of the auditorium, was what made those ethereal stage settings live. In 1991 Warwick University strikingly recreated the 1912 and 1913 Hellerau stagings of Gluck's *Orpheus and Eurydice* as tribute to both Appia and Dalcroze. At last one could understand why at Hellerau in 1913, in the words of American novelist Upton Sinclair, 'a storm of applause shook the auditorium. Men and women stood shouting their delight at the revelation of a new form of art.'

Hellerau's Institute, which survives and is to be given back to the performing arts following the reunification of Germany, was a huge double cube in which a steeply raked auditorium confronted one or other of Appia's 'rhythmic spaces'. These usually included steep stairways raising the upstage actor to a point even higher than the back row while the flat dance floor between was at the same level as the front row. All the rostra or steps (*praticables* in French) were standard pieces precisely repositioned for scenes. They obeyed simple geometric rules and were set in a space controlled by a harmonious geometry evolved by Appia. Sadly, although Appia designed festival stages he designed no other theatre and no sketches for entire theatrical spaces survive. Yet the dream was stated in 1918 in his second preface to *Music and Stage Directing*: 'the cathedral of the future, which, in a free, vast and variable space, will play host to the most diverse activities of our social and artistic life. This will be the ultimate setting for dramatic art to flourish in.' Less clear was what these free spaces would look like once the necessary equipment for Appia's lighting had been installed and the levels introduced for both audience and actors. One is left with the feeling that Appia and Craig's cry for free space, like the post-war cry for escape from the proscenium arch, signifies much about what is to be left behind but tells little of what is to be put in its place.

The second natural partner to Craig, in that he actually proposed a whole family of theatres that seems, at first, as if they would have been perfect stages for Craig's designs, was the American designer, Norman Bel Geddes, born in 1893. As early as 1914 Geddes started publishing breathtakingly beautiful but insanely impractical designs for theatres. To the theatre historian, it is fascinating to see how a scene designer can propose superficially seductive architectural designs which, had they been built, would have failed and would have reduced his reputation. However, precisely because none of them ever was built, yet they were everlastingly reproduced, the Bel Geddes theatres became the theatrical equivalent of

Corbusier's high-rise *La Ville Radieuse*, the inspiration of a hundred third-rate imitations.

Geddes' Theatre No. 6 is a good example of his work. Theatre No. 6 shows a theatre in a quadrant, not unlike Lasdun's Olivier. Geddes set himself a tight city-centre site, 100 feet (30.5m) square with a street on two sides. In this, he got an audience of 800 in a single quadrant with aisles at the sides only, plus a ring of boxes on the outer circumference of the quadrant. The scale, as always in Geddes' work, is enormous. The rows are over 4 feet (1.2m) apart and audience and stage sit under a single huge dome at least 90 feet (27.4m) across and 60 feet (18.3m) high. The back row of seating is nearly 100 feet (30.5m) long with room for over sixty people. Under the stage are five levels of basement and at the foot of vast elevators there is space for huge scene wagons the size of the stage. In Geddes' theatre the stage picture was not to be abandoned but merely freed from its frame and centralised as an island tower within space. The island stage was to be serviced by the elevators, the effect of which would not have been unlike that achieved by spectacular use of the drum revolve at the Olivier Theatre after 1988.

But more importantly there are fundamental weaknesses in the acoustic properties of the quadrant form which the Olivier shares with Theatre No. 6. In the Olivier it proved necessary soon after the opening to introduce a number of corrective devices, including for a short time microphones and loudspeakers in the ceiling, to ameliorate the acoustic problems. In 1992, sixteen years after the opening, work was still in progress. In the much larger Theatre No. 6 what cannot now be questioned is that most of the audience would not have heard a word under Bel Geddes' dome.

A circular stage set in a corner also provides a connection between Bel Geddes and Terence Gray. Terence Gray was an eminently practical man of the theatre who in 1926 created the Festival Theatre, Cambridge, in an old Georgian playhouse, by then a mission hall, which had originally been designed in 1808 by William Wilkins. Wilkins, the architect of the National Gallery in Trafalgar Square, London, was also a theatre manager and built or rebuilt most of the circuit theatres in East Anglia of which the Theatre Royal, Bury St Edmunds, of 1819 survives in a surprisingly complete state. In Cambridge Gray retained the triple tiers of Wilkins' Georgian horseshoe auditorium but took away completely the proscenium arch, the proscenium arch doors and the stage boxes. On the resulting wall-to-wall open stage he built a permanent cyclorama of plastered bricks and, immediately in front, installed a small revolve of only 20 feet (6.1m) in diameter. The front of the stage was a series of broad steps on which a whole crowd could be placed. The result was magical and today the Festival remains tantalisingly recoverable, having slept for over fifty years but remaining still largely intact. The magic had resulted partly from good luck; Gray could not afford a totally new theatre and by using a Georgian

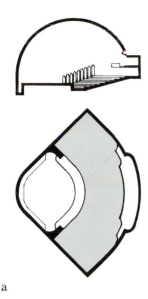

a

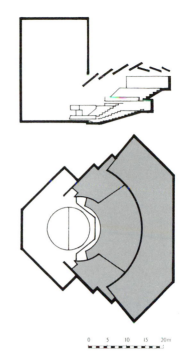

c

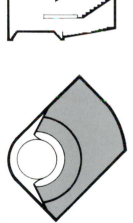

b

0 5 10 15 20m

11 Three theatres in a quadrant – 'a stage in the corner of a room'. All three have been redrawn in a similar style and at the same scale to make comparisons easier.

a 'Theatre No. 6', an unbuilt project by scenographer Norman Bel Geddes dates 1929. This is a development of his 'Theatre for a More Plastic Sort of Drama' of 1914 transferred to a typical American city block. Geddes' theatre has many strange features: 4ft 6ins (1.37m) back to back row spacing and a ceiling form which would have been an acoustic disaster.

b The theatre proposed by Terence Gray in 1931 for London to follow his success at the Festival Theatre, Cambridge, which he had reopened in 1926. Gray was heavily influenced by both Norman Bel Geddes and Gordon Craig. It was the tightness of the site in Covent Garden which accounts for the asymmetry of the design.

c The Olivier Theatre at Britain's National Theatre, architect Denys Lasdun & Partners, which opened in 1976. In strict geometric terms the stage is in the corner of the room, since the side walls if prolonged would meet at a precise 90 degree upstage centre. However, this is not apparent to a seated audience and the cutting off of the side walls suggests rather a 17.3m (56ft 9ins) wide scenic opening.

courtyard space which embraced his open stage he had stumbled on the vital ingredient of verticality which most thrust and open stages lack. In the auditorium there were entrances shared by both audiences and actors down aisles which pierced the lower tier of boxes and led through the pit seating to the stage steps. In this and other matters Gray was heavily influenced by the modern movement in Russia led by dramatist Vladimir Mayakovsky and directors Meyerhold and Tairov.

Gray discovered talented young people and offered them their first opportunities. These included Tyrone Guthrie and Ninette de Valois, founder of the Sadler's Wells Ballet, subsequently the Royal Ballet. On possibly the most successful open stage ever created in Britain, Gray offered an experimental repertoire drawn mainly from Europe and, with his non-naturalist settings, made real much of Craig's dream. It was ironic therefore that in 1926 Craig refused the offer of complete control of Gray's theatre for a season and the opportunity to direct and design productions of his own choosing in a theatre so well suited to everything he stood for.

In 1931 Terence Gray retired from the theatre mainly as a result of the frustration felt when the London County Council rejected his design for a new theatre on a site in central London which he had bought. The design he commissioned was based in a large part on Bel Geddes' Theatre No. 6 although its arc is greater than the 90 degrees Theatre No. 6 shares with the Olivier. Hindsight suggests that Gray may have been fortunate as it is unlikely that the London project would have been as successful as the Festival. It certainly would have changed professional attitudes to the idea, reborn in the 1960s and then thought revolutionary, of building what was to become the Olivier Theatre as 'a stage in the corner of a room'.

Most of the architectural ideas of the new movement rarely got as far as Gray's. Unbuilt theatres abounded, such as Walter Gropius' Total-theatre project of 1927 for Irwin Piscator, the successful and innovative German director and playwright. The Totaltheatre has been well described as being 'endlessly influential and eminently unworkable'. Other practical men of the new movement included those whose fame is largely based on their talents as ring masters creating massive spectacle. Max Reinhardt, having done *Oedipus Rex* in a circus in Vienna in 1910, had a theatre for 3,500 created out of a converted circus in Berlin, the Grosse Schauspielaus which was designed by architect Hans Poelzig who, like Reinhardt, escaped to America on the arrival of the Nazis. The Grosse Schauspielaus has been reproduced in all the text books, a vast gloomy oval with stalactites dripping from the ceiling. However its form, that of a 'U' shape of seating enfolding both a circus ring in the centre and directed towards a pro-scenium stage at one end, was in no way original as on a smaller scale this had been the convention of all circus theatres from those created by Astley between 1780 and 1814 in Britain, France and Ireland. (It was at Astley's in London that equestrian productions of extensively cut plays of

Shakespeare invoked the audience response of 'cut the cackle and bring on the 'orses' which is a reminder that the sell-out to spectacle never goes far enough for some.) Later Reinhardt staged *The Miracle*, a tedious spectacle requiring the construction of most of a medieval abbey in London, first at the Lyceum, where half the auditorium was covered with canvas scenery, and later at the huge trade hall of Olympia. In New York he collaborated with Norman Bel Geddes over an unrealised production of Dante's *The Divine Comedy* which was to be presented on a specially created stage in Madison Square Gardens. Reinhardt remains in the record as a brilliant pageant master but cannot be said to have been an enduring influence on the drama despite the repeated pictorial references to his work in illustrated histories of the theatre.

The repetition of illustrations of rarely realised projects by Gropius, Geddes and Poelzig probably accounts for the impression that the taste of the purifiers in the first half of the twentieth century was chiefly for new uncluttered forms of theatre in which unbroken arcs of audiences in vast 'democratic' auditoriums shared a single space with all-embracing spectacle shaped by the directors who claimed to be the new artists of the theatre. But there was another strand in the new movement that was anti-pictorial and sought not a wider canvas but a narrower concentration on the text and on character. This second group can be further divided into those who saw no need to change the theatre structure itself to create 'a new theatre' and those who were for a return to Shakespearian or even Athenian simplicity of theatre design.

In England the apologist par excellence of the first position was George Bernard Shaw (1856–1950). In the 1890s he devoted himself to attacking the greatest actor-manager of them all, Henry Irving, from whom he would chivalrously protect the beauty and intelligence of his idol, Miss Ellen Terry. To Gordon Craig on the other hand, who wrote a fine book on Irving, Irving was a giant and Shaw a pigmy who would soon be forgotten. But, while Craig battled to realise his visions and failed in Britain, Shaw succeeded and found managers, in Harley Granville Barker and J. E. Vedrenne, who presented extensive seasons of his plays which the English theatre establishment had at first rejected as vigorously as they had rejected the designs of Gordon Craig.

Theatre architecture figures little in any of Shaw's analyses of the theatre. But the nature of the theatre where his work first succeeds is significant and has escaped the notice of many. It is significant in that the Barker/Vedrenne seasons from 1904 to 1907, when 701 performances were given of eleven of Shaw's new plays, many for the first time, took place at the Royal Court Theatre, a theatre which then as now was comparatively small. In 1904 it held slightly over 800 and had, as now, a proscenium arch only 21 feet (6.4m) wide. This Royal Court is the same Royal Court which George Devine refounded in 1956 as the home of the English Stage

Company, with a modern capacity of 450, and which since then has been the single most successful playhouse in Britain for the creation of new work. In 1904 as in 1956 the new drama needed no more than a small tightly focused theatre with the stage at one end embraced by a couple of horseshoe-shaped galleries.

The magic of the Royal Court lies in that it is both conventional in form and little in size so that it can present itself as either a two-space theatre, with the actors' world revealed as the curtain rises, or as a single room, which we the audience share with the actors, and it can do this without any architectural or theatrical flexible devices other than the ambivalence achievable in such a well-proportioned small space. It is not coincidental that one of the names for the Art Theatre movement of the 1920s and 1930s in both Britain and America was the 'Little Theatre movement'.

Another group of purifiers, who were also more interested in words and poetry than in scenography, were the New Elizabethans including those directors whose aim it was to rescue Shakespeare from the flummery of the actor-manager. Somewhat unfairly they criticised equally both Irving's magnificently managed crowds and Beerbohm Tree's more ludicrous attempts at stage naturalism, exemplified by the introduction of real rabbits into *A Midsummer Night's Dream* in 1900. The first influential purifier was William Poel (1852–1914). The last of a succession of New Elizabethans, most of whom worked at the Old Vic for Lilian Baylis who saw the economic sense in simple staging, was the only one to surpass Poel in his achievements, Tyrone Guthrie (1900–73). Both were to change attitudes to Shakespeare and to the theatres in which Shakespeare and the classics were to be performed.

William Poel founded the Elizabethan Stage Society in 1894. In halls and courtyards more often than in theatres, Poel erected his simple Shakespearian platform and, before a standing set with actors dressed in Elizabethan costumes and with little or no variations in lighting, restored Shakespeare's text to the centre of the dramatic experience. Bernard Shaw reviewing Poel's work wrote: 'The more I see of these performances by the English Stage Society, the more I am convinced that their method of presenting an Elizabethan play is not only the right method for that particular sort of play but that any play performed on a platform amidst the audience gets closer home to its hearers than when it is presented as a picture framed by a proscenium.' This is a rare incursion by Shaw into the subject of theatre architecture.

Alongside William Poel stands Harley Granville Barker, both of whom were later described by Tyrone Guthrie as his mentors. Barker, the producer at the Royal Court of the Shaw seasons, became briefly a director of Shakespeare in a long and varied career which early on had included acting for William Poel. Barker created a series of stylised Shakespearian productions, with Albert Rutherston and Norman Wilkinson as designers, at the Savoy from 1912 to 1914. In 1933 Guthrie became director of the Old Vic and in his autobiography, *A Life in the Theatre*, reported that he intended 'to follow Poel and Barker and Shaw, make no cuts merely to suit the exigencies of stage carpenters, have no scenery except a "structure" which would offer facilities usually supposed to have been available in the Elizabethan theatres: stairs leading to a balcony.' (This is the style of staging which, when the 'structures' had been prettified in the 50s to give a greater illusion of Verona, Mantua or Navarre, critic Kenneth Tynan described as 'stylistically falling between two stools which is all the furniture the director usually allows'.)

For Guthrie neither the bare stage of Poel nor the stylisation of Granville Barker seemed ultimately to be the right route. Shakespeare's intermittent realism, whether comical as with Justice Shallow in the Gloucestershire garden or lyrical as in Lorenzo and Jessica's observation that the floor of heaven is 'inlaid with patines of bright gold', seemed to Guthrie to run the danger of being dulled by too austere a style of production. He was looking not for money or machinery but for something more vital than the simple and the abstract. Guthrie needed a new stage and he achieved it by accident.

In 1936 Guthrie directed Laurence Olivier as Hamlet. The Danish Government invited the Old Vic to bring this *Hamlet* to Elsinore to inaugurate an annual festival which would be staged in the open air in the courtyard of Kronberg Castle. After enduring the difficulty of converting the Vic production to an open-air stage – Guthrie had never worked in the open air – the first night approached. The show was to start at 8.00 in the presence of the Danish royal family. At 7.30 the heavens opened. Cancellation was impossible. Within an hour Guthrie moved the production to the ballroom of a nearby hotel: he personally helped arrange 873 chairs around nearly four sides of a central acting area. The evening was a triumph and set Guthrie thinking. The whole event, wrote Guthrie later in his autobiography, 'strengthened me in the conviction which had been growing in each production at the Vic that for Shakespeare the proscenium stage was unsatisfactory. I should never have suggested staging the rather important occasion as we did if I had not already had a strong hunch that it would work. At its best moment that performance in the ballroom related the audience to a Shakespearian play in a different and I thought more lyrical, satisfying and effective way than can ever be achieved in a theatre of what is still regarded as orthodox design.'

Critic Ivor Brown was present at this seminal performance and compared it, in *Theatre Arts Monthly*, with what he saw the following night: 'Next evening we saw the same players on a huge platform built up in many levels at one end of the huge open courtyard of Kronberg. The scene of natural stone was imposing and the grey ghost of Hamlet's father seemed to have stepped straight out of the grey wall behind. But naturalism died at nine thirty. When day waned and the artificial light was turned on, the castle itself became artificial. . . . So it happened that *Hamlet* "on the very spot" became very like *Hamlet* in a modern theatre, whereas *Hamlet* in a ballroom had been strange and different and perhaps more truly Elizabethan.' This adds elements missing in Guthrie's own account including the vital fact that the central acting area in the improvised ballroom was much smaller in size than the purpose-built outdoor stage as well as being out in the centre of the congregation.

In 1948 Guthrie had the opportunity to advance these ideas when he created a thrust stage for the classics in the Assembly Hall, Edinburgh. So successful was it that it has become the home ever since of the major classical drama offerings of the Edinburgh Festival. Next at Stratford, Ontario, in 1953 and at Minneapolis in 1963 Guthrie, with his designer partner Tanya Moiseiwitsch, created what none of the new movement had succeeded in doing: a whole generation of new theatres, new in form and character and yet grounded in an ancient tradition. Guthrie wrote no books other than the autobiography and he made few artistic statements. There were no elegant architectural visions. Rather were theatres created which were new and practical and which have offered thousands of performances of a full range of drama from Shakespeare to pantomime, from musical to Chekhov.

Guthrie encapsulated the essence of these theatres in his description of the first of these, the conversion of the Assembly Hall, Edinburgh: 'One of the most pleasing effects of the performance was the physical relation of the audience to the stage. The audience did not look at the actors against a background of pictorial and illusionary scenery. Seated around three sides of the stage they focussed upon the actors in the brightly lit acting area, but the background was of the dimly lit rows of people similarly focussed on the actors. All the time, but unemphatically and by influence, each member of the audience was being ceaselessly reminded that he was not lost in an illusion, was not at the court of King Humanitie in sixteenth century Scotland but was in fact a member of a large audience taking part, "assisting at", as the French very properly express it, a performance, a participant in a ritual.'

Thus at Edinburgh in 1948 and in the later purpose-built thrust stage theatres Guthrie achieved what Terence Gray had dreamt of in 1932 when writing of the new theatre: 'in these theatres stage and auditorium will be a unity, the audience will once more view the stage from diverse angles so that actors will really be seen in the round; make believe reality will be unwanted and impossible, scenery will no longer seek to reproduce the external appearance of the place of action.' Of all the purifiers who wanted to create a new theatre only Guthrie can be said to have created a new type of building as well as a movement. Architects and scenographers had

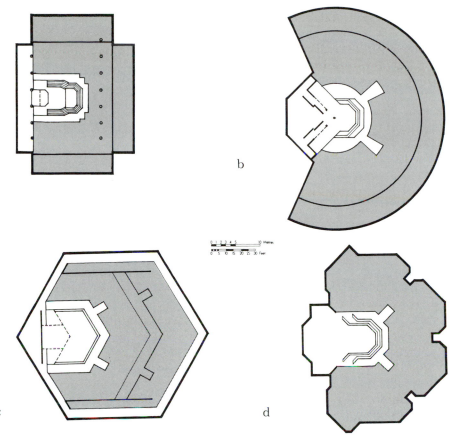

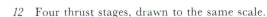

12 Four thrust stages, drawn to the same scale.

a Tyrone Guthrie's first thrust stage, a conversion of a gothic church assembly hall built by William Playfair in 1860. The Assembly Hall, seating 1,200 was first converted into a thrust stage theatre for the seminal production of *The Three Estates* at the second Edinburgh International Festival of 1948. Guthrie directed a range of plays as well as *The Three Estates* in this temporary theatre from 1948 to 1955, excepting for 1953 when his energies were directed toward opening the first tent theatre at Stratford, Ontario.

b The permanent theatre at Stratford, Ontario with 2,262 seats, which replaced the tent in 1957.

c The Festival Theatre, Chichester in England of 1962, a low cost structure designed by architects Powell & Moya which, by reason of its hexagonal form, placed most of the audience of 1,394 to the front.

d The Crucible, Sheffield. Although not completed until late 1971, shortly after Guthrie's death this is a true Guthrie thrust stage theatre, Britain's only one other than the Assembly Hall, Edinburgh. The audience of 1,022 at Sheffield is equally balanced in three sections, to the front and to the two sides of the thrust.

drawn and dreamed. Little of what they had dreamt had been built. The director Guthrie, who could not draw a line, created something new which did endure, revolutionised acting style and restored to audiences the role of 'assisting at' the event. It was this active participation in the act of theatre, enjoyed by ancient Athenians, Elizabethan groundlings and Georgian playgoers, that had been removed from theatregoers in the dimmed auditoriums of nineteenth-century temples of illusion. Guthrie turned the clock back, while most of the modern movement failed to turn it forward.

The Guthrie stage had its detractors, especially in Britain. It seemed at first well suited for pageant plays interspersed with soliloquies and the arrival of messengers from the four quarters, say *Richard II*, Act III Scene ii, when Richard's army evaporates. However, in the comedies or the late plays of Shakespeare the thrust stage encouraged restlessness while in naturalistic plays of the late nineteenth and twentieth centuries the furniture often obscured the actors from the spectators at the sides. Guthrie suggested that all that was needed was for directors and actors to learn 'a slightly different technique' and almost all plays could be translated to the thrust stage. As illustration of the wide repertoire possible on the new thrust stages, once that technique had been learnt, Guthrie singled out in his contribution to *Actor and Architect*, published in 1964, the 1962 production by his successor at Stratford, Ontario, Michael Langham, of *Cyrano de Bergerac*, 'one of the very last plays which you could pull out on to a stage of this kind . . . a musical comedy without music. But it was marvellously directed. The performance was a tremendous success.' At that time, shortly before he was to open the theatre that bears his name in Minneapolis, he maintained that the only part of the repertoire he would not present on a thrust stage would be 'the artificial comedies from Restoration comedy down to the end of the eighteenth century'.

While Guthrie opened Minneapolis in 1963 Sir Laurence Olivier had opened the Chichester Festival Theatre in 1962. The latter is a strangely diluted version of a Guthrie thrust stage. Its comparative unsatisfactoriness is due to the lowness of the ceiling (exacerbated by the technical accretions of thirty years), the shallow rake of the seating, and to the slackness of the geometry in plan which results in the front edge to the stage tapering to a point. This overemphasises the centre line and is as fundamentally unsettling as a central column would be in the portico of a Greek temple. Yet Chichester survives with an independent tenaciousness and with a house style that owes more to scenic panache than Guthrie would have liked and with a glamour given by big stars and a broad style.

Olivier, who directed Chichester for its first four seasons, the third and fourth with the newly founded National Theatre Company, did not love the Chichester thrust stage but accepted that a younger generation craved an escape from the confines of the proscenium stage, at that time erroneously equated with the picture frame of illusion. Olivier's antipathy to the thrust stage, coupled with the fact that Britain's only true Guthrie thrust, the Crucible, Sheffield, did not open until 1971, resulted in a loss of impetus in the development of the thrust stage in Britain. With the building boom of the late 1960s and 1970s the continuity with Guthrie and his philosophical predecessors was lost.

It is difficult to draw a line between 'history' and 'today' in any analysis. The student of English dramatic literature has always regarded 1956 and the first performance at the Royal Court Theatre of John Osborne's *Look Back in Anger* as a watershed. Within a very short time a change in direction was apparent to all. For theatre architecture 1953 and the opening at Stratford, Ontario, of the thrust stage by Guthrie is an event of equal significance. However, that Stratford, Ontario, represented a watershed between 'history' and 'today' was not as quickly apparent as was *Look Back in Anger*. Little changed in theatre architecture in the 1950s and 1960s during which time many inferior theatres were built for reasons which are explained in the next eight chapters. Nevertheless the Guthrie theatres are landmarks: in these theatres, as in Wagner's Bayreuth, a clear line can be traced from radical theory to successful practice. They were successful possibly because they were carefully considered reappraisals of an ancient form, the Elizabethan platform stage. At any rate they have endured while much vaunted later open stages, built in the 1960s and 1970s and once regarded as improvements on the Guthrie thrust, have outlived their usefulness and are now being superseded or redesigned.

As a result of Guthrie's achievement three distinct groups of worthwhile theatres were inherited by the English-speaking theatre of the 1950s and 1960s: first a handful of pre-1830 Georgian playhouses; second about 10 per cent of the 5,000–6,000 major theatres built in England and America between 1870 and 1920, many of a compact size which reflects the continuity in the English-speaking playhouse; and third the select group of Guthrie thrust stages, most of which are in North America.

Part II

Today

Chapter 4

Critics and analysts

The 'today' of the second part of this book is defined as the theatre we have known since 1953. As prologue to 'today' a brief review, with all the advantage of hindsight, is needed of the state of theatre architecture as then perceived.

Tyrone Guthrie had created at Stratford, Ontario, the thrust stage with audience evenly arranged on three sides. The traditional theatre, the 'real theatre' of plush and gilt, velour and cherubs, still survived but was, for the moment, in decline. Not only were hundreds of these theatres being closed and then demolished in the city centres of Britain and America, the commercial developer having been aided by the overzealous planner to wreak more theatrical destruction than any Nazi bomber in Europe or movie mogul in America, but also those that remained were no longer loved. They were run down and, except in the West End of London and on Broadway where they continued to be accepted, were out of favour with theatre activists. To the latter these were the theatres of the well-made play, of drawing-room comedy and of French windows. While the theatre establishment cherished glitter, in London mainly for a certain sort of undemanding straight play, the 'West End play', and in New York for the Broadway musical, those who believed that the theatre deals with the society of the present, and with the playwrights' aims to alter it, dreamt of a new modern theatre as a suitable setting for their new modern plays.

In Germany and in most of central Europe the opera houses and play-houses of almost every city had to be either replaced or restored after the ravages of war. In America every university campus seemed about to build a theatre for its newly emergent drama department and 400 new theatres were completed between 1950 and 1970. In Britain the repertory theatre movement, now enjoying state support through the Arts Council of Great Britain, aimed to build a new playhouse in every city as a more serious alternative to the ever shrinking commercial circuits.

None of the new clients for the design and construction of these new theatres on either side of the Atlantic were commercial managers as they had all the theatres that they could use. In place of commercial theatre managers, whose instruction to architects had always been simple and rarely innovative, the new clients were either many-headed charitable trusts running not-for-profit theatre companies or places of learning. The new clients were not sure where to start. To whom should they turn for advice? All wanted to do the best for their communities, though almost everywhere the budgets were smaller than the aspirations.

Because so few theatres had been built in the preceding twenty-five years there were no existing factories of design, by which is meant specialist architects who did only theatres plus the occasional ballroom and who had their own networks of decorators, engineers and contractors. In Edwardian England if a theatre burnt anywhere in the country Frank Matcham, the non-pareil specialist theatre architect, would have had a representative there the next morning, would himself be stamping the still smoking site by the end of the week and would have had the replacement theatre open within a year. Thomas Lamb did much the same in North America.

In the 1950s many of the new university clients reached for the books of Bel Geddes and Craig and got together with architects who had similar intellectual baggage bought at the Bauhaus. Other less knowledgeable clients asked where experts could be found.

They wondered whether the critics, both drama critics and architectural critics, could advise from their knowledge of the arts of theatre and of architecture. And, if the help from these quarters was insufficient, could there be specialist architectural historians who had analysed theatres past and present and who could therefore advise on the future of theatre architecture? This chapter examines the contribution of the critics, the historians and the analysts.

Drama critics go to the theatre more than anyone else if they live in a major theatrical centre such as London, New York, Chicago, Toronto or Paris. However, their view is particular in the literal sense. From where they sit in the front half of the orchestra the architecture of the space is outside their field of vision. From where they sit all theatres must be roughly the same. This is the first problem, but there is a greater one.

Drama critics do occasionally write about the theatre buildings themselves. But generally they do it only when a theatre is new. This raises a question of critical attitude to the very different arts of acting and of architecture. A piece of dramatic criticism concerns the performance of a particular production of a play. The critic has the difficult task of describing and defining the flight of the theatrical butterfly. The theatre, on the other hand, is the solid setting for thousands of performances of hundreds of productions. When it is new it is sticky to handle and unfamiliar to those whose tool it has to be. Both actor and audience need to ease themselves in and to break down the dauntingly new edifice. Once this has been successfully achieved others can come either side of the curtain and slip on familiar and hence more comfortable clothing.

The drama critic observing a new theatre inevitably provides only a first fleeting impression. Once the architectural and theatrical atmosphere of a theatre is familiar it is taken for granted and no longer appears to warrant any aesthetic analysis. It is also no longer news. Thus the drama critic's opinion of a theatre, which is ironically sometimes quoted for years afterwards, long after the opening production has been forgotten, is usually less well considered than his opinion of the performance. As records of how a theatre serves audience and actors they are rarely any more valuable than those public relations officers' puffs telling patrons and press alike of the perfection of their new playhouse.

Just occasionally critics allow themselves a reflection on the contribution of the theatre to the theatrical experience. For the best and most illuminating instance, it is necessary to dip back into 'history' to illustrate a universal and timeless point with an anecdote which deals directly with the question of where the critics sit. It was recounted by Max Beerbohm in the *Saturday Review* of which he was drama critic from 1898 to 1910. On 12 May 1906, Max Beerbohm started his column with a reference to the 'very faint and hazy notion' he had had the preceding week of *The Fascinating Mr Vanderveldt* at the Garrick Theatre which was and still is a fine theatre built in 1899 by Walter Emden and C. J. Phipps. It is on four levels, stalls, formerly orchestra stalls and pit, plus three circles, has a 30-foot wide proscenium and today holds 750, over 1,100 in 1906. The haziness was caused by the fact that four years earlier Max Beerbohm had offended Arthur Bourchier, the licensee and actor-manager, and had been struck off the first-night list. Since then he had not attended the Garrick or reviewed the work of Bourchier except on rare occasions when he paid for his own ticket. In May 1906, while still on Bourchier's black list, Max Beerbohm found himself somewhat surprisingly short of ready money and could only afford the benches of the pit which at the Garrick Theatre then stretched a long way under the dress circle and which have long been replaced by overpriced 'rear stalls'. Beerbohm reflected: 'Though I had never happened to see a play from the pit and my heart was leaping with the sense of adventure I knew no fear. The pit! There was a certain traditional magic in the sound, there was some secret of joy that I had often wished to elucidate. . . . It was with a glad heart that I had bounded down the stone steps.

'Gradually my eyes accustomed themselves to the darkness and I groped my way to a vacant space that I discerned on the backmost bench. Not until I was seated did I realise that the play had begun. Yes, there, at a distance of what seemed to be 50 dark miles or so was a patch of yellowish light; and therein certain tiny figures were moving. They were twittering too, these figures. I listened intently. I strained my ears, I strained my eyes. And since both my sight and my hearing are excellent, and since, as I have told you, I had read a detailed notice of the play, I was enabled to get some sort of vague illusion – the sort of illusion that one gets from a marionette show.'

Beerbohm discovered he had to guess at what Miss Irene Vanbrugh was saying. The sound 'want – pew' was guessed to be 'I want to help you'. Only two of the cast never failed to make their words easily understood to that displaced drama critic in the back row of the pit. Beerbohm noted 'Mr Bourchier's smile . . . quite distinctly. For the rest, no facial expression was anywhere discernible. Had I been sitting in the stalls [i.e. at the front of the orchestra] I should doubtless have accused Mr Bourchier of "clowning" – of smiling more widely than he ought to in a not farcical part. You may remember that last week I complimented him on having acquired the restraint needed for comedy [in his notice of the play in the preceding *Saturday Review*, a better-placed Beerbohm had written "Fate must be pleased to notice that Mr Bourchier, born a comedian, is ceasing to overlay his birthright with crude buffooneries. It is two or three years since I had seen him act and I was delighted by a very real improvement".] But he must not preen himself overmuch on that compliment. What seems like restraint to the man in the pit may seem like violent over acting to the man in the stalls. And what seems like restraint to the man in the stalls may be a mere blank, a vacuum, to the man in the pit. Everything depends on the point of view.'

Today the question of what is overacting and what is necessary projection in a large theatre has become increasingly important as commercial pressures coupled with demands for comfort makes theatres much bigger. Fifty years later in the 1960s and 1970s there was a revival in Britain's touring theatres, those large Victorian and Edwardian 'No. 1' theatres holding between 1,000 and 2,000 people. Most touring theatres had been closed by film, television and commercial development, but when a city in the 1960s found itself with only a single large touring theatre left, a fresh start was often made. They were generally acquired by the local authority as mixed programme theatres. This meant they presented opera, ballet, musicals, the pantomime and even drama.

The drama included the classics performed by such companies as the Prospect Theatre Company and subsequently the Actors' Company, both forerunners of the later actor-manager companies such as those of Kenneth Branagh, Michael Pennington and Tim Piggott-Smith. Shakespeare was once again 'on the road' in the footsteps of earlier actor-managers Henry Irving, Beerbohm Tree, Frank Benson or Donald Wolfit. But where were the actors of a new generation who could physically and vocally fill these great old theatres? At the Royal Shakespeare Theatre, Stratford-upon-Avon, which was almost as large, there was the safety net of an unusually attentive audience of worshippers at the shrine of Shakespeare. The Old Vic, home in the 1960s of the emerging National Theatre, was much smaller than the provincial Empires, Opera Houses and Theatres Royal.

Prospect and one of its leading actors who was to become famous, Ian McKellen, evolved the required bigger style. At first the national critics who had travelled out into the provinces, but still sat in those familiar front orchestra stalls, found the style of McKellen to be overpowering. But to stand at the back of a full gallery in the 1,600-seat Grand Theatre, Leeds (1878), and hear McKellen as King Richard II on the battlements of Flint Castle, was to realise that the critics in the front rows were watching in close-up performances prepared for long shot. 'Everything depends on the point of view', as Beerbohm had said when experiencing the rear of the pit rather than the front of the stalls.

The success of television drama in England and serious film making in America had also led both to a decline in actors who could fill the large houses and to a shift of taste in the public for a more measured internal style. However, in the 1980s this changed, not least because British classical actors had to cope with the challenge of making contact in the huge Barbican, Olivier and Lyttelton theatres. Meanwhile American actors found many of the new performing arts centers to be of a monumental scale that required the relearning of earlier barnstorming skills with or without the newest abomination, the throat mike. But on both sides of the Atlantic the critics in their front orchestra stalls for the most part failed to see the connection between style of acting and scale of theatre architecture.

If drama criticism is not a reliable source for an analysis of the part played by theatre architecture in the theatrical process, what then of architectural criticism?

Public interest in theatre architecture is a relatively new phenomenon at least in Britain. Certainly there was great interest at the beginning of the nineteenth century when leading architects of the day actively sought theatre commissions and in some instances took part in full-scale competitions. But by the time so many of our present 'old' theatres were built at the end of the nineteenth century theatre architecture in Britain had ceased to be considered a matter of architectural interest. In this respect Britain was different from the rest of Europe where Garnier in France and Fellner and Helmer in Germany, Switzerland and Austro-Hungary were widely feted for building theatres that were regarded as national or municipal monuments. In Britain theatres were regarded simply as commercial ventures. Thus the theatres built between 1871, when the present Old Vic auditorium was built by J. T. Robinson, whose daughter Frank Matcham was to marry, and 1914 and the outbreak of war, were not considered suitable subjects for the architectural critic of the day.

Only in the pages of *The Builder* can one find accounts of the hundreds of new theatres being built by C. J. Phipps, John Briggs, Bertie Crewe, Walter Emden, Frank Matcham, Ernest Runtz and W. G. R. Sprague, all for the most part specialist theatre architects. Of these C. J. Phipps alone was thought worthy of an entry in the *Dictionary of National Biography*, and then largely because of his non-theatre buildings. In America only rarely did theatres merit attention from the architectural establishment; state capitols, churches, museums and even railway stations being regarded as civic buildings more worthy of the attention of the serious 'beaux arts' architects of the day. Playhouses were regarded by an essentially puritan establishment as mere entertainment buildings and hence of a lower order aesthetically. For example very little is known today of the work of J. B. McElfatrick who built nearly 400 theatres in North America.

All this had changed with the new movement in the 1920s and 1930s. The architectural press on both sides of the Atlantic became interested in the unbuilt visions discussed in an earlier chapter. Thus by the 1950s there were books and articles by the score but these still dealt for the most part with ideas rather than with realities. In Britain the interests of the architectural critic were finally engaged in the 1960s by the decision to create a national theatre on the South Bank of the Thames and to give the newly named Royal Shakespeare Company a permanent London home at the Barbican in the City of London. Just as the rebuilding of Drury Lane and Covent Garden at the end of the eighteenth century focused interest on theatre architecture, so the creation of homes for the National and RSC, temporarily housed at the Old Vic and the Aldwych which everybody then thought of as merely makeshift premises, reawakened the interest of both architectural profession and press. Slightly earlier in New York the Lincoln Center for the Performing Arts, consisting of an opera house, a second opera house for ballet and operetta, a concert hall and a theatre, the Vivian Beaumont, all sited on 14 acres close to Central Park, was conceived in 1955, and completed by 1966. The American adventure happened characteristically much quicker than in Britain where the National Theatre Company was temporarily housed at the Old Vic for thirteen years rather than the five originally envisaged.

When Britain's new National Theatre opened in 1976 the mood of the country had begun to swing against modern architecture. Moreover the theatre profession was not as pro-National as it had once been. The committees of the Arts Council which decided the size of the grants to the National and other drama companies disapproved of so large a slice of the subsidy cake going to the biggest of the newly dubbed 'centres of excellence'. In contrast the architectural critics rallied round and the new National received a surprisingly good press. The *Architectural Review* published a special issue in November 1977, edited by Colin Amery, which included a very favourable critique by the doyen of critics of the social dimension in architecture, Mark Girouard, entitled *Cosmic Connections*. Girouard explained: 'The Olivier is cosmic. This is not a pretentious adjective but a descriptive one. The Olivier was designed under the influence not only of individual theatres from Epidauros to the Globe but of classical and Renaissance theories of the theatre as microcosm, a little model of the world connected by its architecture to something bigger than itself. . . . It succeeds; and in doing so it puts an instrument of exciting power into the hands of the producer.'

Amery concluded of the Olivier Theatre that 'here the architect has done his utmost to heighten the sense of drama, here the life of man is to be played out in an emblematic room . . . it will not be the fault of the architecture if the drama does not flourish here.' Few actors who worked there in the first dozen years would agree with that forecast. But the architectural press retained a solemn tone of voice. There was a lot of talk of humanity although what they were talking about now appears to be built on a superhuman or epic scale. No critic of the 1970s speculated on how an epic theatre which might be wonderful for *Oedipus Rex* would be difficult to work for *Twelfth Night*, for a farce or for a new play dealing with contemporary social realities and that if pressed into service for such plays a broad stage would engender a broad style.

The translation of the National and of the RSC from the warm embrace and tight focus of the smaller and more human-scaled Old Vic and Aldwych to the wide open spaces of the South Bank and Barbican was a rerun of what had happened at Drury Lane and Covent Garden as recounted by John Byng and Richard Cumberland (see pp. 34, 35). The new Olivier and Barbican theatres failed to achieve the hoped-for closer contact with the audience because, while the picture-frame proscenium had been abolished, at the same time the scale of the auditorium had been increased and the stage widened. It was the sheer volume of air across which they had to communicate at the Olivier that disconcerted the actors who universally preferred the older theatres.

When actors fulminate against new theatres they dislike they rarely find the words with which to make their dissatisfaction clear to architects. A productive dialogue between theatre and architect has rarely taken place. This is largely due to the lack of critics to lead the debate. Fortunately of late architectural criticism of theatre in Britain has been passed to the few theatre people with lighting and technical backgrounds, such as Frederick Bentham and Francis Reid, who had shown an ability to write entertainingly about theatres in specialised theatre journals. As a result they have occasionally been granted space to discuss these matters in the architectural press which otherwise concentrates on the exterior and, in respect of the all-important auditorium, accepts the promoter's or the architect's claims instead of testing them against different works and different audiences.

Books on theatre architecture are obviously worthwhile sources of advice for those wishing to build theatres. There are three sorts of such book. First there are the academic books which take the reader on a tour of theatre throughout the world down the ages, its plays and its theatres. These books have two-dimensional diagrams of the different patterns of theatre (e.g. Greek, Roman, Shakespearian, classical, Restoration,

Georgian, late Victorian, etc.) which tend to leave one with the feeling that for every sort of play you need a different sort of theatre. Others identify different types of theatres simply by the topographical relationship of audience to actor (end stage, in-the-round, traverse, arena, thrust, etc.). Both sorts, the historical and the topographical, are often written by scene designers who teach scene design and who concentrate heavily on the different ways in which plays can be staged in different sorts of theatres, rather than how the audience enjoyed them or the actors responded. The best of the American titles is by stage designer Jo Mielziner (1902–76), *The Shapes of Our Theatre* (1970). But the reader should be warned that the date of publication resulted in this being in part a defence of the 'multiform' stage compromise forced upon the author by the vociferous building committee for the Vivian Beaumont Theater (1965), made up of apparently equally weighted advocates of 'open thrust' (Mielziner's phrase) and of proscenium staging, who were blind to the fact that the demands of thrust and proscenium staging are irreconcilable.

The second category is the planning and technical book of which the best in Britain is Roderick Ham's *Theatre Planning*, published in succeding editions in 1972 and 1987, for the Association of British Theatre Technicians. In 1990 the Arts Council published *The Arts Council Guide to Building for the Arts* by Judith Strong which summarises Roderick Ham's work, adding much about the legal and financial framework for the design and construction of theatres, new or old, in Great Britain. In America there is nothing of comparable stature except the specialised *Space for Dance, an Architectural Design Guide* by Leslie Armstrong and Roger Morgan, published by the National Endowment for the Arts in 1984. Such books are necessary for the architect or engineer seeking advice on how to carry out a design. But they are not books which you read to decide what sort of theatre architecture you need. A different tone is needed to debate the 'what' rather than the 'how'.

An empirical approach has bred the third sort of analysis of theatre architecture. It is the select category of those who have worked on a vigorously comparative basis. While the volumes created by Richard Leacroft in Britain and George Izenour in America in the last twenty years are well known, their antecedents are not.

The tradition of the *parallèle*, comparative studies of theatre architecture illustrated with consistently styled and scaled drawings, was established in the eighteenth century with two publications which have already been referred to in the section on theoreticians of the eighteenth century. But their value today lies as much in their comparative presentation as in their philosophies. The first was the *Parallèle de plans des plus belles salles de spectacle d'Italie et de France avec des détails de machines théâtrales* by Gabrielle Pierre Dumont, which was published in Paris in 1774 and which originated the notion of theatrical parallels, while the second was Pierre Patte's *Essai sur l'architecture théâtrale* published eight years later, also in Paris, in 1782. In the nineteenth century the parallel was perfected in two great publications, the first being the sumptuously produced *Le Parallèle des principaux théâtres modernes d'Europe* by Clement Contant and Joseph de Filippi, published in Paris in 1860 and republished in facsimile by Benjamin Blom in New York in 1968. This had magnificently engraved parallel plans and sections of thirty great theatres, from the opera at Versailles of 1770 to the then recently completed Covent Garden Opera House by Barry of 1858. The second was *Modern Opera Houses and Theatres* by Edwin O. Sachs and Ernest Woodrow published in three volumes in 1896, 1897 and 1898 with parallel drawings of fifty-five great theatres built between 1875 and 1897. Almost every country in Europe was covered and all theatres illustrated in parallel had been already built except for a projected opera house in St Petersburg. The theatres are reproduced in plan, section and elevation and there is a consistent text on each one of them which provides a critical analysis and certain standard measurements. A third volume, with 880 illustrations, covers many other theatres and such issues as town planning, the details of proscenium arches, staircases in the foyers, stage machinery, the steel cantilever and even an analysis of 346 theatre fires in the nineteenth century, their causes and how future buildings should be altered to avoid their recurrence. This too was republished in facsimile by Benjamin Blom in New York in 1968. A study of at least Contant and Sachs is advised if the more recent work of Leacroft and Izenour is to be understood fully.

Leacroft, an architect, who spent some years as a scenic artist at the Leicester Theatre Royal before joining the Leicester Polytechnic where he taught architecture, had created a technique of drawing clear axonometrics of all the theatres he studied. Examples of these are reproduced on pp. 32 and 33. In 1973 Richard Leacroft wrote *The Development of the English Playhouse* which is as full a history as the title suggests but which stops firmly in 1922 and the design of the present auditorium of the Theatre Royal, Drury Lane. It was published by Methuen and has thirty axonometrics and isometrics. A second book, *Theatres and Playhouses: an Illustrated Survey of Theatre Building from Ancient Greece to the Present Day* was also published by Methuen in 1985. This has a further sixty isometrics. The text in both cases was carefully researched by both Richard and Helen Leacroft though that for the latter was edited down to half its original length and as a result appears peremptory in some of its judgements.

George Izenour also wrote two books. Both are physically huge, daunting in scope and very expensive. The first, *Theatre Design*, was published in 1977 and the second, *Theatre Technology*, in 1988, both by McGraw Hill.

Izenour had a team of draughtsmen and through them developed a technique of drawing long sections through populated auditorium with a strange internal perspective imposed upon them. There are also hundreds of other useful illustrations. However, the text turns out to be in no way a dispassionate analysis of different styles of different theatre architects with different aims, as are both of the books by Leacroft. Instead the Izenour philosophy, of theatre design as rational seating geometry in the image of Wagner's Bayreuth, is presented as if it were the only route to heaven. Such special pleading by an engineer belongs in a later chapter.

Chapter 5

Film and television

Film has always had a greater influence on theatre architecture in North America than in Britain. The reason is that while in Europe the outbreak of the First World War in 1914 put a stop to the building of theatres, which did not restart until the early 1920s, the same war, in which America did not join until 1917, increased rather than decreased American national prosperity. Prosperity almost always leads to bigger and better places of entertainment. However, the American theatre had to cope with a different and ultimately more damaging threat: the moving pictures. First came the vaudeville theatres in which the silent movies got second billing below the popular stage acts. Then to house moving pictures the Americans created the picture palace in the mid 1920s. It is possible to pinpoint almost precisely the moment when priorities changed and vaudeville died. Prior to this the cinema and the live actor coexisted in the same building. It is necessary to go back to this point in the history of cinemas if one is to understand how the architectures of the cinema and of the theatre interact.

In 1913 Scottish-born American architect Thomas Lamb designed a theatre on 116th Street in Harlem, New York City, which was then a prosperous middle-class neighbourhood. This theatre, which survives today intact as a First Corinthian Baptist Chapel, looked like a legitimate theatre and was decorated in the Adams style. The auditorium had triple-stepped boxes at the side and a deep balcony, the whole set behind a façade which was supposedly a one-third replica of the Doge's Palace in Venice. But the Regent was built not as a legitimate theatre but as a vaudeville also showing movies. After a false start 'Roxy' Rothapfel, who was later to build both the great Roxy cinema on Broadway, destroyed in 1961 after a lifespan of scarcely thirty years, and also the still surviving Radio City Music Hall, took over as manager. An orchestra was engaged. Magnificent uniforms were bought for the staff and the Regent reopened with *The Last Days of Pompeii*, a silent movie with orchestral accompaniment personally selected by Roxy. There was the duet from *Aida* for the love interest, *Lohengrin* plus choir for the frenzied scenes after the eruption of the volcano. The press was ecstatic. The *Motion Picture News* of 6 December 1913 had 'a single criticism to be entertained, and that has nothing to do with the performance itself. This concerns the price of admission. It should be 25 instead of 15 cents.'

Roxy led the picture palace boom. Many equally flamboyant entrepreneurs followed. But by 1932 and the opening of the Radio City Music Hall it was almost all over. And yet in under twenty-five years more theatres, as Americans like to call their cinemas, all bigger and better, were built than in any preceding theatre-building boom in America or elsewhere. In addition hundreds of legitimate theatres were converted to moving pictures. Sadly even more closed altogether and with the advent of the talkies in 1927 the entire legitimate and musical comedy theatre circuits of America went into terminal decline leaving only a handful of live theatres in the very biggest cities.

Almost all the new movie palaces had flytowers. But an examination of their gridirons shows that they were hardly used. The reason is not only that the moving pictures were ever more enticing than vaudeville, even before the introduction of talkies, but also that the new picture palaces holding 2,000 to 4,000 (with reasonable legroom compared to earlier theatres) were simply too big for the vaudeville artists who, like those in music hall and variety in Great Britain, required a rapport with their audiences which is impossible to achieve in these vast houses. The great stars, for whom a reverential audience might refrain from pin dropping, could hold a capacity audience 'in the palm of their hands' but these stars were themselves appearing before cameras for much larger fees than a live audience could sustain at the box office, however big the theatre.

But when the talkies came the orchestras and singers who had given 'class' to the evening were disbanded. Although these giant picture palaces were hardly ever used by live performers, they confused students of theatre then (and still do) as to the distinction between the theatregoing and the cinemagoing experiences. In the 1920s the image on the silver screen was proportionally smaller and did not dominate the auditorium as it does today in modern cinemas where decoration is considered an unnecessary distraction. On the contrary, in the 1920s the architecture not the film was the dominant element. Said picture palace owner Marcus Loew, 'we sell tickets to theatres, not movies', a diametrically opposed view to that of Brooks Atkinson, quoted in the Introduction, that theatres are merely places for people to 'assemble and enjoy the show'.

The theatre architects themselves had managed to change gear in moving from the design of legitimate theatres before 1915 to the design of movie palaces from 1915 to 1930. It was not just that they were bigger. Despite being superficially similar to legitimate theatres in that they had proscenium arches, a large curtain, balcony and florid plasterwork just like the later legitimate theatres, these picture palace auditoriums had changed in a few years to become fundamentally different.

The difference was twofold. The description of the character of these exotically decorated theatres – some were Moorish gardens, others French palaces – as being 'an acre of seats in a garden of dreams' was apt. The architect's job from entrance through the huge lobbies to the moment when the lights dimmed was to dazzle and to impress those who had paid 10 or 15 cents, and to transport them in their imagination to a fantasy world. They may not have been educated in artistic appreciation but they knew 'class' when they saw it. Such an audience of the people was to be put in awe of what was placed before them, the architect's job being not very different from that of the creator of a rococo church.

Responses were to be conditioned. The audience was not in celebration of its own community, as in a live theatre, but in communion with something outside their experience, a polychromatic architectural orgy which framed a monochromatic silver screen on which the new gods and goddesses appeared. This audience was awestruck and passive, not active and involved.

If the mood and purpose of auditorium architecture had changed, so had the form itself. All the seats now had to face one way for technical reasons concerned with the brilliance of the picture under projection conditions. This made individual members of the audience aware only of their immediate neighbours. Side boxes disappeared and in their place were huge box-like decorative follies, framing not live people but dead statuary, as well as providing useful space for the organ pipes of the 'mighty wurlitzer'. The paramount need for seeing the projected picture from the best possible position made the middle of the house better than the front or back. As a result the highest-priced seats were in 'loges', under which soubriquet boxes made a brief return to theatre architecture relocated in the prime position which was at the front of the balcony. Behind the loges, the balcony audience (in conventional seats) need not be aware of the audience in the orchestra, as the interaction of the audience one with the other as well as with the performer was not relevant any more in a mechanical art form.

The audience was to be aware first of the palace in which it was sitting, and second of the screen. Sightlines were calculated to the screen framed by the proscenium arch which resulted in a focus above stage level. This has the result that today the downstage performer on the stages of these erstwhile monster movie palaces is only just visible on a grazing sightline over the heads of those seated in front. A second consequence is that all the audience can see of other members of the audience in the erstwhile movie palaces is the back of the heads of those in front, which, as Peter Brook and others have observed, is hardly the most interesting part of anyone's anatomy.

Nevertheless many people's perception of old (pre-1915) legitimate theatres in America was and still is confused with their perception of those

13 The Ohio Theater, Columbus, Ohio, 1928. 2,897 seats on two levels in a style
described by the architect, Thomas Lamb, as 'faithfully carried-out Mexican
baroque'. Since 1969 it has been the house of the Columbus Association for the
Performing Arts with an eclectic policy of dance, opera, broadway musicals and
'headliners' as well as moving pictures. Such a programme is typical of those movi

alaces that have been recycled as Performing Arts Centers.

This photograph is by Hiroshi Sugimoto who produces an accurately luminous image by opening the camera's shutter for two hours during the screening of a film an empty, darkened auditorium.

later and ridiculously overdecorated movie palaces. In the 1950s and 1960s serious theatre workers reacted so strongly against all that plasterwork that the architectural and theatrical merit of the older theatres and of the few post-1915 real theatres, typified by the extant mid-size Broadway theatres, was almost totally ignored for a quarter of a century. Somehow all were simply lumped together as 'irrelevant' to modern theatre.

Meanwhile afficionados of the movie palace formed a society to preserve everything, irrespective of its quality. In America the Theatre Historical Society, whose members would kill for plasterwork, is almost exclusively concerned with movie palaces, not live theatres, despite its title. However, the League of Historic American Theaters, which in 1987 published the excellent *Directory of Historic American Theaters* (of surviving pre-1915 theatres) edited by John W. Frick and Carlton Ward, does, partly by virtue of its chosen cut-off date, distinguish between real theatres and those movie palaces which made a token provision for vaudeville. In Britain and the rest of the world, florid picture palaces were much more of a rarity and so the opportunity for confusion did not arise.

The relevance of this confusion to recent theatre architecture is that some modern architects were unable to distinguish the difference in form between a cinema and a proscenium arch theatre. For example in theatres as important as the proscenium arch theatre at the National in London, the Lyttelton, the sightlines in the balcony were, as in the movie palaces, calculated to ignore the presence of the audience in the stalls. For the actor this has had the result of creating two distinct levels of audience, one above and one below the natural eyeline which is frequently, as at the Lyttelton, occupied by glazed control rooms. The cause was that the design of proscenium arch theatres had become oversimplified as a question of sightline formulae and the wrong ones at that. The design of such theatres is not simply the business of arranging a lot of people to face a stage so that all can see and hear perfectly. That the problem is more complex had not been perceived in the 1960s: the building committee of Britain's National spent 90 per cent of its time discussing the open-stage theatre (the Olivier) because everybody thought they knew what a proscenium arch theatre (the Lyttelton) should be and that therefore it did not merit debate. Architect Denys Lasdun's own oversimplification, quoted by Peter Lewis in *The National Theatre: a Dream Made Concrete* published in 1990, says it all: 'There are plays where actor and audience confront each other. The characteristic of confrontation is very straight forward. You need a rectangle and the audience, frankly, just facing. That is the essence of the Lyttelton Theatre.'

A second major influence on theatre architecture has been the rise of television. Just as the movies closed live theatres in the 1930s and 1940s when the talkies supplanted legitimate live theatre, musical comedy and vaudeville (or music hall as it was called in Britain) as popular entertainment, so in the 1950s and 1960s most of the remaining live theatres and some of the cinemas closed as a result of the challenge of television. But on this occasion the audience did not move from one sort of auditorium to another; it stayed at home.

Yet ultimately television may well be seen to have had a beneficial effect on live theatre. While the cinema screen replicated the framed picture of scenic illusion of the late nineteenth and early twentieth centuries live theatre television did not because in television the edges of the picture are less significant.

With television the viewer is encouraged to look into the picture at the character in close-up, whether a politician, actor or light entertainment performer. Television focuses down on character or personality while film on ever wider screens opens up to the panoramic. As a result those familiar with the intensity and intimacy of television are no longer prepared to sit as Max Beerbohm did at the back of the pit at London's Garrick Theatre in 1910 and watch a far distant flickering image. If television watchers are to leave their comfortable armchairs and go to the theatre they want either to see spectacle that cannot be created within the confines of their small TV screen or to be close to a live performer. Therefore as a consequence of television the modern theatregoer, except when attending the latest mega-musical, is increasingly receptive to small focused spaces whether in the round, environmental, or with thrust or sparsely furnished end stages. Film going encouraged conservatism in theatregoers and hence dull theatre architecture in the 1920s, 1930s and 1940s. Television, on the other hand, has encouraged audiences to accept directness in presentation in the intimacy of small theatres and hence less reliance on illusionary staging technique. However, this may change with the introduction into the home of high-fidelity, big-screen television.

Chapter 6

Historic theatres and found space

Until the mid 1970s old theatres were generally unloved. In Britain there were so many churches, country houses and even railway stations under threat that conservationists, who were predominantly upper class, donnish or plain eccentric, concentrated on great architecture conceived for great people and thus gave the impression that conservation was somehow elitist. Britain has had an official listing system since 1944 which offers limited protection to 'buildings of special architectural or historical interest'. In England there are now three categories – Grade I, Grade II Star and Grade II – with a simpler system in Scotland. But until recently there was a reluctance to list theatres built after 1860. The reason why late Victorian and Edwardian theatres were passed over for so long is worth examining.

The magic of theatres lies largely in their interiors and even then they do not come to life until lined with people. The incandescent glow from the stage lights up capital, cornice and caryatid, as well as the craning faces of the gallery goers which the painter Sickert caught so well. But an unlit, empty and disused theatre is a gloomy place to all save theatrefolk or to those who have trained their imaginations. In addition the later Victorian and Edwardian theatres rarely had a convincing street facade, while inside the architectural connoisseur found only an illiterate and apparently ill-considered jumble from the plasterworker's catalogue. Thus authorities such as Niklaus Pevsner and Sir John Summerson hurried past the high-street theatre. Thus, as a cumulative result of the enemy bomber, of the greed of the commercial developer and of the neglect by the architectural historian, London in the mid 1960s had lost nearly all its fifty or so suburban theatres and music halls. Elsewhere in Britain most cities found they had retained only one or two of their half dozen old Empires, Palaces, Royals or Alhambras. In their places were offices and shopping malls.

In the United States the equivalent landmarking scheme of most states did not allow the landmarking of buildings not in use, and so hundreds of theatres were torn down without a chance being given to conservationists, largely because they were dark. The National Register of the Federal

Parks Commission was highly selective and roughly equivalent to Britain's Grade I. As a result few theatres have ever made it on to the national list which does offer better protection than most of the state landmarking systems. The Canadians, once awakened in the 1980s to the little that remained of their theatrical heritage, have been much more assiduous in its rescue.

The theatre profession was even more lukewarm. Politically committed directors of theatre companies and their playwrights saw in the old theatres evidence of a compartmentalised social structure, each level for each class in a multi-tier auditorium having its own entrance. They failed to see that there had been few more effective architectural devices to bring together the social classes in a single space than eighteenth- and nineteenth-century theatres.

Directors of plays also saw bad sightlines to a proscenium arch from which they yearned to escape. Few were prepared to use the theatricality of the old theatres as a tool in the way that Brecht did in Berlin at this time when, for example, he allowed his chorus in *The Caucasian Chalk Circle* to lean against the theatre's proscenium arch and, in this precisely ambivalent position, interpose between us, the audience, and they, the actors, telling their story up there on the stage. To this day nothing would persuade the Berliner Ensemble to exchange their ancient and intensely theatrical Theater am Schiffbauerdamm, which they have occupied so successfully since 1949, for the best modern theatre money could buy.

From the point of view of the audience the old theatres were associated with cramped and badly run bars, rude box office staff imprisoned behind wrought-iron guichets and uncomfortably close-spaced seats. Only one group, the actors themselves, knew instinctively the value of the old theatres, but even then they had much to dislike in the tiny subterranean and usually ill-lit dressing rooms with their old furniture, dirty mirrors, cold water and non-existent green rooms. Unfortunately it did not occur to the actors of the 1950s and 1960s that the architects of new theatres when emptying out the cracked baths and dirty bath water would almost always throw away the baby of theatricality.

In the 1990s it is hard to imagine the situation of twenty-five years ago when few understood the architectural and theatrical potential of the traditional proscenium arch playhouse. The new was all the rage and the old was out of fashion. Today the whirlygig of time brings in his revenges and the conservationists on both sides of the Atlantic have the upper hand.

One of the reasons why conservation movements are now so anxious to restore almost any old theatre is because they arrived too late to save many of the finest. It is thought that in Britain there were just over 1,000 theatres in use between 1900 and 1914, leaving out the simpler music halls, early cinemas and flat-floor halls with a barely equipped stage at one end. By 1982, when a self-appointed vigilante group chaired by this author published *CURTAINS!!! or A New Life For Old Theatres*, Britain's first gazetteer of pre-1914 theatres, evidence was found that 85 per cent of the 1,000+ theatres in use at the end of the nineteenth century had been demolished or irretrievably altered. Of the remaining 150 it seemed to the *CURTAINS!!!* committee in 1982 that 98 were in use and, of the remaining 52 disused theatres, at least half were sleeping beauties which should, if at all possible, be reawakened. Since 1982 some have been restored as suggested and only a few more lost.

In America the situation was comparably worse. The base from which the reduction was made was larger, there having been between 2,000 and 3,000 major 'legitimate' theatres in the boom years before the arrival of moving pictures. By the 1960s almost all the city-centre theatres built before 1915 had vanished leaving only those later and more flamboyant movie palaces as the recipients of much misplaced nostalgia.

In Britain in the late 1980s there was also a clearly discernible reaction against modern architecture as a whole. The new theatres, especially the larger ones, had not been well received by either audience or actors although the magnificent new foyers and easily accessible bars had been welcomed. It was a reaction which had started much earlier amongst such people as playwright Somerset Maugham who wrote as early as 1955 in the preface to *The Artist and the Theatre* of the old theatres and of 'the glamour which put you in a comfortable state of mind to enjoy the play you are about to witness. The theatres they build now are severely func-tional: you can see from all parts of them what is happening on the stage; the seats are comfortable and there are abundant exits so that you run small chance of being burnt to death. But they are cold. They are apt to make you feel that you have come to the playhouse to undergo an ordeal rather than enjoy an entertainment.' In 1955 many thought this the senti-mental nostalgia typical of an author whose plays seemed always to feature French windows. Today these words written in 1955 read as a prescient criticism of the theatres of the 1970s which had not yet been designed, let alone constructed. However, the theatres opened since 1980 and those now on architects' and designers' drawing boards are very different from the modern theatres of the 1950s, 1960s and 1970s against which Maugham was the first to inveigh.

The balance is now more even. Theatre architecture has progressed while the conservationists themselves have put a foot or two wrong. In Britain many old theatres have been tarted up in saloon bar or boudoir restorations with Wilton carpet where once was sawdust, brass balustrades where once were iron handrails, wallpaper for tile work and gilding which glitters under the modern intensity of reflected stage lights instead of glowing as it did under the original gas light. Nevertheless councillors are proud of the glitter as evidence of the millions that have been spent on their local Alhambra, Theatre Royal or Lyceum. However, theatregoers sometimes discover that glitzy restorations are often a justification for a hefty hike in prices, especially in what were once the cheapest areas of the house. But what riles most is not the architecturally artificial atmosphere newly created but the pretence that this is how it was in some good old days gone by. Such gaudy 'restoration' is about on a par with the recreated Dickensian snug in ye olde inne or the sanitised authenticity of a Disneyland.

The historical argument for more sensitive restoration which produces a more accurate evocation of a theatre's past is not easy. Theatre is an ephemeral art and the fact that a century or more ago Booth played here and Sarah Bernhardt there smacks to most audiences and many theatre people as sentimental antiquarianism. Cost is a doubtful ally as an authentic restoration of a fine old theatre may not cost less than either a glitzy restoration or a new theatre on an empty site. The more esoteric arguments that do stand up include the argument that in a sensitively and more authentically restored old theatre the audience will accept a higher density of accommodation than they would either in an overgilded restoration or in a brand new theatre. This density, together with the atmosphere created in a well-restored old theatre, can increase not only the box office takings but also the heightened sense of expectation in an audience and hence the likelihood of theatrical success. Actors, too, are wary of the bright as a band box theatre unless, of course, it is full. John Gielgud wrote of the old Old Vic, in the physically run-down days of Lilian Baylis when there was no money for Wilton carpet: 'It is warm, alive and it has a tattered magnificence about it. It smells and feels like a theatre, and is able to transform a collection of human beings into that curious vibrant instrument for the actor, an audience.' Would he have felt the same about the present highly efficient restoration and glittering decor of which Jonathan Miller said to this author 'there's nothing wrong that a blowlamp or some paint stripper cannot put right'?

Both the authentically restored theatre and the glitz plaster and gilt version share one advantage over the modern theatres of the modern movement. At a conference on theatre space held by the International Federation for Theatre Research in Munich in 1977, Richard Küller presented the conclusion of his experiment on measuring the capacity of the audience to be aroused at the start of a show. With electrodes connected to the brain, the arousal rate of those who had been seated in a room abounding in colour and pattern (with a high 'information rate' to use the behavioural scientist jargon) was compared with the capacity to be aroused of those who had for an equal time, say fifteen minutes, been seated in a dull black or grey room with little decoration. Those who had been in the festive space (= an old theatre) laughed quicker and cried quicker when exposed to stimuli (= theatre performance) than those who had been in the darker decoration-free space (= a 'modern' theatre). Actors who have

tried to warm up an audience in many a new theatre and have compared
this with their experience in good old theatres did not need a behavioural
scientist to tell them this, but some architects did and still do.

There is another profession close to that of acting where the experienced
performers can recognise what will best assist them in their art: that is
politics and, in particular, the effect of place on public speaking. Britain's
party political conferences are a unique ritual which, because the audience
is the party faithful who have chosen to come, have a peculiar theatrical
atmosphere of their own. Television has not quite taken over as in America.
However, the sessions are long, the speakers numerous, and so they have
little time to grab their audience's attention. Labour and Conservative
parties generally alternate between Brighton or Bournemouth, where they
meet in faceless new conference centres, and Blackpool, where the venue
is the Empress Ballroom in the Winter Gardens built by Frank Matcham
in 1899 in the same opulent multi-tier style as he used for his theatres of
the same period. In a BBC interview on the subject of oratory conducted
by Melvyn Bragg in 1988, Michael Heseltine MP, one of the most charis-
matic of modern Tory politicians, spoke as any seasoned actor would of
the difference between the two sorts of venue. 'I would say at once if I
have a claim to be able to make public speeches that if I have a choice
of venue it is the Winter Gardens, Blackpool. There is nothing like it: the
feeling of the audience in that building, tiered up there, towering over you.
And you can see them there, rank upon rank of them, often standing in
the big packed meetings of the Winter Gardens. Whereas in these new
buildings the hall, the carpeting and the chairs, it's all been toned down
to remove any excesses of language or of tone. You have to fight, really
fight, to try and get through to the audience. The Winter Gardens, it's
there with you.'

The fair-minded will reply that this is a criticism of particular new halls
and that the excellence of the old does not prove that a new space cannot
be equally as exciting. Suppose that an architect, who has studied the
spirit of these old theatres, not to imitate them but to emulate them, and
who knows how to cluster the audience around the performer, is able to
achieve a fine new theatre as good as the old ones in its spiritual quality
and possessing infinitely more agreeable accommodation backstage for the
performers and in the bars and foyers for the audience, can any convincing
arguments remain in favour of the old? This author believes there are at
least two which deserve to be noted and puzzled over.

The first was advanced by Joachim Herz, then newly appointed director
of the Komische Oper in East Berlin, at the same Munich conference of
1977. At a televised debate at the stage of the Cuvilliés Theatre, a group
including this author debated theatre space old and new for two long hours.
Suddenly towards the end August Everding, Intendant of the Bayerisches
Staatsoper at Munich, which occupies both the Cuvillies and the neo-

classical Nationaltheater that Munich had reconstructed rather than replaced after the Second World War, threw Herz this difficult question: 'You have been director at Leipzig of a fine modern theatre, your present theatre is an old theatre restored, which do you prefer as a director of productions?' Herz thought for a few minutes and then answered in words as recalled by this author: 'We live today in an age of dissonance. The mid eighteenth century and the end of the last century were ages of consonance. Then society was confident of its values and believed in progress. In the 1950s and early 1960s we were confident. At such times it was natural to want to match the performance on the stage to the building in which stage and auditorium were placed. But now as in earlier periods and as in the 1920s and 1930s we are no longer confident of aims and values. Now there is no motive for matching style of theatre production and of architecture. Therefore in this age of dissonance I would prefer the stimulation and the contrast of producing new work in old theatres.' That was in 1977 – the reader must judge whether the same would be true today.

The second reason is the one implied by much of what has been achieved by Peter Brook, though never explicitly stated. This is the presence of ghosts in old theatres.

Since moving to France in 1970, Peter Brook's work has probably been equally divided between the disused theatre he occupied in 1974, Les Bouffes du Nord, which lies behind the Gare du Nord and was built in 1876, and a series of peripatetic performances round the world. The string of works created for and by his international company have been performed in a variety of 'found spaces', that is space that had not been designed for theatrical performances, whether palace, village clearing or quarry. Little or nothing would be done to these spaces, and when it was it consisted of the almost imperceptible retouching, or 'distressing' as they say in the antique furniture trade, carried out by Brook's remarkable designer Chloe Obolensky, who is now famous for her designs for *The Mahabharata* and who is one of Brook's most important collaborators.

In contrast to Gallic improvisation in Paris in 1974, the process of finding a New York space in 1987 with the right resonances for *The Mahabharata* and adapting it so that it would have the same texture as Brook's rapidly and cheaply improvised Bouffes du Nord became a multi-million dollar matter. After a long search they finally settled on the 1904 Majestic Theatre, decidedly not a movie palace but rather a J. B. McElfatrick legitimate theatre of great quality, close to the Brooklyn Academy of Music. As in Paris, Brook and his party pulled back the corrugated iron and crept into the deserted theatre with their flashlights, thus re-enacting once again the legend of the Sleeping Beauty. At the Majestic, as before in Paris, they knew immediately that they had found the right space. But this was not Paris in that there were more regulations and authorities to be satisfied. Architects and engineers were engaged. Stage level was raised 6 feet (1.8m) above the old so as to bring half of the acting area through the proscenium arch right up to the dress circle (or first mezzanine) which had been extended down towards the new acting area with a further six rows. The resulting theatre space was larger than that of Les Bouffes du Nord but with a reduced capacity, 900 in 1988 compared with 1,800 in 1904.

At the Majestic, Chloe Obolensky and technical director Jean-Guy Lecat excelled themselves. Both Brook's *Mahabharata* and his subsequent *Cherry Orchard* demonstrated the intense theatricality of the space in different ways. The cynical Michael Kimmelman in the *New York Times*, 25 October 1987, had suggested that the Majestic was 'the architectural equivalent of the intentionally worn look of a Ralph Lauren jacket'. Brook protested to this author that 'we did nothing really'. But Kimmelman was accurate in saying that 'the Majestic is largely but not entirely an authentic ruin with what used to be the theatre's boxes intentionally distressed or touched up to look elegantly old and worn by a crew of skilled scenic designers.' Theatre people accept that art conceals art and that apparent spontaneity is often a painstaking creation. At the Majestic many puzzled over the elaborateness of the artifice. To understand why, one has to look below the elegantly romantic surface.

Brook claims that early in the 1970s theatrical imagery, which is so realisable within a proscenium arch theatre, became less important to him than theatrical energy. In his rediscovered theatres in both Paris and Brooklyn he uses theatrical associations of the old theatres he has found, both as images in themselves and as a source of energy. His success suggests that an old theatre may be a sacred place and that the ghosts of past productions are a reality and, if friendly, are a benign presence. Slap on too much new paint and too much gilding and those ghosts will leave. One is reminded of the eccentric architect who once said that you should never let a brass band play in a concert hall as it ruined the acoustics for future concerts. It is just possible that he was right. Certainly when the Rose was rediscovered in 1989 few would have disagreed with journalist Lesley Garner who noted in the *Daily Telegraph* of 17 May that the Rose, standing no more than a few inches above the mud, was alive: 'Theatre exists in voice and movement, in the communication of ideas and emotions between performer and audience. This focussing of power can be felt in certain auditoria as though the intensity of human emotions is still trapped between stage and seating. You can feel it in the Greek theatres like Epidaurus, which have an almost tangible spirit of place.'

Les Bouffes du Nord and the Majestic naturally had a sense of theatrical place since they had once been theatres. They were 'found spaces' only in that they were disused theatres found by theatre people and reconverted to theatre use. Of a different order are the spaces which have never been

SECTION, BEFORE   SECTION, AFTER

14 and 15   The 1,800 seat Majestic Theater, Brooklyn built by J. B. McElfatrick
in 1904 and rescued by director Peter Brook and designer Chloe Obolensky in
1988 for a season which started with their productions of *The Mahabharata* and *The
Cherry Orchard*, shown here in a photograph from *New York*, 7 March 1988. The
sections below are from *Progressive Architecture*, April 1988. The architects for the
revival of the old Majestic were Hardy, Holzman, Pfeiffer Associates.

theatres and which have nevertheless been converted into theatres with surprising success, such as the sadly defunct Roundhouse, a circular nineteenth-century steam-engine shed converted to theatre use in London in the 1960s, a library in New York, now The Joseph Papp Public Theater, Schechner's Performing Arts Garage also in New York, which was just that, a garage, and Mnouchkine's Cartoucherie de Vincenne, the ammunitions factory outside Paris that has provided very different, very chic environmental spaces for shows as diverse as *1789, La Tragédie de Sihanouk* and *Richard III.*

Ariane Mnouchkine, interviewed in 1989 for *Theatres* by Gaelle Breton published in 1989, made the general case for 'found space' in explaining why 'for us La Cartoucherie is almost the ideal place. Of course the ceiling is rather low, and the truss rods sometimes get in our way, but it is a house, a theatre, a large gracefully shaped umbrella made out of solid material that can be sculpted, painted, arranged and veneered. . . . Why does a factory often make a better theatre than any other place? Because it has been built to house creations, productions, works, inventions and explosions! La Cartoucherie is the opposite of the "black box" theatre – the famous multi-purpose technical box which in fact bristles with limitations. A few years ago, directors were saying: "Give us a neutral space and we'll handle the rest!" I'm not sure if they would still say the same thing today. I say an empty space, but an inspiring empty space that can be filled with images.'

To many architects this preference for space that is not purpose made seems at best incomprehensible and at worst an insult to their profession. (It is said that at a meeting of the National Theatre building committee in the 1960s, Denys Lasdun suggested that Peter Brook would prefer a bombed site in Brixton to anything he, an architect, could design. Brook answered 'Yes'.) To the experimental and the avant-garde, the 'found space' clearly advertises that theatre played here is going to be different from theatre played in a normal theatre building. The audience gets a buzz from the feeling that the players have come to town and taken over this particular structure. In addition the redundant church, munitions factory or whatever will have its own ghosts from the past plus the good will of a community relieved that a use has been found for a fine old building. And yet neither this argument nor Mnouchkine's love of factories quite adds up to a convincing set of reasons for preferring the 'found space' to the purpose built.

It is possible that there is also a more mundane explanation. This is that the opportunity to comprehend immediately the character of an existing space and its dramatic potential is what attracts the theatre director and stage designer as opposed to the architect. Architects' plans are notoriously difficult to understand and when new theatres are envisaged from the ground up theatre directors feel that they have to give complete trust to an alien profession. Proposals for the new theatre are expressed in an often impenetrable foreign language although there should always be a friendly theatre consultant to act as go-between and translate the different argots. In a 'found space' the director, with the help of his or her stage designer, can quickly envisage what is possible. The architect for its conversion to theatrical purpose then becomes more the facilitator than a distinct creative force. Thus the theatre director and his or her group find it easier to control the design of 'found space' than the design of the purpose built.

If one considers the attraction of deserted theatres imaginatively reused, one soon becomes aware of a poetic dimension alongside the practical. David Freeman, founder in the late 1970s of Opera Factory of London and of Zurich and director of many imaginative, innovative reinterpretations of both opera and drama classics in the 1980s, summed up to this author his motives for endorsing the adaptive reuse of an old theatre in preference to either a conventional restoration or the creation of a new theatre: 'I seek in one building both the sensuality of the old and the flexibility of the new.' For Freeman conventionally restored theatres are dead museums while most new theatres have the soul of a hospital. And so, like Brook, he seeks the ruined theatre which will retain its mystery as well as permit unconventional staging of plays and operas both old and new.

The 'found space' solution, namely the adaptive reuse of a deserted theatre or of any building, is undoubtedly a valid alternative to the complex and difficult task of creating a new theatre from the ground up. (The two merged in 1992 when in Addison, Texas, artistic director of Center Theater, Kelly Cotten, and his architect Gary Cunningham claimed not to have built a theatre but 'our own found space', thus signalling a new meaning for an already difficult to define phrase.) The following chapters examine how people from the different worlds of architecture and of theatre approach the design of a new purpose-built theatre.

Chapter 7

Directors and designers

Directors often preside over the opening of a theatre they had little hand in creating. They are interviewed enthusing over what must be the best theatre of the age/city/country. The press office swings into action, producing 'puffs' in a centuries-old theatrical tradition. Even the grandest of arts correspondents trot out the untested superlatives. Usually the director is secretly appalled at the size, complexity and sheer unreadiness of the theatre but his professional training enables him to exude confidence. In contrast another professional skill, that of not being afraid at the last moment to adjust, alter or even abandon a whole mise en scene, is of no use whatsoever. Decisions taken years ago by others or, occasionally, by the director himself, perhaps when his or her mind was on more immediate matters, are now, literally, cast in concrete. It is all too late. All must then be for the best in the best of all possible theatres.

In 1976, when Britain's National Theatre opened, Public Relations Officer John Goodwin was pouring oil on unfinished stage machinery. He could look up and see on his noticeboard an enlarged photocopy of the prayer of Walter Kerr, erstwhile drama critic of the *New York Times*, which was printed in *Thirty Plays hath November: Pain and Pleasure in the Contemporary Theatre* published in 1969. 'O Lord give me successes that are not simply successes but contain just enough quality to let me feel I haven't wasted my life. Give me long enough runs to pay my bills and then, when I am rich, get me into repertory. . . . Let me be praised, let me be paid, let me be proud . . . [give] me the fortitude to survive my collaborators. Humbly, I ask all this and Sardi's too. But dear Lord . . . whatever else you give me out of your unbounded generosity never, never, never give me a building.' Goodwin's master, Peter Hall, had been on the building committee of the National Theatre in the late 1960s but had taken little part in its planning until the early 1970s. In 1973 he endorsed what had been done – he had little option – and, perhaps because all the decisions had been taken on the larger theatres, concentrated on breathing life into the previously abandoned Cottesloe. Hall and his head of design, John Bury, were opening somebody else's theatres. Ironically, they had themselves conceived another theatre in which to date neither of them has worked, the Barbican in the City of London to which the Royal Shakespeare Company was to transfer its London base some six years later in 1982. Hall and Bury opened a theatre conceived by Sir Laurence Olivier and his building committee while Trevor Nunn and his team were to open the Barbican conceived by Hall and Bury. (The use of the word 'conceive' identifies the creation of the sketch designs and models for a stage and auditorium and its translation on to the architect's drawing board rather than the subsequent business of architectural detailing.)

The design of the Barbican auditorium and stage had evolved between 1965 and 1968 through models which emerged from the Royal Shakespeare studios in Stratford. In 1968 the completed design was presented to the press by the architects, together with Hall and Bury. The situation was different at the National where Olivier the director had always been more eclectic in his relationship with stage designers. Thus as the Olivier and Lyttelton theatres evolved there was no equivalent to Bury. The stage design element in the National Theatre architect selection committee had been represented by John Piper who was rather more distinguished as an easel artist than as a scenic artist. The building committee appointed in 1964 had two stage designers: Roger Furse, doyen of romantic designers whose career had started in 1934, and Tanya Moiseiwitsch, whose collaboration with Tyrone Guthrie had been crucial to the evolution of the Guthrie thrust stage theatre. The building committee at the National was very much a gathering of eloquent and distinguished men of the theatre trusted by director Olivier, while the Barbican Theatre had been developed by a more effective sort of committee, the committee of two. What they had in common was that neither director was to work in the theatre he had created, Olivier having had to retire tragically in 1973 owing to ill health while at the RSC Hall had already stepped down in 1968.

Thus we shall never know whether Olivier and Hall would have recognised problems in either the Barbican or the Olivier which were, in a sense, of their own making. At the Barbican the RSC have complained bitterly about a building planned to the brief of Peter Hall who should perhaps have paused to consider the psychological effect of burying the backstage of the Barbican entirely below ground. Olivier as actor might have discovered that a contributory cause of the Olivier Theatre's unwieldy scale was his absolute decree that, while it was to have an open stage and no proscenium arch, under no circumstances were spectators to look across the acting area and see the audience opposite. In this way the fundamental quality of open stages was abandoned, that of the audience being constantly reminded of themselves, as Guthrie had noted at Elsinore (with, ironically, Olivier) in 1936 and at Edinburgh in 1948. In its place the notion of a stage in the corner of a room was embraced with the disastrous result of an auditorium with too great a volume for too few spectators and a stage too wide and too often lacking in focus unless either filled with expensive scenery or emptied save for one or two actors positioned dead centre.

In New York in the late 1950s an equally distinguished committee of leaders of the theatre profession had dug its own grave at the Vivian Beaumont. By the time of its opening in 1965 the prime movers were no longer in control, having been fired in typical Broadway fashion. Herbert Blau and Jules Irving were contracted to open a theatre conceived by Elia Kazan and others. The architect was Eero Saarinen who in 1958 had been invited to collaborate with stage designer Joe Mielziner. Together they designed a stage and auditorium to a brief confusingly administered by another oversized building committee. That brief had been all too accurately summed up by the chief executive of the Beaumont at the time, Robert Whitehead, who wrote in the *New York Herald Tribune* of 30 August 1959: 'What we will try to get is a compromise between the 18th century proscenium theatre where the action is set behind a frame and a Roman theatre [he referred to an illustration of the antique amphitheatre at Vaucluse, France] where it comes out into the audience.' To the inherent confusion of compromise must be added Whitehead's misunderstanding of the dramatic and architectural nature of both eighteenth-century and Roman theatre.

Thus, if one examines the role of the director in creating those theatres regarded as pinnacles of the English-speaking pyramid, there is little evidence of follow through, of director welcoming actors and audiences into a theatre on the design of which he or she had collaborated with the architect. The committee and the passage of time – in the case of the Barbican as long as seventeen years from conception to opening night – decreed discontinuity.

There are other examples. At the Nottingham Playhouse in 1963 John Neville and Frank Dunlop opened the theatre with a stage specified by Val May. A few years later, Val May puzzled his successors at the Theatre Royal, Bristol, by tearing out the raked eighteenth-century stage, complete with working machinery, and substituting a flat scenic stage with an expensively high gridiron. The latter would have been more appropriate to late nineteenth- and twentieth-century picture-frame proscenium theatres than to the Georgian Theatre Royal, Bristol, whose theatrical character had always been so dependent on a raked stage with acting forestage extending out into the auditorium. The forestage and hence sightlines have still not been restored but the scenic stage behind the proscenium is once again semi-permanently raked with a false stage, raked at 1:12, and set expensively upon the unnecessarily flat stage of 1972.

Throughout the 1960s and 1970s the professions of both theatre and architecture were equally frustrated by the fact that the length of time it took to create a building exceeded either the professional lifespan of a director at the top of his profession or the likely stay in a particular city of an ambitious younger director. In post-war Britain only one director of stature other than Tyrone Guthrie became so obsessed with a particular approach to theatre architecture that he got together a team of designers and architects to create a theatre and a team of directors and actors to work in it. The man was Michael Elliott (1931–84) and the theatre he created, the Royal Exchange, Manchester, opened in 1976.

At the age of 28 Elliott had founded the 59 Theatre Company in 1959 at the old Lyric, Hammersmith, a venture that was as short lived as the title suggests although the team of co-director Caspar Wrede, designer Richard Negri and lighting designer Richard Pilbrow were to collaborate in the West End and on classics such as the Vanessa Redgrave *As You Like It* at Stratford-upon-Avon in 1961. Having been passed over in 1962 when the Old Vic Theatre Company was transmuted into the National Theatre Company, Elliott upped and left London for Manchester to create the 69 Theatre Company in temporary premises. This later became the Royal Exchange Theatre Company when the theatre of that name opened in 1976. Between 1964 and 1970 he had sat on the building committee of the National Theatre and it was largely this experience which led him to doubt the conventional wisdom. On the BBC's Third Programme in 1973 Elliott mused, 'visiting the several brand new regional civic theatres, or as one leans on the parapet of Waterloo Bridge pondering the huge mushrooming concrete of the new National Theatre, all one's doubts centre round one question – was this the right theatre to build now?'

Elliott suggested that Britain had refused to learn from the continent of Europe. Should we be putting up any more of these buildings at what Elliott considered to be 'near the end of a major theatre building boom'? He continued, 'isn't it time we stopped lumbering our grandchildren with our mistakes – understandable mistakes, but mistakes nevertheless? Don't we need something different, something less expensive, less daunting, less expressive of civic or national pride, more reflective of changing taste – something perhaps less permanent? In future shouldn't we try to attain a certain lightness and sense of improvisation, and sometimes build in materials that do not require a bomb to move them? In short, shouldn't we *stop* building for posterity?'

Elliott quoted Guthrie's experience in starting with a conversion of 'found space' at the Assembly Hall in Edinburgh, followed by a tent at Stratford, Ontario, before the present permanent Festival Theatre was built. He quoted the success of London's low-cost Roundhouse and Young Vic in attracting young theatregoers. In addition to advocating the search for light, warmth and immediacy in architecture he suggested that a small company with a single auditorium would avoid the polarisation found in the large civic repertory theatres between the main house and the studio, 'between the large expensive grand, square and boring on the one hand and the intimate, cheap, informal, exciting left wing on the other'. He abhorred 'huge, inflexible, hard to demolish buildings' which engendered 'huge, inflexible, hard to demolish institutions'.

All this had led him to his own solution: the 700-seat three-level theatre in the round which was technologically totally contemporary (and still is seventeen years later) but was also a strong evocation of the Elizabethan theatre. This exotic theatre structure was set in the middle of the huge Royal Exchange, a mammoth building in which cotton futures had been traded at the turn of the century when Manchester was still the textile capital of the world. Richard Negri, Elliott's trusted designer, conceived the essence of the structure which architects Levitt Bernstein, assisted by engineers Ove Arup and theatre consultants Theatre Projects, turned into reality.

In the evolution of theatre architecture, the Royal Exchange theatre structure is crucial not simply because it is an original and magnificently engineered theatre in the round but because of its verticality. The three levels – Elliott once wished for four – give it a splendid elegance which allows the actor to stand proud, 'wrapping the audience like a scarf around the neck on a cold winter's day', as the tall Elliott once said. Too many theatres are conceived flatly in two dimensions with that part of the audience seated aloft largely ignored as second-class citizens. Michael Elliott's team had experimented for fifteen years in various theatres including five or six annual exercises at Wimbledon School of Art and Design, where Richard Negri ran the theatre course, and in a temporary trial structure in the Royal Exchange itself. Thus the theatre designed in 1974 and opened in 1976 was probably the most carefully considered innovative theatre ever constructed in the English-speaking world with the possible exception of the Arena Stage, Washington. The latter opened in 1961 and was designed by architect Harry Weese after his client, Zelda Fichandler, had experimented for eleven years in various buildings with the artistic possibilities (except possibly verticality) of the arena stage form.

After his experience on the National building committee Elliott had been passionate in his advocacy of impermanence and 'the importance of more transitory and of less permanent buildings. From a palace you can rule an empire but you will not find a manger anywhere but in a stable.' Claims for the efficacy of theatre simplicity are familiar, especially in Britain, but what is unique about the Royal Exchange is that for once the energy of experiment was tempered with the wisdom of experience. The result was one of the least institutional of theatres which nevertheless has become central to the cultural life of the city of Manchester. Elliott's early death in 1984 robbed the world of theatre of a philosopher who practised successfully what he preached eloquently. Such men are rare.

The Royal Exchange is Britain's best-known theatre-in-the-round. There are a handful of other dedicated directors, who, in the belief that theatre-in-the-round is the straightest route to theatrical heaven, have succeeded

16 An actor's view of the Royal Exchange Theatre, Manchester in its first year of operation, 1976. The theatre was conceived by director Michael Elliott and stage designer Richard Negri. The team which turned a vision into reality was led by architects Levitt Bernstein Associates.

in creating their own theatres. In the late 1980s Peter Cheeseman exchanged Stephen Joseph's 1952 conversion of a cinema in Stoke-on-Trent for a purpose-built theatre-in-the-round. In Scarborough, where Joseph founded his first theatre-in-the-round company in 1955, Alan Ayckbourn now holds sway. In London Sam Walters opened his new Orange Tree Theatre in early 1991. There are further examples in North America where theatre-in-the-round has a longer pedigree stretching back before Zelda Fichandler in Washington, DC, to the Penthouse Theater in the University of Washington, Seattle, designed for Glen Hughes in the early 1940s. None has quite the brilliance, or the vertical quality, of the Royal Exchange.

Generally when directors call for an original solution to the problem of designing a contemporary theatre one is wary of the outcome. This is because directors live most of their lives in the present: the present play, the production weekend in ten days time and possibly the next season only six months hence. Although directors must plan ahead to balance their budget and to employ their actors, they still have to make the right decision on the field of battle. The director is the field commander who must lead and, if necessary, countermand his or her own carefully laid plan of battle. Decisions in the field are reached in a totally different way from those reached at headquarters. Unfortunately this has not inhibited architects and building committees, genuinely impressed with the director's latest triumph on the field of battle, from making the mistake of inviting a master tactician to decide strategy. In such a situation the director generally has had little time to plan what he or she will be doing in five years time or indeed to guess what resources will be available. Inevitably when asked about the design of a theatre the director retreats into generalities and asks for the maximum extent of every technical feature in the hope of being granted half.

Just occasionally directors get all that they ask for: in the late 1970s Peter Stein had designed for him the ultimate adaptable theatre. This was a high-tech conversion of 'found space', Eric Mendelsohn's Berlin cinema of 1927. The cost, DM 82 million in 1981, for a single adaptable theatre space lacking rehearsal rooms, workshops, etc., exceeded the total cost of Britain's National Theatre with its three auditoriums and full support facilities. And yet within less than a decade Peter Stein was bored with what was the biggest mechanical box of tricks in Europe, including seventy-eight 7m by 3m (23 feet by 9 feet 10 inches) hydraulic platforms, and resigned from the position of director although in 1990 he was still occasionally working there.

In Britain the ideal had been rarely attained until the National and the Barbican were built. In 1922 Harley Granville Barker had set out in *The Exemplary Theatre* the requirements of a modern theatre company with a classical repertory. When coming to the architectural requirements Granville Barker went straight to the core of the problem. 'A double question is involved: the physical focussing of attention and the relative importance of one's own concentration upon the play and of being in touch with one's neighbours.' He rejected both the circus, (by which he meant the in-the-round solution) and the frontal theatre with long straight rows facing the stage in which 'people sat blinkered like horses. However excellent the performance the whole affair would be as flat as if – however excellent the dinner – the diners sat at a long table all facing one way.'

This is good sense. But then Granville Barker demanded the building of a theatre which in a single auditorium would provide both Shakespeare and also classical Greek actor-audience relationships as well as the picture-frame proscenium. He concluded ominously 'a theatre can undoubtedly be so designed as to provide, not only the picture stage, but a platform with footlights abolished and suitable entrances for Elizabethan plays: it can provide, too, for the converting of a part of the stalls into an arena for a Greek chorus. The architectural problem is not an easy one – but it can be solved. An effectively disappearing proscenium should not be hard to contrive.'

Although Granville Barker never achieved his own theatre the impossible dream of a mechanically adaptable playhouse, initially as a response to the demand for authentic staging conditions for different parts of the classical repertoire, had been dreamt. Nearly seventy years later the truly adaptable theatre has turned out to be as elusive as the philosopher's stone. Architects and theatre design consultants, one after the other, have claimed they have achieved the adaptable multi-form auditorium. But usually all they have done is to have trundled around massive blocks of seats which, because the rake and general characteristics of the seating are unaltered, give a sameness to each and every arrangement. There is also a limit to flexibility in the proscenium zone; you cannot change a theatre such as the Royal Shakespeare at Stratford-upon-Avon into a thrust stage by adding a few rows at each side of the stage where select members of the audience sit uneasily on benches like reluctant ice hockey players. Equally one cannot convert the single rake of the essentially modern Loeb theatre at Harvard into a Shakespearian thrust simply by splitting the front ten rows and repositioning them on wagons each side of the acting area. At Stratford-upon-Avon the centre of gravity of 95 per cent of the audience remains unchanged while at the Loeb the lack of any adjustment to the vertical relationship of audience to actor makes the seats on the sides of the so-called thrust irredeemably second class.

'Adaptability' and 'flexibility' are dealt with in greater detail in Chapters 8 and 9. Here the point is simply that it is often the director of the theatre who asks loud and clear for the very adaptability that so obviously doesn't work. In 1962, at a conference held at Manchester University in England, Tyrone Guthrie rumbled three years before its opening the inherent fatal compromise of the Vivian Beaumont demanded by its artistic directorate.

Guthrie had studied the plans for this while he was collaborating on the design of the new thrust stage theatre at Minneapolis which was to carry his name: 'We stewed over the plans of the big American National Theatre which is going to be built at the Lincoln Centre. This does attempt to combine the two (proscenium and thrust). You press an electronic this and pull a something else that and lo and behold! a whole lot of seats shuffle out of sight and disappear into thin air. An apron stage thrusts itself forward and you are in another kind of form. On paper it is extremely ingenious . . . but my belief is that it is neither as good as it could be as a proscenium theatre, nor as good as it can be as an open stage; that in order to get the flexibility of changing between the two, you have to spend a great deal of money on buttons and machinery and so on, and when it has all occurred it is still a compromise, an exceedingly clever compromise but unmistakeably a compromise.' Guthrie was right about the Beaumont where the moving parts locked up solid within a decade and which never really succeeded as a thrust stage but only as an inordinately wide scenic theatre (the machinery was removed in 1992). In Britain, at the outset of the design process Lasdun wisely dissuaded the building committee of the National from their original idea of a similarly adaptable theatre.

Before setting out to solve the problems presented by the artistic director the architect may meet another character who could play a role in the design process. Director or building committee will often turn to a resident stage designer as one who, as a fellow designer, must be first cousin to an architect and understand the aesthetics of architecture, and, because of working with actors and creating a world for them to inhabit, must also understand the aesthetics of theatre. Enter therefore the stage designer as middleman (the involvement of the stage designer's cousin, the lighting designer, who often translated him- or herself into a 'theatre consultant', is kept for a later chapter).

Surprisingly the stage designer has rarely taken a positive role in theatre architecture. Gordon Craig wrote about the art of the theatre but did not design any theatre buildings. Norman Bel Geddes drew and drew but saw none of his theatres realised. In the eighteenth century a distinguished family of scenic designers, the Galli-Bibienas, did create theatres and often led architects to great effect. But such success is rare. Jo Mielziner wrote eloquently of the design of theatres in *The Shape of Our Theatres* but fared less well when judged by the reality of his role in the design of the Vivian Beaumont Theatre. Mention has already been made of the achievements of John Bury at the Barbican, Richard Negri at the Royal Exchange and Tanya Moiseiwitsch at the Sheffield Crucible after the death of Tyrone Guthrie. But after that the list dries up and about the only other stage designer to play a vital role in the creation of a new theatre in recent decades has been John Napier. In 1979 Napier, who in 1976 had been responsible with Chris Dyer for the variant on the Stratford main stage which carried the balconies through the concealed proscenium arch and round behind the acting area, sketched the potential for conversion of the auditorium shell of the old 1879 theatre, then a rehearsal and conference space, into what in 1986 became the Swan under the guidance of architect Michael Reardon. Why is it, these exceptions apart, that the stage designer does not often succeed in the world of theatre architecture?

The most likely reason is that designers, like directors, live in a different time frame from architects and theatre consultants. But in addition their visual aesthetics are fundamentally different to that of the architect. The stage designer works from a number of givens and although he will rarely admit it thrives on limitation. His or her starting points are the text, the stage on which he must design and the approach of the director to the production. The stage designer works at the edge of what is affordable and of what is realistically possible. It would be nice to rebuild the theatre for every show – and stage designers of the mega-mechanical musicals fashionable in the 1980s tried to do just that. But generally budgets do not allow and the wise stage designer accepts the theatre as it is just as the easel painter generally accepts that the canvas is rectangular and will hang vertically in a frame.

Stage designers or scenographers are thus quite different from theatre designers or architects. The theatre designer or architect designs a theatre for a range of scenic expression. It must not only serve different stage designers but also the actor and the audience in different moods for different plays. The stage designer on the other hand has a specific design problem and must obey the sort of technical equivalent of the Aristotelian unities: a particular occasion, a particular play, a particular production and often a particular building. The architect and stage designer have more to talk about when it comes to repertory storage, mechanical systems, etc.

Stage designers also take time to respond to new spatial challenges. The reaction of leading British stage designers to the Olivier and Barbican theatres in the late 1980s, some five or more years after their opening, underwent an extraordinary change. At first the designers had been appalled at the problem of filling these wide open spaces. In April 1983 Ralph Koltai was quoted in *Plays and Players* thus: 'The Barbican is a problem. So is the Olivier but it is a bit better now [the stage had been raised 1 foot 1 inch (330mm)] . . . I would rather be at the Aldwych which has its problems than in the Barbican.' Koltai forgot that the only balcony the Royal Shakespeare Company could build for Juliet at the Aldwych that would have been seen by everybody in the audience was one no more than 3 feet 6 inches (1.1m) high and located downstage centre. Koltai continued on the Barbican: 'this theatre was largely conceived by Peter Hall and John Bury in the '60s in relation to their work in *The Wars of the Roses* at Stratford. Now 20 years on it's no longer like that.' By this

Koltai meant that the directors of the Royal Shakespeare were no longer predisposed towards epic theatre and consequently no longer yearned to be liberated from the confines of the proscenium arch. Instead they were asking of the stage designers that they create the focus that the new wide theatres appeared to lack. In the late 1970s and early 1980s tighter production budgets meant smaller armies or crowds of citizens. Ironically the money for people had run out just when the classical theatre was moving out of the Old Vic and Aldwych where as in old Drury the words of the Chorus in *Henry V*, 'a crooked figure may in little place attest a million' still ring true. The same budgets were also limiting the amount of scenery that could be built for the bigger stages. As a consequence productions in the first few years of the big national theatres looked thin and stretched. A new scenic approach had not yet emerged.

In 1984 director Richard Eyre said of the designer of the National Theatre's *Guys and Dolls* and *The Rivals*: 'John Gunter has made clear that there is no point being puritanical in that Olivier space. It is almost a vulgar place so it's no use being timid.' Others equally brave followed and soon British stage designers, confronted with unfamiliarly wide canvases, were emulating their European counterparts in their preparedness to express the play or opera with a broad brush. Those large theatres, originally designed to bring the English classics and new works to a new audience, turned out to be wonderful locales for musicals and expressionist theatre in the European style, very different from the hugger-mugger and very English improvisatory style of *Nicholas Nickleby*, shoe-horned into the Aldwych in 1980 and subsequently spread all round the Booth Theater on Broadway. *Nickleby* was an extremely successful synthesis of actor, audience and stage architecture unachievable in the more efficient but colder and wider Barbican. The latter was, however, a most effective breeding ground for *Les Misérables*.

In New York the Vivian Beaumont, which had been in terminal decline ever since its opening twenty years earlier, sprang back to life in the late 1980s not with new plays but with a series of brilliantly bold set designs by Tony Walton: half Chicago for *The Front Page* and a revolving liner for *Anything Goes*, both too big for moving to Broadway. The open stage had become, paradoxically, a designer's theatre. That this was not anticipated seems surprising in retrospect. Even Elliott was off target when he wrote in the *Architectural Review* of February 1972 of the Sheffield Crucible thrust stage on its opening in 1971: 'The actor's position in the auditorium is very powerful but there is little scenic possibility, it is an abstract platform.' At Sheffield, after only five years, the moat, which separated the stage from the audience and swallowed the beam of light so none should spill on to the feet of the front row, was filled in and has remained so for almost all the time. Scenery spread to cover the entire 40-feet (13m) wide area with light spilling everywhere as indeed it always had at its precursor, the

Assembly Hall in Edinburgh. And at Manchester's Royal Exchange Michael Elliott, who had at the outset insisted puritanically that the old wood block floor which extended equally over foyer and acting area was not to be covered, reversed his earlier philosophy to create a *Moby Dick* in 1984 which was described as 'the ultimate in theatrical illusion'. The theatre became a realistic Nantucket whaler, the mime so convincing that the audience ducked to avoid the splash when the longboat capsized, and, at the close, marvelled at a great white whale, created by an inflatable stage cloth, which almost swallowed the theatre.

Until the Guthrie thrust stage theatres had been used for some years, the British theatre establishment continued to believe that scenery's natural habitat was behind the proscenium arch and that if there was no proscenium arch, as there could not be in an open stage theatre, there would consequently be little or no scenery. Indeed three years after its opening one of the architects of the Chichester Festival Theatre confessed in a debate recorded in *Actor and Architect* edited by Stephen Joseph and published in 1964: 'At the beginning we simply didn't expect scenery. We always did expect props – pretty big ones even – and some sort of permanent set that could be changed from season to season. I suppose after that it becomes a question of where you can draw the line – painting the set a new colour? Changing it between the plays? The chance is that within a year your building will be used quite differently from what you had expected.'

The stages of Chichester, Sheffield and the Royal Exchange were all originally intended to limit the designer. At Stratford-upon-Avon's Swan Theatre, the RSC management deliberately omitted any sort of scenic get-in door in the fond but doomed idea that thereby they could ban scenery from the Swan. This is but one example of the sort of self-denying ordinance that management and directors have attempted in response to the call of Robert Edmund Jones, the distinguished American scene designer who wrote in 1941 in *The Dramatic Imagination* that 'the best thing that could happen to our theatre at this moment would be for playwrights and actors and directors to be handed a bare stage on which no scenery could be placed, and then told that they must write and act and direct for this stage. In no time at all we would have the most exciting theatre in the world.' The idea that a theatre should be able to function with its stage bare recurs from generation to generation: in 1990 Stephen Sondheim stated on BBC Radio that 'any show should be able to work without scenery. Scenery should be extra value.'

Were Jones and Sondheim right? Scenery can never be abolished, nor should it be. But neither should its needs be paramount. Precisely because the good stage designer will revel in any scenic opportunity it is dangerous to let him or her loose on designing a theatre. The designer's first instinct will be to push back the boundaries of the area he or she can command.

In the 1960s the scenic designers' intervention may have consisted largely in wanting the auditorium painted black so as to heighten the effect of his or her designs which seemed diluted in the traditional plush and gilt of a proscenium arch theatre. (One or two designers did succeed in getting their theatres painted black although most of these have now been lightened, the sombreness having been seen as a mistake.) But soon designers were wanting unlimited scenic opportunity to do anything anywhere. In 1976 the French stage designer Pierre Chaix had written: 'the spectacle should no longer be confined to the stage but should invade the entire space.'

However, fashions changed and good sense prevailed. In the 1980s British designers began to realise how lucky they were not to have inherited a free space with unlimited scenographic potential. In the 1970s the directors of the Glasgow Citizens had welcomed the suggestion of a move to a bigger stage in a theatre with better sightlines – and indeed there was a short-lived scheme for rehousing them in just such a draughty hangar. Ten years later they realised how much of an asset was the old Royal Princess's Theatre of 1878 with its three wrap-round levels of seating and its 25 feet 6 inches (7.8m) wide proscenium. It is highly significant that Britain's most sensationally theatrical company, under a direction renowned both for 'divine distractions of decadence' and clarity in presenting the classics, should occupy the playhouse with the narrowest of prosceniums (only a few inches wider than Bristol's Theatre Royal and even narrower than Michael Price's very different but equally emotionally charged Goodspeed Opera House, Connecticut, of 1887 which has a 27-feet (8.2m) wide proscenium and only 414 seats). With the tightest of budgets the Glasgow Citizens stage has never seemed small, except when designer/director Philip Prowse, or fellow designers Maria Bjornson or Stewart Laing, have wanted it to be.

One designer, William Dudley who had created the environmental promenade *Mysteries* and *Larkrise* at the Cottesloe, successfully and accidentally turned theatre designer with his realisation in 1990, also in Glasgow, of director Bill Bryden's dream: 'We build a ship – a liner – in fact and at the end of the evening it is launched.' In the engine shed of shipbuilders Harland and Wolff Dudley created, in steel, a liner that was launched into an infinity of smoke at the end of the slipway once that half of the audience seated in three galleries formed by the steel ribs of the hull had left to help remove the timber supports prior to the launching. This ship/theatre, long and narrow with opportunities for staging the length of the vessel, held 550 seated and 350 promenading, about the same number as that for *The Mysteries* when transferred to the Lyceum ballroom/theatre in 1985. Wrote Dudley in the programme for *The Ship*: 'During the last 1000 years, the most successful European theatres have all pretty well followed the same lines and been the same size. The Shakespearean theatres, the small Victorian music halls, the Spanish courtyard theatres, all have the same dimensions, with a horseshoe of galleries above a pit-like space in the middle. All the best theatres – the theatres that actors love to act in and audiences to be in – have the same approximate size and basic ground plan. If you take away the nautical aspect, that's what I've done here in *The Ship*. . . . It's certainly the most ambitious thing I've ever designed. And after . . . well, if you take it off its slipway, it would make a very good theatre.' It is hard to argue with that, though few who saw this short-lived tour-de-force would have realised the direct design descendancy of this towering four-floor steel structure, from the Globe through Georgian theatre, penny gaff and the promenade theatre works created by Dudley and Bryden at the Cottesloe, or recognised that what was launched each night was not so much a liner but a courtyard theatre. William Dudley is that rarity, a scene designer who successfully designed a theatre structure.

But generally to entrust the design of a theatre which will not open for three, four or five years to those directors or designers who exist for the day or for the production is to risk cocooning in concrete the fashionable ideas of the moment. If a theatre is to last for longer than the single generation envisaged by Elliott in his gloomier mood, it is necessary to seek a more enduring design philosophy than that provided by those magicians of the moment, the designer and the director.

Chapter 8

Architects, engineers and the multi-purpose

In Chapter 2 it was recorded that in 1740 actor, playwright and theatre manager Colley Cibber had complained that at the Queen's Theatre in the Haymarket, designed by Sir John Vanbrugh in 1703, 'every proper quality and convenience of a good theatre had been sacrificed or neglected to show the spectator a vast triumphal piece of architecture'. However, the theatre profession's present distrust of architects stems from as recently as the second quarter of the twentieth century. In America at this time the architects began to be briefed not by actor-managers but by the owners of chains of theatres designed to maximise box office receipts. In these grand new theatres the actor or vaudeville performer could see that the money had gone into the entrance lobby and into the plasterwork of the ever larger auditorium rather than into the ever smaller backstage with ever less congenial dressing rooms. The latter were even being constructed underground to take 'advantage' of new methods of mechanical ventilation. In Britain far fewer theatres were built between the wars. But there was one which was to become a *cause célèbre*, the new Memorial Theatre at Stratford-upon-Avon which opened in April 1932.

The first Stratford theatre of 1879, a strange cross between the Castel Sant'Angelo in Rome and the architectural excesses of King Ludwig of Bavaria, was totally unlike any other British nineteenth-century theatre. It burnt in March 1926 shortly before the opening of the annual season. Bernard Shaw sent a telegram to the chairman: 'Congratulations. It will be a tremendous advantage to have a proper theatre.'

After a competition, fund-raising in America and a lot of committee meetings, the final design of the architect Elizabeth Scott, an avowed modernist, commenced construction in 1930. The director of the theatre, William Bridges-Adam, had told the *Observer* in 1928: 'The need is absolute flexibility, a box of tricks out of which the child-like mind of the producer may create whichever shape it pleases. It should be able to offer Mr Poel an Elizabethan stage after his heart's desire. It should be no less adequate to the requirements of Professor Reinhardt.'

What Stratford got would have pleased neither the advocate of the bare

Elizabethan stage nor the master of crowd spectacle. The result was a turkey and put back the cause of Shakespeare at Stratford for a generation. The architect had not lacked advisers. These had included Britain's most eminent producer, Sir Barry Jackson, and the leading modern stage designer, Norman Wilkinson, who had served Granville Barker so well with his uncluttered designs for Shakespeare at the Savoy just before the First World War.

It was mainly in the auditorium that the Stratford Memorial Theatre in 1932 differed from the present building which retains Scott's 'jam factory' façade and fine foyer almost unaltered. The original auditorium was smaller than it is now, holding 1,000 as opposed to the present 1,576. The balconies each held 200 less and the front of the circle was one row further from the proscenium arch than it is today. There were no side boxes or slips. The ceiling and auditorium walls, which survive today under later accretions, were painted cream and everywhere else was panelled wood, a variegated effect justified by each timber having been mentioned by Shakespeare.

The *Architectural Review* thought it wonderful and devoted a whole issue, June 1932, to the Stratford Theatre. Three virtues were identified. First, perfect sightlines: 'we are in a theatre in which the auditorium is in a broad arc. No pillars interrupt, there are no boxes; from every seat the stage can be seen . . . it provides everything that spectators need for seeing including very comfortable seats.' Second, the acoustic calculations: 'The shape of the theatre resembles a giant horn and is so designed that the players can be heard in all parts of the stage and the sound distributed evenly through the auditorium. The splays and the ceiling of the proscenium, together with the forestage when in use, act as reinforcement to the source of sound.' Third, the modernist use of natural materials in decoration: 'Though new theatres continue to appear in constant succession throughout the country, each newcomer, with a very occasional exception, represents no more than another step along the tiresome path of motif ornament and meaningless decoration. Since Palladio built his theatre of Vicenza there has been no development other than an increasing tendency towards vulgarity and overelaboration. . . . In the new theatre in Stratford-on-Avon materials are used with intelligence, selection is governed by fitness of purpose and designed by the nature of the material . . . the interior has a charm that could never result from the application of ornament.'

Now for a theatre person's point of view. Norman Marshall quotes in *The Other Theatre*, published in 1947, that shortly after its opening actor-manager Baliol Holloway believed: 'What we eventually got when the architects, pressure groups, quacks and empirics had finished with us was the theatre, of all theatres in England, in which it is hardest to make the audience laugh or cry.' After acting on the stage two years later he added,

'You can just about see the boiled shirts in the front row: it is like acting to Calais from the cliffs of Dover.' Later he defined more precisely the problem of 'the acreage of blank walls between the proscenium arch and the ends of the circle which completely destroy all contact between actors and audience. It is doubly hard on the actor that the audience does not realise this and is aware only of the actor's comparative ineffectiveness.'

The theatre was finally put right or at least made useful. Within three years of being appointed co-director, Anthony Quayle called in architect Brian O'Rorke and in 1951 they added a row to the front of the circle and one row of stepped boxes down the side. In 1962 the boxes advanced further while the newly raked stage created by stage designer Henry Bardon thrust forward in a shape that would become familiar in the subsequent work of John Bury. In 1976 the gallery also moved down towards the stage in steps which strengthened the architectural focus on the actor. In that year, under the tuition of John Napier and Chris Dyer, the auditorium was actually extended round the back of the acting area representing the apogee of the attempt to convert a proscenium theatre into an Elizabethan courtyard.

The lesson of Stratford-upon-Avon's story is twofold: firstly that, despite the fact that the client did say clearly what he wanted, he did not get it although he thought all was well until the opening night, secondly that the architect thought she had created what she had not: a focused intimate theatre. The theatre profession, when roused, is more vociferous than the architectural profession and the nation accepted the theatrical view: it was all the fault of the architect.

It is clear that at Stratford-upon-Avon in 1930/2 there had been a breakdown in communication between the two professions. In an earlier chapter it has been suggested that the two are in harmony when there is a consensus on the nature of theatre and no dialogue is necessary. But it is also worth remembering that in the ages of consensus theatre architecture was the responsibility of specialist architects, who were often builders themselves. Indeed their 'specialist' skills were simply theatre-building skills, 'specialist' not being a word in use in the English language before 1856. Hence the concept of a 'specialist' architect would have had no meaning until the second half of the nineteenth century. If you wanted a theatre you went to a man who built theatres (an architect who did theatres) just as if you wanted a railway engine you went to a man who built steam engines (an engineer who did steam engines).

Only in one earlier period, at the end of the eighteenth century, did theatre architecture attract the grand architects of the day who had not built theatres before. Fortunately for the architects there was, for the first time, the money available to build grand new theatres. Fortunately for the theatre there was also the money to rebuild or remodel the bit that grand architects, such as Holland, Wyatt and Smirke, invariably got wrong: the auditorium. Too often theatres built by distinguished generalist architects are not only more extravagant than those built by specialist architects but also have to have their auditoriums expensively rebuilt within ten or twenty years of opening.

In London at the end of the eighteenth century as at Stratford in the 1930s, the work of the grand architects was not successful in the eyes of either the audience or the acting profession. In 1822, a mere ten years after its opening, Benjamin Dean Wyatt's competition-winning and architecturally popular Theatre Royal, Drury Lane, had its auditorium replaced. Much the same happened up the road in Covent Garden where Robert Smirke's theatre of 1809 had to be progressively and increasingly fundamentally altered in 1812, 1813 and 1819. The verses of William Combe describing the reaction of Dr Syntax, a fictional tourist, to Smirke's Covent Garden echo down the years:

'I think' says Syntax looking round
'It is not good, this vast profound;
Too large to hear, too long to see
Full of unmeaning symmetry.'

The theatre profession's unease with the work of Wyatt at Drury Lane, Scott at Stratford-upon-Avon, Saarinen at the Vivian Beaumont and Lasdun at the Olivier and Lyttelton theatres are four examples of what can happen when distinguished architects impose a grand new solution on familiar old theatre problems. All were architects who believed that they could rethink the nature of auditorium architecture in their first attempt to design a theatre. Almost as dangerous are those who believe they are not changing anything, simply organising more effectively the elements of auditorium architecture which they perceive in other theatres, past or present, to be either random or merely decorative. This attitude too often forces to the perimeter of the space all the necessary components – stage lighting, acoustic surfaces, side seating, etc. – where they may be better organised architecturally but at the cost of drawing the eye outwards to the architecture rather than inwards to the actor. If before the show the eyes are drawn to side walls or lofty ceiling, where the leaves of the lettuce may be prettily patterned as in a spinner when the water has been removed by centrifugal force, what chance has the performer to draw the audience's attention to his part of the room? Most failures in auditorium design over the centuries have been too wide and too high or have failed to use every architectural device to draw the eye down to the front 15 feet of the acting area which should appear to float miraculously out into the audience chamber. Fail in this and the result is that the performer is pushed to the periphery of the architect's carefully articulated auditorium. The worst cases incur Cibber's wrath that all has been sacrificed 'to show the spectator a vast triumphal piece of architecture'. Today such theatres are photographed for the architectural press without either audience or actor. Architecturally they are the equivalent of monumental art galleries which seem to have been designed for the huge canvases of Rothko or Rauschenberg but in which a watercolour or a domestic-sized oil painting is lost in a vast void.

Fortunately there are a few first-time architects and some successful specialist theatre architects or theatre design consultants who listen to their clients and are prepared to study the principle of auditorium design as well as meet technical requirements. As a result there are a number of recent theatres in both Britain and America which have benefited from a healthy dialogue between the theatre and architectural professions. Nevertheless all must be on guard against a breakdown in communications. The breakdowns often happen at the outset. Sometimes they are due to the architect wanting to devote slender resources to the architectural externals rather than the theatrical internals. In other instances the cause is the architect's taking the modernist stance, alien to most theatrical precedent which generally was 'loose-fit', that the outside of the building must express its internal arrangement and vice versa. This can mean that the shape or detailing of the auditorium is sacrificed in the name of architectural 'truthfulness' of the whole.

More often the breakdown is the result of functionalist fallacy. This trap has engulfed those architects of recent generations who were trained to believe that form follows function. Such architects required that theatrical needs be written down in the form of a quantified specification: so many seats, so much legroom, perfect (always) sightlines, so many lighting bridges and a proscenium arch of this or that width. Features that cannot be measured were excluded or rather left to the architect unaided. The requisite qualities of the theatre were always described as 'intimate', 'of human scale' and so forth. Just occasionally there would be an attempt to measure these qualities. Thus for the opening of the Chichester Festival Theatre in 1961 it was suggested that a theatre would be intimate if all the seats were within 66 feet of the stage. (Why 66 feet? The old 'chain' of four rods, a translation of the European 20m, or, more likely in Sussex, the length of a cricket pitch?) In 1970 Jo Mielziner made 'field tests to determine the maximum acceptable distance between performers and the most distant row of the audience' and concluded 55 feet (16.8m) for Julie Harris in drama, slightly more for Gertrude Berg in a 'rather broad comedy' and 100 feet (30m) for Ethel Merman in anything. In the late 1960s Laurence Olivier made tests on furthest seats with Richard Pilbrow and others and thought that at over 65 feet (19.8m) it wasn't worth the audience buying a ticket. But neither Mielziner nor Olivier went on to think of how density, either in respect of space allotted to each audience member or as a consequence of superimposing tiers of audience, has a considerable bearing on how many can be accommodated within the agreed maximum distance.

Distance of furthest seat apart, a measured description of those theatres which the profession loves, such as Wyndham's or the Old Vic in London, the Lyceum or the Booth Theater in New York, would certainly condemn them as badly planned. These theatres have a number of seats with bad sightlines, a majority with short legroom plus rotten front-of-house lighting positions, etc. Yet in these theatres shows succeed in a way they do not in the newer theatres that have been built to functionally correct specifications.

Too great a reliance on function generally signals the failure on the part of architect and theatrical client either to engage in a more philosophical discussion on the nature of theatre, or to use the empirical approach of comparing and visiting theatres of all ages which all agree to be successful. To retreat behind a functional specification and leave aesthetics to the architect is like instructing the architect hired to design your new home the precise size of the rooms you need but allowing him or her to make all the decisions on furnishings and decorations.

An extreme example of this was the creation of the Kalita Humphreys Theater which opened in 1959. In the late 1950s director Paul Baker and his building committee decided to invite Frank Lloyd Wright to design a new playhouse for Dallas, Texas. After the briefest of consultations Baker and the building committee were invited to Taliesin to view the design and a model. Limousines greeted them at the airport, costly wines were served, and they were lodged in the guest apartments by a gracious Frank Lloyd Wright. Back in Dallas they realised the sheer impracticality of much of the theatre he had so grandly designed – for example the actors were to pull the scenery up ramps from the workshop to the stage as the architect disapproved of elevators – and the banality of the auditorium, with its flat rake and immensely wide acting area, 70 feet (22m), for an auditorium seating less than 500, plus non-existent lighting positions. Baker listed his concerns as tactfully as he could, mailed them to Lloyd Wright and returned to Taliesin. No limousine at the airport. On arrival he was directed to the servants' entrance and after being shown to a bare room was offered no food. At a brief meeting the next day it was explained to him that clients did not question the designs of the master architect. Baker returned and the theatre was built with only the few minor modifications that could be negotiated with Lloyd Wright's staff. The management, with the connivance of the site architect, had to conceal the scenic elevator behind 'temporary' scaffolding whenever Lloyd Wright visited, explaining that the builders were still working in that area. In 1959 the theatre opened and since then improvements have been attempted. However, so contrary is Lloyd Wright's theatre that every attempt to attend to the needs of audience and actors screws up the architectural concept and vice versa.

In the late 1980s in Britain public attitudes to architects changed most markedly. Prince Charles' campaign to open up a debate has made those who commission buildings less reverent towards the over dogmatic master architect. Prince Charles focused on the aesthetics and the liveability of architecture, qualities as vital in a theatre as its functionality. As a result clients and architects have begun to make greater efforts to talk to each other. But in the theatre there is still some way to go and much opportunity for misunderstanding.

One danger area continues to be the architectural competition, whether open or closed. It has been a tradition in Britain that the best architects do not enter competitions unless these are to be judged by their peers, i.e. fellow members of the Royal Institute of British Architects, who have an entrenched right to organise open competitions. The client, who pays for the winning entry to be built, gets little look in and it is no secret that in 1930 Elizabeth Scott's designs were not the first choice of the governors of the Stratford Memorial Theatre. The closed or limited competition in both Britain and America is rather different, in that a shortlist of architects is invited to contribute designs for a nominal fee which enables the client to take his or her rightful place as chairman of the jury. However, even then clients will find themselves very much in the hands of their architectural assessors.

There is a second danger inherent in the competition system. In order to produce attractive models and artists' impressions, the architect must design in considerable detail and in some haste the main auditorium, which must be the heart of the building. It is then very difficult to change this central element later. Thus the most critical part of the theatre is frozen much too early in the design process. If an architect is appointed before any ideas are put down on paper there is a much greater chance of a productive dialogue, though all who have engaged in building a theatre with a strong-willed architect will recall how there is rarely more than half an hour in the architect's response to suggestions from either client or consultant between 'it's really too early to go into that sort of detail' and 'I think it's too late now to question fundamentals of the design'. The difficulties of dialogue are not one-sided. The architect will be unwise to listen only to the leader of the client body, whether the artistic director or resolute chairman of the building committee, and not just because of their comparative impermanence as has been suggested earlier. The architect should realise that, for all the media emphasis on the role of the director as creator of a theatrical production, theatre is essentially a team game. Similarly the theatre professional meeting the architect needs to understand that to be successful the senior architect like the director must lead a large team.

Architects are team leaders in two senses. Within their own offices they will have partners, associates and production men who churn out the hundreds of contract drawings. There will also be some bright young men and women, the pick of the architectural schools, who are anxious to work with a good architect on an interesting project. It is often the latter who will be producing the sketch solutions to design problems which the leading architect will select or discard in the quest to pull together a coherent answer to a complex problem. Theatre people would be wise to spend some time with the younger and intensively creative members of the architect's team.

The architect is also a team leader in that he or she heads a design team of engineers, acoustic consultants, cost consultants (in Britain quantity surveyors) and theatre consultants. The roles of the latter two are dealt with in the next chapter. Here a note is necessary on the role of the engineers and their occasional and dangerous tendency to take over.

Electrical engineers are the least dangerous as their task is routine except in the theatre area where the key electrical role is generally taken by the theatre consultant who may also be responsible for the architectural lighting. More central to theatre design is the mechanical engineer responsible for heating, ventilation and, most probably, air conditioning or 'comfort cooling' which is air conditioning without any humidity control. The reason for this is that today both performers and audience demand that our theatres are enclosed, cool and quiet. One cannot get fresh air by simply opening a window as of old because of the possible intrusion of traffic or aircraft noise, problems not encountered in Elizabethan or Georgian London. One cannot achieve the simple extraction of foul air by lighting the gas sunburner in the centre of the auditorium's ceiling, the prime purpose of which was to draw used air upwards and out by simple convection, general illumination being only its secondary task. It is no longer possible simply to close the theatres in the hot months of July or August, as they were in London and New York right up to the middle of this century, because now these months are when managements make most money from theatrical tourists. The managers, audience and actors demand silent, efficient air conditioning in our new theatres and often in our restored old theatres. Quite simply there is nothing more expensive and nothing more necessary. And if it is to be silent the necessary air-handling machinery must be well sited on ground or 'grade' level rather than on the roof where noise will be imparted to the whole structure. It is all very technical and to all but the design team somewhat tedious. This is not a technical book but it would fail as an *aide-mémoire* to anybody ever considering the creation of a new theatre or the restoration of an old one if it did not point out that the solution of the ventilation problem is one of the costliest and most difficult elements in any theatre design.

Good engineers, whether mechanical, structural or electrical, are like good theatre technicians. Their job is the 'how' rather than the 'what' of design. But they cannot do this job unless they not only understand the problem as presented to them but also are sympathetic to the aesthetics both of architecture and the theatre. What is disastrous is when engineers or technicians redefine the goals of architecture or of theatre. In the 1950s, 1960s and 1970s just this happened in North America. There was a shift in the aim of theatre architecture that came not so much from the client or architect but from the engineers. These were the men who opened the trapdoor of the functionalist fallacy and left it open. They arrived in the architect's office with convincing degrees and qualifications in stage engineering, acoustics or scenic technology (never acting, singing or dancing). They offered to 'fix the nuts and bolts of seeing and hearing'. They protested that they were simply providing a technological armature for the couturier architect. One might rather say that the technical tail began to wag the design dog.

Finite angles in both planes were proposed as limits for acceptable sightlines in the auditorium. Side walls, which in earlier ages had been lined with humanity, would now be modelled only as directed by the stern science of acoustics. Ceilings, originally in the theatre called 'the heavens' and for centuries both an expression of the soaring of the human spirit and a lid to the theatre space which helped focus attention downwards on the actor, were dug up by the stage lighting expert. One widely read consultant, George Izenour, who was an exponent of 'theatre design as an embodiment of rational seating geometry', went so far in *Theatre Design* as to suggest that 'the magic can be left to the artists and the poets – once the lights are switched off, the audience doesn't have to see where it is sitting.'

Today this is recognised as nonsense, but in America of the 1950s and 1960s the fallacy at the root of all this remained undetected. The functionalist fallacy was the product of confusing the criteria of what makes a good theatre through emphasising the seeing and hearing by the spectator of the performer to the exclusion of everything else, especially the sense of community and of involvement. It is these which distinguish the live theatre, and therefore live theatre architecture, from the passive cinema which has a quite different set of design problems. This the engineers did not understand.

One of the reasons why engineers such as George Izenour briefly became central to modern theatre architecture was because they offered engineering devices which would vary the volume of a theatre auditorium and also, if necessary, convert a theatre into a concert hall before your very eyes. Massive moving ceilings were designed. Orchestra shells unfolded. Fan-shaped theatres 2,500 or 3,000 seats wide with generous legroom metamorphosed into 900-seat playhouses, or rather were supposed so to do.

Building committees were greatly attracted by the engineers' promise that one building could serve many different purposes. The architect, who had been handed the detailed design for the auditorium by the engineer, was also relieved as he could then direct his energies to designing the lobby and facade or to gaining a reputation for being good at cutting cost. The results in North America were dehumanising and ultimately unsuccessful if success is measured either by how well a theatre is liked or by how often a theatre is used. Few of the resulting theatres had any architectural merit or theatrical interest. The technical ingenuity of the solution to the problem of substantially altering the volume of the auditorium had masked the fact that the problem should not have been posed in the first place. Jo Mielziner left no doubt about his views on some of his fellow countrymen engineers: 'During the '60s, engineering firms devised astounding mechanical systems that changed the very shape of an auditorium, pitched the floor, tipping the ceiling and cutting off balconies, pivoted the halls, and rolled banks of seating across the floor and stage. . . . The Multi-Use Auditorium is one of the most serious mistakes in the history of theatre design. The notion that any single design can be used for all purposes is nonsense.'

Here a pause is necessary to clear up semantic confusion over words and phrases such as 'flexible', 'adaptable', 'multi-use', 'multi-purpose', 'all purpose', 'multi-form', 'uncommitted', 'black box' and 'courtyard'.

The American phrase, 'multi-use', as applied to auditoriums by Jo Mielziner, is much the same as the British 'multi-purpose' and the vaguer 'all purpose'. The purposes referred to are not different ways of staging plays but different uses for the one auditorium, theatre or hall. On American campuses in the 1950s and 1960s there was a call for a single building which would serve for symphony concerts, graduation ceremonies, even visiting Broadway shows of the 'bus and truck' variety as well as for the annual opera. In democratic spirit all 2,000 or 3,000 students would be accommodated, all with equally good sightlines. In vain did the architect or consultant, as men of integrity, protest to the building committee that, in the words of Mielziner, 'however well an auditorium suited the combined needs of the choral society and the music school opera it cannot possibly be used for intimate drama as well'. Nevertheless the universities and high schools built just such memorial halls the length and breadth of America.

In Britain neither the need was felt nor were the resources available for such monsters. Yet the 'multi-purpose' continued to be built at a smaller scale: insipid, flat-floor halls which were dim descendants of the great town halls of the end of the nineteenth century. The latter often had superb acoustics, a florid style and a sense of occasion for many purposes though certainly not for drama. Recently the newest all-purpose, no-purpose halls have been the sports halls, which are theoretically convertible into entertainment 'venues' but in fact have neither the atmosphere nor the facilities to support any other than the most heavily miked performer or self-contained fit-up theatres complete with seats and stage. It is the latter that the Royal Shakespeare Company and the Royal Exchange, Manchester, perversely choose to transport around Britain's sports halls rather than play theatres built for the purpose.

'Multi-form' theatres are quite another thing. These are the theatres that claim to be 'adaptable' or 'transformable' from one theatre form to another: proscenium into thrust into arena or theatre-in-the-round. Their origin can be traced back to Walter Gropius' unbuilt Totaltheatre which not only was never built but was hardly typical of the purifiers between the wars, each one of whom had a different vision of the new ideal theatre to be substituted for the nineteenth-century picture-frame proscenium. Those between-the-wars purifiers rarely espoused the multi-form philosophy.

Once again it was America that first had the money to build such whizz-bang multi-form theatres. Often it was the same engineers who had offered the multi-use auditoriums with their variable volumes, who now suggested they could, in a single theatre, create a range of different theatre forms, all equally valid.

Engineering has rarely solved the problems of providing different styles of actor/audience relationship. When engineers announce a technical innovation that will do everything caution is needed especially if they claim to have solved, as no one else ever has, the problems of either multi-use or multi-form theatre architecture.

Occasionally magic results from a technical innovation. In 1981 director Trevor Nunn, composer Andrew Lloyd-Webber and producer Cameron Mackintosh had scoured London for a theatre in which to stage an experimental musical, *Cats*. They looked at spaces which were not theatres and were despairing when someone thought of the New London which had been dark or had managed only limited seasons since its opening, a decade earlier. This theatre had a revolve hitherto unused except for trade shows which was 60 feet (18.2m) in diameter and had 206 of the theatre's 911 seats screwed down on one half of it. Designer John Napier blessed the inspiration of the late Sean Kenny who, together with architect M. J. Percival, had conceived this eccentric and hitherto unloved theatre, and the rest is theatre history. Without the huge revolve device *Cats* might never have happened in the form that was so much part of its original success, 'now and forever'.

Another engineering device which resulted in a multi-use theatre succeeding in a way which might have surprised Mielziner has been the air pallet. This is a development of the British hovercraft invention but its first theatrical application was to move scenery wagons in large American theatres. The 1983 Derngate Theatre in Northampton, England, which holds 1,000 to 1,600 people depending on form and purpose, achieves its transformations from concert hall into proscenium theatre, into flat-floor hall for banquets or trade fairs, into arena for speaker or boxing, by moving not only large blocks of raked seating on 'cushions' of air but also seating towers which can accommodate two or three levels of audience. Both seating and towers are moved by two people as they hover half an inch above the stage or auditorium floor. Derngate surprisingly and uniquely vindicates the multi-use approach although it ought to be remembered first that its medium size is appropriate for the scale of the moving parts and second that the one purpose unsatisfactorily served is conventionally staged drama, the proscenium arch format seemingly distancing the actor who is framed by endless masking curtains. A similar theatre to Derngate opened in Cerritos, California, in 1993.

In the 1960s the newly formed Association of British Theatre Technicians, on which theatre architects have always been well represented, had decided that 'multi-purpose' meant 'no purpose' and also that 'adaptable' or 'multi-form' theatres did not work and were a bad thing. At the same time they decided, with semantic precision, that 'flexibility' was, unlike 'adaptability', a good thing. What 'flexibility' means to its supporters must be left to the next chapter which will introduce the theatre consultant and describe some concepts of flexibility and of uncommitted space. But first there is another engineer to consider, the engineer of room acoustics. This is the acoustician who started life in the concert hall but soon strayed into theatre design as part of the architectural and engineering team who would create the multi-use or multi-purpose auditorium.

In America from the 1950s onwards the acoustician was also busy solving a problem related to adaptability that perhaps ought not to have been set either. The apparently inexorable 'dollar equation' was determining that opera houses, playhouses and concert halls were to be bigger than they ought to be. The commercial economics of touring Broadway musicals in the 1960s, 1970s and 1980s meant that these shows, if they were to be profitable, had to be played on the road in auditoriums seating 2,000, 3,000 or 4,000 when on Broadway they had been created originally for more intimate theatres seating 1,000 or at most 1,500. In addition, all over America local opera companies were being created which presented short seasons of operas with local choruses plus imported stars and rented scenery. For the latter big box office capacities were needed because of small or non-existent subsidies. Meanwhile, the success of first-class regional orchestras in the older concert halls suggested that their new halls should be larger. The arguments were not only commercial but also social: a vital young new audience had been created through the long-playing gramophone record and it seemed sad to deprive them of the experience of attending concerts by building the hall too small.

The pressure for bigger auditoriums of every sort resulted in the rise of the acoustician. The acoustician said to the architect and to the client quite simply that if the required large auditorium was not of this or that shape, which he or she had determined, then the audience would not hear. Since the client wanted capacities larger than those for which successful precedents existed and since the architect was not an expert in the science of acoustics both felt that they had better knuckle under. Some acousticians offered their own brand of infinite flexibility. Wrote Richard Talaske in *Halls for Music Performance* in 1982: 'first rate facilities can be rapidly changed to accommodate a variety of events from music to drama by the use of such devices as moveable walls or ceilings, demountable orchestra shells and adjustable sound absorption. It is easily possible to shift the emphasis from romantic to baroque during a brief intermission and three or four hours later to have a stage fully rigged for drama or opera.' This is acoustics as alchemy. And even if the result were to be acoustical gold what of the architectural consequences of a concert hall masquerading as a theatre or vice versa?

Nobody was brave enough to say the client had asked them to design a hall with too great a capacity for its purpose, as those who did so would be fired. Architects and acousticians also have a laudable ambition to succeed in solving any problem posed. This was so obviously a difficult problem which, if successfully tackled, would surely lead to further similar commissions. Having little previous experience of theatre design most architects cheerfully offered to carry out the client's brief as stated. A few managed to tame the acoustician and work closely with him or her. Most sold out. The results were often multi-purpose auditoriums which look like acoustical models carved out of soap. The large modern concert hall was also all too often a failure until Russell Johnson and his collaborators scored significant successes in Calgary, Canada (1985), Dallas, Texas (1989), and Birmingham, England (1990). The City of Birmingham Symphony Orchestra conductor, Simon Rattle, jested that the architect's role at Birmingham was reduced to 'choosing the colour of the seats'.

The upsetting of the balance between architecture and engineering in the mid twentieth century was not only the consequence of trying to build multi-use or 'adaptable' auditoriums but also the result of clients asking for theatres with too large seating capacities, too much comfort and hence with too great volumes. It is therefore scarcely surprising that in the late 1970s American communities started to prefer adapting movie palaces into opera and concert halls rather than risk a modern theatre. Fortunately braver attitudes prevail today. Nevertheless one still is suspicious when told that a new theatre will have generous space for everyone, perfect sightlines, adaptable acoustics and technology sinisterly described as 'state of the art'.

Chapter 9

Committees, consultants and flexibility

The clients of new theatres or renovations are now invariably unpaid committees rather than actor-managers or commercial managements. Almost all new theatres in America and Britain are thought of as cultural institutions serving the community and are financed from the public sector or by private subscription or both. Therefore there is no alternative to forming a committee to whom the community's money is entrusted.

These committees, whether running touring or 'receiving' theatres taking in shows or operating creative theatres originating their own productions, have rarely built a theatre before. So they are first-timers as well as being many-headed. Add the fact that many architects and engineers have never built a theatre before either and it is surprising that many of the new theatres work at all. This is not the way you build a car.

However, some committees can be unexpectedly resolute and business-like, homing straight in on the right solution. In his autobiography, *A Life in the Theatre*, Tyrone Guthrie tells of the telephone call in June 1952 from a stranger, Tom Patterson, inviting him to fly to Canada to discuss the creation of a Shakespearian festival at a small railway junction in Ontario with no theatre. The town was called Stratford, the name being its sole asset. Guthrie was offered expenses and a small fee. He flew out the next day, and after an hour or two looking round the town met the committee. Guthrie continues: 'in the course of 30 years I have had experience of many sorts of committees and boards who manage theatrical enterprises. I expected that this one would consist mainly of artistic and excitable elderly ladies of both sexes, and a sprinkling of business men to restrain the artistic people from spending money. There would also be an anxious entity from the town hall, briefed to see that no municipal funds were promised, but also to see that, if any success were achieved, the municipality would get plenty of credit. The point about this sort of committee is that the artistic ones have extremely definite views, but so conflicting that it is easy for a tiny minority of business men to divide and conquer. Prudent, sensible, business-like council prevails. The result is that nothing would ever get done. In Britain the average age of members is 73.

'My first surprise at Stratford therefore was to find that most members of the committee were young. I was almost the oldest person present [Guthrie was 52 at the time]. The second surprise was to find that the males outnumbered the females by about 5:1. The women spoke seldom, but when they did their remarks were usually briefer and more practical than those of the men.

'The greatest surprise was now to come. . . .'

Guthrie explains how then and there all the major decisions were taken about the character of the season, of the acting company (two productions only for the first year) and of the nature of the theatre that had to be created from scratch. This was to be a temporary tent with a thrust stage which later could be converted into a more permanent structure if the festival and the shape of the theatre proved to be a success. Guthrie ended with the words: 'all this was carried through in one evening, not bad going.'

Contrast this with Michael Elliott, speaking on the radio in 1973: 'I served on the building committee of the National Theatre and I remember those endless and agonising meetings as though they had taken place in the shadow of the ruins of some newly shattered tower of Babel. Every illustrious and experienced voice spoke in a different language, not only from his fellows, but different from his own a month before or a month after. We could all speak of very personal dreams of private theatres that held our fancy that week, but to analyse objectively the purpose of the National Theatre over the next century and design an appropriate house for it, that seemed for a long time almost impossible.' Elliott once added as an aside to this author that after a few months he himself vowed not to talk and not to drink the scotch that was placed on the table, but that the next day he always woke up with a sore head and a sore throat.

A committee generally starts with a feasibility study. This assesses the practicality of attaining a new theatre, its size and character, and the design options open. Enter then the theatre consultant who, ideally, combines the skills of management consultant, stage and auditorium designer, theatre planner from box office to dressing room, and technical expert for the specialist areas of stage lighting, stage rigging, theatre sound and intercommuncation. The theatre consultant's voice is expected to be that of experience and reason. And at the door may be other 'theatre experts' who are members of government agencies or professional bodies and who proffer additional advice whether asked or not.

The voice of reason? One must pause. Reason and the theatre are strange bedfellows. The ability to say what the community needs and what sort of theatre is likely to be successful is almost certain to involve more faith than reason. A statement of needs is little more than a 'snapshot' of a particular place at a particular time. A snapshot is essentially ephemeral while a building is not. If and when the theatre consultant has convinced him- or herself that a theatre can be achieved he or she is probably going to need the skills of a revivalist preacher saving souls to persuade others that a realistic route to a worthwhile theatrical heaven lies ahead. Vision will be the first requirement.

Vision is difficult to analyse. Calling for a visionary study is not unlike the prayer of the confused minister who asked God that where He saw a spark to water that spark. However, a prominent and determined citizen who wants a theatre badly, like Tom Patterson at Stratford, Ontario, and who has gathered together a committee who listen to the right professionals, can survive ordeal by feasibility study. The committee that is too logical too early will probably argue itself into a corner and out of a theatre.

One of the committee vices to be avoided is cumulative brief writing. This is what happens when, to keep the support of every constituency on which the project depends, the leader keeps adding to the architect's brief this or that feature which is regarded as essential by this or that group. Britain lacks a lot of post-war opera houses for this reason. In Edinburgh, in Cardiff and in the Midlands, modest projects have been defined, re-defined and then so loaded with 'necessities' that they easily outstreak any conceivable budget. Every step along the road which ultimately deprived the community of the proposed facility seemed logical at the time, but the cumulative effect of all that logic and reason was to kill the project. A similar fate overtook the proposed Toronto Ballet Opera House in 1990.

Another way for the committee to kill a project is by practising what in America is called by the new euphemism 'value engineering'. This is jargon for cost cutting, the two sympathetic sounding words meaning precisely the same as the more familiar but more brutal pair. It is the process that has to happen when the true cost of a project is realised too late. A committee can admire other theatres, choose an architect and enthuse over a model of the proposed best theatre of its type in the world with one side of the brain engaged, and then, faced with realities, switch to the other side and ask for 25 per cent of the cost to be cut, believing fondly that this will result only in less fancy wallpaper and fewer stage lights but essentially the same building (taken to extremes this can result in a theatre, the capital cost of which has been so carefully controlled, that the seats and carpets wear out in eight years). A solitary schizophrenic may respond to treatment but a committee can easily start playing Hyde to its own Jekyll without realising the monstrosity of its double.

One might think that the cost consultant, or in Britain the quantity surveyor, can save the committee and its design team from having recourse to 'value engineering' as a result of its own folly. Yet this can be so only if the cost consultant is employed early enough and educates the committee in realistic costing.

The committee must understand that the cost consultant produces costs with different degrees of accuracy at different stages of the design process.

An early guide, before a line is drawn, can be established by taking from the building programme, or schedule of accommodation, the net usable area of the proposed theatre, multiplying by a 'grossing factor' that allows for wall thicknesses, ducts, ventilation, plant and the 'circulation' which includes the corridors, staircases and exits necessary in a public building. This gives a gross area. The gross area can then be multiplied by the yardstick of an average cost per square foot or per square metre, arrived at by analysing recent comparable buildings and making adjustments for local factors as well as for the passage of time.

A second and subsequent method is to measure the areas off the early sketches of the proposed building. However, a really accurate figure cannot generally be reached until the design has been worked up in greater but not complete detail. Such a figure is arrived at by the process of elemental costing, when the cost consultant or quantity surveyor calculates more precisely what it will cost to build that design by quantifying the bricks, the timber, the equipment and the slates – provided of course that the building industry behaves as predicted when the final designs are put out to bid. Only when the bids are received is the actual cost established by a contractor who tenders to build the theatre for a specified sum, or who, as contract manager, undertakes that the sum of separate tenders for each part of the building process will not exceed the agreed budget.

Most committees contain the business men to whom Guthrie referred. They are often amazed both at the grossing factor, which is much larger in a theatre than in a block of offices, and also at how expensive per square foot or per square metre a theatre is compared with the essentially much simpler commercial buildings with which so many business men are familiar. It is the cost consultant's job to explain early on to the committee the realities of the cost of a theatre, so that architect and theatre consultant are not thought of as extravagant, and so that the cost per square foot or square metre is not thought of as being attributable to expensive finishes or to extravagant stage equipment but to the sheer inherent complexity of any theatre building.

It is now necessary to describe the newest member of the design team, the theatre consultant. He or she is a specialist theatre designer and/or theatre technician who did not appear until the decline of the specialist theatre architect. In the post-war German theatre-building boom technical theatre consultants, whose expertise was generally confined to ever more elaborate stage machinery, abounded. In Britain and America in the late 1950s the new art/craft of stage lighting was born. If advantage was to be taken of the new technologies that had become available then all but the most technically minded stage designers or directors would need help to realise the full potential of stage lighting to direct the audience's attention, and, in an age when painted canvas no longer convinces, to provide illusion of time and place. The successful lighting designer had to be both an artist and a technician to understand both the 'what' and the 'how' of creation. This was thought an appropriate background for the design of stage and auditorium. As a result a few lighting designers formed theatre consultancies in the late 1960s. Those that succeeded included those of Jules Fisher and Roger Morgan in America and Theatre Projects Consultants, which Richard Pilbrow formed in 1967 in London, to work in Britain, North America and across the world, and of which this author has been a director since 1973. Initially services offered were confined to the design of stage lighting, stage engineering and stage sound installations. But, aware of the vacuum that existed in theatre architecture, consultants extended their services to provide expertise in theatre planning in general and in stage and auditorium design in particular. And, in the pragmatic 1980s, the one-stop theatre consultants added feasibility studies and arts administration consultancy to the services on offer.

The theatre consultant claims to help the situation at the outset when the brief, the 'what' set out in architectural terms, is being prepared. Often he is appointed before the architect and is regarded as the protector of the theatre interests against architectural excess, who will direct the little money available to the stage technology. However, the theatre consultant who has persuaded the committee that a multi-level, and hence more theatrically concentrated, auditorium is the greatest priority, preferable to a simpler and cheaper single-tier auditorium, knows how difficult it is to get either cost-conscious committee members or theatre technicians to accept that the creation of a theatrical atmosphere in the auditorium is more crucial to the success of a theatre than either a graceful building or the latest 'state of the art' technology.

Clients are generally more attentive to the theatre consultant or a specialist theatre architect if he agrees to offer them something 'flexible'. The call for a stage which can transform itself through a range of actor-audience relationships – Greek, proscenium, thrust, in the round – which is what Jo Mielziner called a 'multi-form stage' – will strike the committee as good value for money. It will also save the committee making up its mind on what sort of an actor-audience relationship it really needs. Therefore the theatre consultant's biggest challenge after the reconciling of budget with appetite, either of building committee or of architect, is how to contain this call for 'flexibility'.

In the previous chapter the concepts of 'multi-purpose' (= no purpose) and 'multi-form' or 'adaptable' were reviewed as illustrations of misplaced enthusiasm on the part of the engineer or engineering-based theatre designer. Here it is the less technologically ambitious concept of 'flexibility' that requires examination. Flexible is an easy word with sympathetic connotations. The successful theatre dubbed 'flexible' is generally one that is substantially of this or that form but is detailed in such a way as to provide flexibility in its form as an added bonus.

The simplest and best-known example of this is the flexible proscenium zone of most modern proscenium theatres. Here there is an orchestra lift with three positions: at its lowest level it provides an orchestra pit; at audience level the space for two or three additional rows of seating and at its highest level, stage level, an extension of the acting area on an apron stage which is not a thrust because, like the orchestra pit or additional rows of seating, it extends the full width of the auditorium rather than thrusting out into it. Nobody can deny that this arrangement is desirable in an auditorium presenting both drama and musical theatre. On occasions such flexibility of the floor is matched by flexible side walls to the proscenium zone which allow the option of stage boxes for audience or areas for scenery each side of a fixed proscenium arch.

All this is familiar. But when the requirement extends, as Harley Granville Barker demanded, into providing the alternative of a full thrust with more than token audience on each side, the designer of the theatre and his or her client is seeking after 'adaptability' rather than 'flexibility'. Or so the words are currently used. And, as previously suggested, adaptable or multi-form theatres generally compromise all the forms on offer and hence fail.

There are two further forms of flexible theatre which have been promoted by theatre architects or consultants and these are the 'black box' or 'uncommitted' theatre space on the one hand and the 'courtyard' on the other.

In the 1950s and 1960s the building committee, when asked to choose between so many theatre forms, often decided to have two theatres and chose one fixed form, generally proscenium, for the larger of the two and an empty space where everything was possible for the second and smaller. These empty spaces were christened 'black boxes' because they were box-shaped and because they were generally painted black in the erroneous belief that black is neutral. In the black box anything was thought to be possible. However, unless the resources and time were available to create a new environment for each production the sheer anonymity of such spaces turned out to be a liability rather than a theatrical asset. Not only was the atmosphere depressing, audience and actor having to be wound up for any spark to be struck, but also if these neutral spaces were painted black and were equipped with flexible seating 'podiums' or wedges of two- or three-stepped rows of seats, each rearrangement was somehow drearily the same. The topography of the space may have changed but the mood, by reason of its lack of character and its inability to distinguish formality and informality, remained unchanged. Some of these 'studio theatres', to use the description more often used in Britain than 'black box', settled down into one semi-fixed format, end stage or three-sided acting area with minimum flexibility. This was the solution which attracted the licensing authorities and fire marshals who, in some situations, had to relicense the theatre on each occasion the layout changed.

In 1977 with the opening of the Cottesloe, the third auditorium of Britain's National Theatre, the phrase 'courtyard theatre' was re-coined by this author who was also the author of the design concept of the Cottesloe. The word was chosen as explanation of a theatre which had to be for some the epitome of simplicity, for others the height of sophistication to allow experiment in the very nature of theatre; for some a theatre where scenery was unnecessary, for others a place where scenery could be placed anywhere; for some a showcase for new plays which if successful would transfer upstairs to the bigger theatres, for others a theatre which would always stand in contrast to the established way of things; for some a showcase for the fringe, for others a television studio; etc., etc.

In *The Stage* in March 1977 this author wrote: 'The response to this brief is to turn this large empty space into a form of "courtyard". Galleries were introduced on three sides of a central, much smaller, empty space. Two objectives were thus achieved: the increasing of capacity, by papering the walls with people on three levels (one row seated, one row standing) and the reducing of the free space to a smaller more manageable volume. . . .

'At one end is a reasonably sized stage that can be used scenically. The middle level of the galleries is at foyer level and, since the linking of stairs between the three levels is within the theatre, everyone aiming to sit at the lower level must pass through an upper level thus removing any feeling of an hierarchical layout. . . . Since stage level is the same as the "first" of three audience levels, all that need be done to achieve the flat floor throughout is to lift and remove the encircling rostra of the first level, fill up the central space to stage level and take away the seats to a subterranean store. As complete a transformation, is the placing of the stage in the centre of the courtyard, with two or three rows of seats around it.

'A series of sketches would also show the more formal options: end stage, arena, thrust, traverse, etc. However, such a series might be misleading because the point about a courtyard is not that the stage area can be altered through a set of fixed options, but that the place and character of the space within the courtyard can be varied infinitely: every level, every direction being available to either actor or audience. . . .

'The Cottesloe is a clean slate. It is now up to actors and artists to do just what they like with it. Push it around, even re-paint it if they do not like black, which is relatively easy because almost every inch can be reached with a pair of domestic step ladders. The only limitation on what can be done, is the theatricality inherent in the courtyard form, a form at once ancient and universal, a form which may suggest some fresh ways of achieving a theatrical relationship. . . . Only by leaving a lot to the user can the designers of brand new theatres encourage the improvisation and the vital response to problems of theatrical relationships . . . so much for design philosophy.'

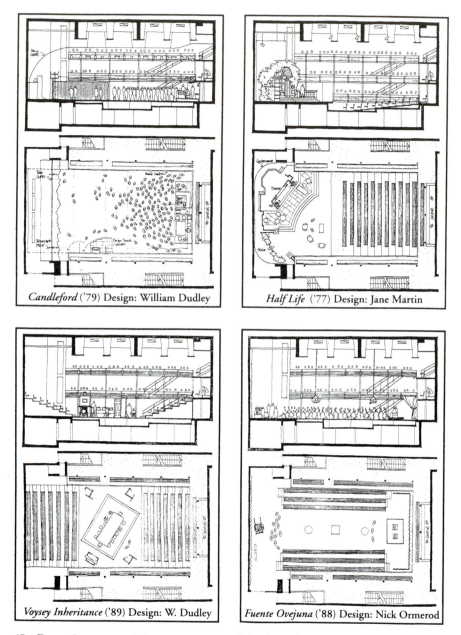

Candleford ('79) Design: William Dudley

Half Life ('77) Design: Jane Martin

Voysey Inheritance ('89) Design: W. Dudley

Fuente Ovejuna ('88) Design: Nick Ormerod

17 Four of many possible arrangements of the Cottesloe Theatre, the third experimental 'courtyard' theatre of Britain's Royal National Theatre, architect Denys Lasdun & Partners. The 'courtyard' concept with three fixed levels of seating surrounding on three sides a flexible space, was originated in 1973. The Cottesloe opened in 1977. It predates both Tricycle Theatre, London (1980) and the Martha Cohen Theater, Calgary (1985) illustrated on pages 165 and 131.

By the 1980s some courtyards were rightly rejected as being simply theatres with bad sightlines at the side because these were being used exclusively as end-stage theatres. Courtyards were also confused with multi-tier horseshoe opera houses simply because they were multi-level and had the side walls of their auditoriums animated with people. But for some of their instigators, including this author, their main attraction is the sense that they are modern expressions of the traditional playhouse, for which a continuity in scale and form has already been claimed, and are descendants of the Rose and of Drury Lane, prior to its end-of-the-eighteenth-century elephantiasis, of the minor and provincial theatres up to the 1850s as well as of later small proscenium theatres such as the Royal Court. These are all theatres which have supported the playwright and the actor over the last hundred years. In addition the true courtyard does not lend itself exclusively to proscenium style of production; there must always be the real possibility for the actor and the action to escape into the centre of the space.

How that escape is to be achieved is crucial. If there is the money to pay for mechanics the engineer or technical theatre consultant will offer a system of lifts, pallets and retractable seating to shunt acting area and seats around at minimal cost in time and labour. This will mean that the theatre can rapidly achieve A, B and C but not D and E, because the engineer was told, before the theatre was built, that the latter two arrangements did not qualify for expensive engineering. On the other hand the beauty of a tight budget and no mechanics is not only can all requirements be met – A, B, C, D and E – by man-handling rostra and floors but also, and more important, X and Y audience/actor relationships which were not even thought of until the theatre was complete and the production of a certain play in a certain way contemplated.

Which is the more flexible, the theatre with the purpose-built machinery or the one with the hole in the middle filled by old-fashioned rostra? The answer must depend on what you mean by or require of 'flexibility': flexibility to create the modes most likely to be demanded easily, quickly and hence cheaply (in terms of operating cost) or flexibility to do anything theatrical within the architectural context provided. For every situation the theatre consultant must balance the two: for theatres used predominantly for touring productions created for, say, thrust or end stage, the mechanical system is preferable, despite the limit to the permutations; while a studio or courtyard theatre, in which experiments are to be made in actor-audience relationships, should go for the flexibility of no mechanics, despite the consequent labour costs. The latter was the fortunate fate of the Cottesloe, conceived in 1973, by which time almost all the money available had been spent on the National's two larger and much more technically sophisticated theatres.

The limiting of the size of any theatre is probably where the theatre consultant will best be able to serve the art of theatre in the initial dialogue with any committee. Committees always include, as Guthrie suggested, men and women who may not understand art but sure do understand 'the dollar equation'. They will be there to ensure that the theatre is neither too expensive to build nor too costly to operate. Whether it is a resident theatre that creates its own shows or a touring one that books in shows, they will aim to maximise income. In the latter case they will be aided and abetted by the Broadway or West End producer, who is not involved in raising the finance to build the theatre whatever the size and who is anxious to spend as short a time as possible in their city while playing to as many people as possible. There will be talk of 'an economic size'.

There is in fact no such finite thing as 'an economic size'. An economic size is different in one country from in another or in different ages in the same country. It will certainly change within the lifespan of the building. The matter gets more complex at the larger end of the scale when the preparedness of an audience to continue to attend live performances where the actor is no bigger than the thumbnail of an outstretched hand, as is the case from the back row of any theatre seating over 2,000, must be assessed lest that member of the audience, having once experienced long-shot theatre, decides to stay at home for close-up video. The factors that make up the 'dollar equation' are so complex that the case for ever enlarging the theatre to an 'economic size' soon collapses. How different are the measurable matters of art such as the distance over which one can see the expression in the performers' eyes or even on their face! The distance over which a Mozart aria can be projected is also measurable if one excludes either radio microphones or the rare voices to which scale appears not to apply.

The business man on the board or the theatre manager who believes a bigger take makes more economic sense must also be reminded that the cost of producing a play, opera or ballet does not remain constant, whatever the size of the auditorium, leaving the income to increase as the size of the auditorium increases. Such an argument fails to take into account every-thing from the increased cost of bigger sets, of more ushers or of building maintenance to the fact that in the bigger house more experienced and hence more expensive performers may be needed to create the same effect as can be attained in a smaller space by younger and hence less well-paid actors, singers or dancers. This author has heard managers of a successful new 350-seat theatre complain that the theatre is great but if the architect or consultant had really understood the problems of theatre they would have provided 450 seats. When one has heard the manager of the new 450-seat theatre ask similarly for 600 seats, of the 600-seater 750 seats, etc. the conclusion becomes obvious. How much more shrewd are the West End or Broadway producers who launch their new untried shows in as small a theatre as they dare – for instance the spectacular musical *Phantom of the Opera* in the 1,200-seat Her Majesty's Theatre in London which, only a few years earlier, had been declared uneconomic for any musical, let alone one of the most lavish recently staged anywhere in London – so as to give them the best possible chance of success.

However, producer Cameron Mackintosh (no relation) did not gross over £200 million world-wide with just four musicals in nine years (*Cats, Les Miserables, Phantom of the Opera* and *Miss Saigon*) by always playing small theatres. Once the shows are established in theatregoers' minds through ineffable marketing they will pay high prices for a touring version despite their effect being diluted by reason of the sheer size of the 3,000-seat plus memorial auditoriums or monster movie palaces played 'on the road' in North America. The producers, directors and designers who create the mega-musicals are under no illusion that they need the smaller and usually older theatres of the West End or Broadway in which to originate and nurse to maturity their creations which subsequently stride across continents.

Thus the need for smaller, more focused theatres for original work applies at all levels. And so, despite the lure of big grosses for full houses for blockbusters, the consultant has a duty to explain to the committee that you do not build a church for Easter Sunday. If success is to be won for anything but the predictable at the end of the week, a less than full audience must not rattle around. Only if the consultant or architect can create a climate where such matters are discussed at the outset will he or she ensure that actor-audience relationship in the proposed theatre does not suffer from the commonest and most deadly handicap of all, that of the auditorium being too big. The commercially successful Irish playwright Dion Boucicault, wrote in the *North American Review*, CCCXV, October 1889: 'The popular places of public entertainment have always been medium sized or small. The stature of the actor should determine the size of the stage on which he appears, and the distance at which his features can be perfectly seen may determine the proportions of the auditorium. The measure of the spectator's eye may be taken as a standard for his ear, for within that scope the actor will be heard: the two senses are, so far as theatre is concerned, of equal capacity. . . . There is a limit to the genius of the actor as regards its reach over his audience; and no auditorium should exceed in size that limit.' Boucicault's advice was sound but consistently ignored, especially in North America, for the next century.

Chapter 10

Actors and audiences

So far there have been few star performers in this account of theatre architecture in the last twenty-five years, other than the geniuses such as Tyrone Guthrie, Peter Brook, Ariane Mnouchkine and Michael Elliott who have created theatrical environments which have not only served their own purposes but have also inspired others. There have been many villains who must be hissed off to clear the stage for the heroes of this piece: the actor and the audience. For it is these two groups of people who are essential for theatre to exist, who are there when everyone else has gone home, round to the pub, or returned to their drawing boards or calculators. Except for the ushers and stage management they are the only ones to sit it out, to be the indispensable elements in making theatre for three concentrated hours. Everyone else, including too often the critics in the front few rows, is a voyeur.

How rare it is for more than lip service to be paid to the needs of either actor or audience! How little time is spent trying to analyse what actually happens when theatrical congress takes place, what has happened when the actor can say, genuinely, to a member of the audience 'you were a wonderful audience to play to'! There are many secondary factors – day of the week, price of the ticket, whether the audience has dined before, the presence of coach parties, etc. But the primary factor is 'place' and if this phenomenon is to be satisfactorily explained an empirical approach is likely to serve better than theorising.

In May 1989 RSC director Adrian Noble was reflecting upon his difficulties in getting a laugh when directing *Twelfth Night* in Japanese at the Ginza Saison Theatre in Tokyo. This theatre was new, it was well-equipped. At first he thought the reason why the audience did not laugh was because in Japan laughter in public places is thought impolite and therefore the audience had better hold their programmes up to their faces and giggle quietly behind their fans. In a letter to this author he recalled that he changed his mind when he realised that the problem lay elsewhere: 'The seats were very comfortable to sit in, but designed with a very high back, so that one disappeared into the chair, as on an aircraft, and had no sense of the surrounding audience at all. I am sure this contributed directly to a sensation not dissimilar to watching the television, and for a comedy like *Twelfth Night*, was very destructive, as it made it extremely difficult for the audience to become welded into one group.' He noted that when Peter Brook was at the same theatre a few months earlier with his production of *Carmen* he had built a structure which covered all the seats in the auditorium and then introduced more rudimentary and less comfortable seating with a stronger potential for group identity.

A theatrical genius, such as Brook, touring one of his own productions, may be permitted such a radical solution as flooring over a brand new auditorium. Others who would harness the place to the play are unlikely to be allowed the privilege of rebuilding any theatre for an individual production unless, that is, there are millions of pounds or dollars available to create the sort of 'theatrical experience' which is now part and parcel of the mega-musical. Rather is it necessary to build up through experience an understanding of how the architecture of the house aids or thwarts the actor-audience relationship and with this knowledge design better theatres.

A good starting point is to tour a production and stay long enough in each theatre (in Britain generally Monday to Saturday) to assess the part played by the architecture of the house, so as to discount the elements of unfamiliarity or Monday night malaise. An observant producer or director who moves around the country in which a tour takes place, and also around the auditoriums in which the production plays, will start to identify the part played by the playhouse. With a production that only ever plays in one place it is much harder to disentangle all the factors involved.

A discussion centred on the experience of playing the same production in different theatres is also the best starting point for a dialogue with actors. But only the most experienced actor will find it easy to identify precisely the architectural elements that make for success. There are two main reasons for the difficulty. The first is that the enduring physical world in which they are playing is less real to the actors than the ephemeral world of the production in which they are engaged. It is not merely a question of the set being better lit than the auditorium. The actors must be sufficiently confident or 'played in' to be able to observe the process of actor-audience connection, and to discover whether they are breaking glasses in the gallery bar or hearts in the rear stalls – they will know soon enough if they are pleasing the critics in the front row.

The second reason is that actors subconciously regard the architecture of the house as yet another obstacle to be conquered if their performance is to suceed – hence the familiar nervous question 'could you hear all right?' asked of a visitor backstage after a first night or preview. The actor may not know even whether the audience was large or small in certain theatres and for interesting reasons.

This author recalls an occasion in 1965 at the Royal Lyceum Theatre in Edinburgh, an 1883 theatre then holding 1,300, when a leading lady was convinced that the theatre 'must have been three-quarters full' when it certainly was not.

The mistaking of 350 theatregoers for the 975 needed for 75 per cent attendance, by one who had been in the business for over thirty years, says a great deal about the architecture of the Lyceum, Edinburgh. The 25 per cent capacity audience had given the impression of 75 per cent capacity, for a comedy, *The Importance of Being Earnest*, for which the actors would have had every opportunity to gauge the response and hence the size of the audience.

The illusion of a greater capacity had not been confined to the actors. For the audience to laugh rather than to rattle around at what was demonstrably a commercially unsuccessful occasion, the theatre must have seemed to them fuller than it was. The reason was that this house has, as many other turn-of-the-century theatres have, four levels of audience with, on this occasion, a few full front rows at every level concealing many more empty rows behind. For an auditorium to feel fuller than it is is precisely the effect that one does not gain in a modern democratic theatre with but one or two levels of slightly curved rows of well-raked seating facing the stage and without side boxes or more galleries. In such modern theatres a three-quarters full house can feel at best half full, at worst half empty. This is the reverse of what you feel at the Lyceum, Edinburgh, which Tyrone Guthrie in 1962 dubbed 'one of the best intimate proscenium theatres'.

A rigorously commercial view might be that what the theatre feels like at less than half capacity is of no relevance: the architect should only plan for success. But this is a thin argument. Even in a commercial theatre success must be won for all but the smash hit. Word of mouth for a show presented in a theatre that feels gloomily empty when not full, is not going to do the show's commercial prospects any good. More important in any theatre where art is at least as important as commerce, new work will be essayed and the theatre, which may be full for a star in *Hamlet* or for a sure-fire comedy, should, when less than full and when the management is 'nursing' a show, support the actor rather than advertise short-term failure.

Clearly the actor prefers a warm responsive multi-tier auditorium to a cold uniformly raked single-tier theatre which looks more like a cinema or a worn lecture hall. Warm responsive auditoriums of more than 150 or 200 seats generally have a gallery or number of galleries which wrap around the space, so as to enfold the performing area in a welcoming embrace. The problem of such traditional theatres, which preserve the continuity of character already noted from the days of Shakespeare to the present, is that inevitably some seats are going to have less good sightlines than others. How is the audience going to accept the paradox of bad sightlines being necessary for a good theatre? Even those who may accept that bad sightlines are inevitable will certainly prefer that others, not they, sit in those seats.

The popularity of such theatres, and hence implicit acceptance by audiences that sightlines need not be perfect, often surprises architects and designers of theatres. Certainly the question 'do you want a seat from which you can hear and see everything on the performance space?' will produce a simple answer. But time and time again audiences who have sampled a variety of theatres will generally pick out the older theatres or, where a choice exists amongst wildly divergent modern theatres, the most characterful and architecturally interesting spaces. All these theatres which the audience prefers have some seats with bad sightlines. How are members of the audience going to be persuaded to sit in them?

There is a simple answer. You cannot persuade a member of audience to sit in a bad seat for the good of others. You can possibly persuade him or her to accept it if there is no other seat available and the alternative is missing the show. But that argument only applies to the smash hit and the corollary is that if that all seats in the auditorium are sold at the same price, then, if the house is not full, all those interesting side positions close to the actor remain unsold and what audience there is sits dead centre, leaving the sides ominously empty.

In Chapter 1 it was explained that theatre in the seventeenth, eighteenth and nineteenth centuries appealed to a wider section of the population than does theatre today. A major factor is that in these centuries theatres had a price ratio, top to bottom, of 8:1 (at the London Coliseum in 1911 the price differential was regularly 15:1, 7/6 to 6d – compare this to a 6:1 ratio at the same theatre today, for example a range of best seats in the stalls or the first circle to worst in the gallery of £40 to £6.50 for American Ballet Theatre in July 1990). The commercial managements of London and New York find it very difficult to accept price differentials even as wide as 6:1. They narrow the differential, grossly overcharging the gallery although demand often outstrips supply for the expensive seats. If the house is less than full they try to fill the good empty seats by discounting them to students, to those who 'queue on the day', to purchasers of 'twofers' (two for the price of one) or to the patrons of the ticket booths that are so popular in both New York and London. As a result in commercial theatres on both sides of the Atlantic, as in transatlantic planes, you can find in a single row those who have paid widely different prices for the same product.

Such indiscriminate opportunism on the part of the manager drives away the old 'gallery goer' who used to be able to book a cheap seat in advance. It is also unhelpful to the designers of theatre space. The architect needs managements who understand the advantages of those galleried multi-tier theatres which audiences and actors evidently prefer. Both audience and actor will be happier if the patron who pays $50 gets $50 worth of comfort and sightlines while the one who pays $6 gets $6 worth. The committee commissioning a new theatre who, either on commercial or 'democratic' grounds, insists to the architect that everybody gets $25 worth will finish up having themselves a homogeneous lecture hall or cinema rather than the sort of theatre that everybody likes.

In 1989 the United States Institute of Theater Technology held its annual conference in Calgary. This included a session on the design, management and use of multi-tier courtyard theatre spaces which was summarised in the summer 1990 issue of *Theatre Design and Technology*. The session took place on the stage of the Martha Cohen Theater for which this author had prepared the original design some eight years earlier. The director of the theatre since its opening in 1985 was Michael Dobbin who introduced the session from the front of the stage, facing an audience of 150 scattered through a 420-seat theatre. The Martha Cohen has four levels of seating: pit plus, on the perimeter of the pit, three enfolding circles of audience, one above the other and none more than three rows deep.

Dobbin first established that he liked the theatre. 'The three components of theatre are, in the simplest form, the original idea generated by the creative artist (i.e. the playwright), the interpretation by the director, the actors and the designers and the third, and probably the most important, the community of the audience combining with the community of the artist. This theatre provides us with the latter without any struggle. It doesn't matter what you do up here. You can leave every worklight in the place on and perform in sweatpants up here and the same sense of community is created as if we had all the other elements combined which in many older spaces are used to form the sense of community. It's natural in this space.' In describing the Martha Cohen he contrasted it with 'the things that we as audiences at any rate come to have thought of as being theatres when we sit in rows looking at the backs of other people's heads and yearning for a row further forward from where we are in order that we might see past the heads and see what's on the stage.' So far so good.

The physical consequences from the superimposed gallery reaching round to the edge of the acting area Dobbin defined thus: 'When the house is full and the stage is used in the full format in both its depth and its width the movement within the house is palpable and that active and interactive relationship between the audience and actors is what I believe to be the essence of theatre. If I walk from this side of the stage to that side of the stage, automatically here following me would be a movement because those people there [pointing at one end of the top gallery] can't see me here unless they stand up and lean against the rail. I see this as an asset.' When in 1976 the Royal Shakespeare Theatre extended its side seats through the proscenium arch around the back of the acting area

18 The Martha Cohen Theater, Calgary, Alberta, is one of three auditoriums in the Calgary Center which opened in October 1985. It seats 400 to 450 depending on audience arrangement. Generally the theatre is used in formal end stage mode, a three level semi-circular structure in space, the form of which owes something to the Royal Exchange, Manchester (1976 – see p. 93), the Theatre Royal, Bury St Edmunds (1819 – see p. 163) and to the Cottesloe at Britain's National (1977 – see p. 122) in respect of the inherent flexibility of the centre volume. In May 1990, for Michael Dobbin's production of the Leonard Bernstein's *Candide*, the room was 'completed' with a three quarter auditorium on stage shaped to match the fixed auditorium. Both were faced with canvas to help convert this space into an almost in-the-round environmental theatre.

John Barber of the *Daily Telegraph* tried these side positions and wrote 'the best are peaks in Darien and the worst offer only squatter's rights'. The same could be said of the top gallery at Calgary.

Dobbin was not only artistic director but was also responsible for the entire theatre. He then took us into the box office: 'It's taken us five years to explain to the audience that when you sit here and pay $22 you are getting $22 worth. When you sit up there in the second row and pay $5 you are getting $5 worth of seat and sightlines. That, as you can imagine, is an extraordinary task to communicate to the public. So when we are normally selling at 85 per cent or 90 per cent to subscription and a casual buyer arrives and the only seat that's available to them for the first visit they've ever made here is a second row bench seat behind the side rail on the top gallery you then have to communicate to them what it's about, why it's like that and what it means and can mean to them to participate in that active way. But often they get out the door before we can get to them and sometimes we never see them again.'

The moral must be that ticket pricing is not something the marketing department sticks to the seats as a consequence of their evaluation of the market. Seat pricing is rather an integral part not only of the design of the space but of its management. Designer William Dudley, whose experience ranged from *The Mysteries* and other promenade productions at the Cottesloe to *The Ring* at Bayreuth, took a radical view at the same conference of the prejudices of box office managers: 'They like a nice simple tidy little drawing which they can sell off. The fact that they are the cutting edge of selling to the audience that go into this sort of theatre makes ticket selling a bit different from a movie house. That's what's got to change, not the notion that this form of theatre is the most exciting.'

Audience behaviour may indeed be an integral part of performances in which audiences and actors are free to interact physically in the same space and this interaction can be continued outside the auditorium. For the Lincoln Center's production of *The Road* at La Mama, New York, in 1988 those members of the audience who chose not to stay and dance with the cast during intermission found another actor had instantaneously transformed the bar in the lobby into a sleazy Liverpool nitespot in Thatcherite Britain.

But both the Cottesloe and La Mama are in sophisticated cities where theatregoers can pick and choose. In Calgary, as in most North American cities, the audience has to be wooed once or twice a year 'on subscription'. If they have not been persuaded to book for all or most of the shows before the season opens they will go to a concert, out to dinner or stay at home and watch television that third Thursday every month from September to May. Danny Newman, the subscription king, may feel he has given the American legitimate theatre a sound base of a loyal audience putting their money where the theatre can bank it to earn interest. Others, including Gregory Mosher, director of the Beaumont, New York, from 1986 to 1991, feel it is one of the worst things to have happened to the American theatre: artistic programmes controlled by marketing men always asking for a homogeneous product and as a result there being no chance to grab an opportunity during the course of the season for a new play or a different actor. With subscription it is difficult to play in repertoire, impossible to pull out a failure or to run a success.

But is this an accurate picture of the average subscriber? Who talks for the audience? The marketing man? The chairman of the playgoers' club who is usually the most conservative of the playgoers? Will the curious, the young, the audience any theatre needs if it is to produce vital and challenging work, take out a subscription? And if they have not and therefore are not considered to be regulars are they going to have any voice in either the choice of plays or the way in which they are presented?

What happens is that the marketing man draws an ever more accurate picture of what he regards as the typical theatregoer who must be asked each year to buy culture and therefore has to be wooed with increasingly anodyne leaflets which look more and more like covers to romantic novels. The marketing man has also worked out that there are so many A/Bs in the town who might buy a subscription and soon suggests that the income and expenditure account of the theatre would look much better if more people came to fewer productions given longer runs. Theatregoing soon becomes a rarer event for a larger audience rather than a regular event for a more involved audience. Theatregoing is thus drained of much of the immediacy and inevitably this starts to affect how theatres are designed and how they are used simply because it is too easy to identify the tastes and preferences of the typical subscriber.

The commercial theatre is no better. Hits now run for a decade or more when twenty-five years ago a year was a long run, and seventy years ago six months in the same Broadway or West End theatre was the mark of great success. A vast new audience for live theatre may have been discovered by the producers of the smash hit but at the cost of the regular theatregoer in the major cities who went once a week to his local commercial theatre. London and New York used to offer fifty or more West End or Broadway theatres to visit regularly as a succession of new shows opened. Today in both the not-for-profit and commercial theatres theatregoers are much more inclined to arrive for their night out secure in the understanding of precisely what awaits them. The risk is ebbing away. Marketing rules, is it OK?

Some theatres are putting on a fight against the deadly hand of marketing men with their certainties of what the public wants and their increasing control, along with that of the commercial sponsors, over artistic policy. In Glasgow the Citizens Theatre has never touched subscription or sponsors or indeed any more complex ticket pricing than one price for the fit and employed and a second for the young, the old or unemployed. The policy of the directorate has been like that of Diaghilev: to put on shows they like and hope the audience turns up because it shares their preferences. The audience does and for twenty-one years has patronised a programme largely of unknown classics, new plays and only a few that they have ever heard of before. The Glasgow audience has supported the Citizens in greater numbers than the audience of those British repertory theatres which, in times of the reluctant granting of subsidy, of jaded sponsors and of all-powerful marketing men, have moved down market, eschewed classics and put on potboilers. Of course the success of the Citizens is more complex than it might at first look. Giles Havergal, as the senior of the three directors of the Citizens, summed up his own marketing strategy in an interview with Michael Billington in the *Guardian*, recorded by Michael Coveney in *The Citz*, published in 1990: 'I'm like the madame of a brothel. I have my girls on one hand and my clients on the other and the delicate art is to bring them together.'

Such refreshing frankness is relevant to theatre architecture. The theatre planned by the marketing man will have homogeneous seating for a homogeneous audience. Old theatres with their galleries or new theatres with their flexibility, which sometimes involves moving the regular seats of regular subscribers, are inconvenient to the box office manager, as Dudley suggested. And yet perhaps it is no coincidence that the most loyal audiences are found in the quirkiest theatres, whether new or old. Every time one hears an audience of children and adults alike bellow: 'Oh no we won't' in reply to 'Oh yes you will' from villain or comic in an old-fashioned pantomime in an old-fashioned British theatre, one recovers hope that the audience of the future may still be alive and not all, as they grow older, metamorphose into tired business men silently waiting in their comfortable seats with perfect sightlines for the newest mega-musical to be more stupendous than the one before.

There are hopeful signs on both sides of the Atlantic that subscription may have done all it is going to do to theatregoing. Summer festivals abound and the new ones do not preach to the converted as do Bayreuth or Stratford-upon-Avon which run the risk of becoming too much the church and too little the brothel. In summer theatres, or on a visit to off-off-Broadway or the Edinburgh fringe, the unexpected is embraced. The audience is *en fête* and prepared to run risks. This is beginning to wash over into mainstream theatres which today are liable to be bolder in commissioning new stages and auditoriums with interesting new opportunities for new actor-audience relationships. Or so one hopes.

It is now time to turn to the precise physical relationship of audience and actor in most theatres. There are two topographical questions. The first asks whether the greater part of the audience should sit out front with only a few seats placed at the side to connect, in capillary fashion, actor to audience or whether the audience should be placed equally on three sides of the acting area, as in a thrust stage, or on every side as in an in-the-round theatre. This question is endlessly debated. But the second question that is scarcely debated at all concerns the vertical plane rather than the horizontal plane. Should the audience be positioned below or above the actor's eyeline, which is generally regarded as 5 degrees above the horizontal measured from the standing actor of average size?

Few books on theatre design consider this second question while the first has been the subject of endless popular debate since Guthrie created the thrust stage and since in-the-round escaped from the university closet. All text books on theatre history include diagrammatic representation of theatre forms, presented in two dimensions on the horizontal plane, showing the difference in encirclement between Greek, Roman, Baroque, eighteenth-century picture-frame proscenium, etc., etc. It will therefore be a fresh approach to start here with questioning the vertical relationship. This might lead to a reappraisal of the actor-audience relationship in the horizontal plane.

When an audience looks down on the actor it is more likely that its attention will have been precisely predetermined by a director who has organised the pattern of production. The audience looking down will then be contemplating the performer critically as did the director at the rehearsal. If the attention of the audience wavers the actor is in a weak position. There was indeed one sort of eighteenth-century theatre laid out just like this, the operating theatre, of which one survives at Guy's Hospital, London. Each row rises steeply above the one in front and hence the sightlines are perfect to the operating table where lies the 'performer': a corpse laid out for dissection by the surgeon.

If, on the other hand, the audience looks up to the actor, the actor is in control, can elicit responses and can manage the audience because he or she is, quite simply, in the dominant physical position. Actors as well as stand-up comedians generally prefer this. Actors also understand the need for a raked stage so that the dominant position is not confined to the front edge (unfortunately they are often opposed in this by a rare consensus between theatre technicians and architects who find raked stages inconvenient).

A good theatre partakes of both relationships. Ideally the audience is, and for centuries was, divided with half below the eyeline of the standing actor (horizontal plus 5 degrees which also balances the 1 in 24 rake of almost all stages built until the start of this century) and half above that line. This was the rule of the past and, it is suggested, should be the rule in all theatre architecture irrespective of the relationship in the horizontal plane.

In a very small theatre this can be achieved with no stage riser, that is with the first row of seats at stage level. If the rows have 300mm or 1 foot increments, for better sightlines over the row in front, there will be three rows before the horizontal plus 5 degree line is reached. Simple mathematics reveals that if there is no stage riser or just a minimal one, and if there are more than six rows in an auditorium where the back rows are longer than the front rows, then the actors are going to start to feel that they are acting in the bottom of a well because more than half of the audience are going to be above their eyeline. The designers of the Royal Exchange, Manchester, which has three levels of seating, the lower one of which starts at the same level as the acting area, alleviated the problem of acting at the bottom of a well in a large (700-seat) house in a most ingenious fashion. There the first row reclines on low benches the height of oriental cushions, the second on low stools only slightly higher and only the third on conventional theatre seats, the cumulative effect of which is to bring two extra rows further below the actors' eyeline which is not reached until the sixth and last row. This means that at Manchester everybody on the lowest level, nearly half the audience, are on or below actors' eye level.

The critics in the front rows of any theatre may not be aware of the 'acting at the bottom of the well' problem but the actors are. If they feel that most of the response is coming from above they can only counter with 'chin up' acting. Harley Granville Barker deplored this specifically in *The Exemplary Theatre* published in 1922. 'For plays of the so called realistic school of the nineteenth century little is needed but a picture frame proscenium and an auditorium made for some intimacy of effect; and there must be no gallery which will elevate the actor's chin to an angle of disadvantage in the eye of the stalls, or exhibit little more than eyebrows and hair parting to the patient gods.'

And yet for the classics or for music hall (vaudeville) entertainment communion with the gods could be turned to positive advantage. Shakespeare offers opportunities for asides to the underprivileged wherever they are sitting. In the 1880s Little Dot Hetherington at the old Bedford Theatre sang 'The boy I love is up in the gallery', making the whole audience aware of its vertical displacement. More recently Barry Humphries as Dame Edna Everage memorably employed an hydraulic extending platform at the curtain call to raise himself vertically 25 feet above the apron stage at Drury Lane and throw gladioli at his/her 'paupers' in the top gallery. And Ian McKellen, who of all British actors now at the height of their powers has the greatest experience of touring, acknowledges his debt to the variety performers he watched as a schoolboy at the Hippodrome, Bolton, 'working the house'. This is a technique perfectly illustrated in his 1990–1 performance as Richard of Gloucester for the National Theatre Company. In the soliloquies he searched the house, up and down, side to side, until he caught your eye before, confident in your compliance, he found another's eye, and hers over there, and then, having broken down the audience into a collection of individuals, fused them back together again into what Guthrie called 'that great single collective personality'.

Seating that is too steeply raked and, as a consequence, has a centre of audience gravity too far above the actor's head is a major fault in too many modern theatres. This inevitably makes it more difficult for the actor to move an audience to tears or laughter. The Greek influence is partly responsible: at the Olivier Theatre the balance and sightlines were markedly improved when the stage was raised 1 foot 1 inch (330mm) after the first five years although even then probably 80 per cent of the audience remained above the horizontal plus 5 degrees actors' eyeline. Other causes of over-raked theatres producing the well effect, both in Britain and America, include the slavish following of the rules for calculating sightlines, which say that each member of the audience should see over the head of another member of the audience two rows in front to the feet of the actor, with obviously disastrous consequences in any large single-rake auditorium. A second contributing factor is the experience of directors in small fringe theatres where there are rarely more than five rows. From such theatres they attempt to import the freedom of having no stage riser into larger theatres without realising that what is right and appropriate in the small theatre will produce that bottom-of-the-well effect in a theatre seating over 150 or 200. An example of this has been the Cottesloe, which, in so far as its end stage arrangement is concerned, originally had over 50 per cent of the audience of 400 below the horizontal plus 5 degrees actors' eyeline when it opened in 1977. As designed, the 'stalls' (or pit) rose with gentle steppings in eleven rows from a traditional 3 feet 3 inches (1m) below stage level to stage level at the back of the pit. There was originally a complete ring of seats directly below the surviving two galleries that enfold the entire pit/stalls. All the spectators in the pit and in the lowest ring of seats were below the horizontal eyeline.

However, after a few years directors favoured a steeper rake of seats from the same starting point to the middle gallery some 8 feet 6 inches (2.6m) above stage level with row increments of 1 foot (300mm) rather than 4 inches (100mm). The seating capacity was reduced and the centre of gravity of the audience moved upwards converting the Cottesloe to an analytic rather than actor-dominated theatre in its end stage format. This did not affect the endless options open in its other forms – promenade, environmental in-the-round, traverse, etc., although it was interesting to note that the 1989 awards-winning production by Richard Eyre of David Hare's *Racing Demon* raised the actor above the front three rows of audience which surrounded a long cruciform-shaped traverse stage. This elevation gave the actors valuable audience support from below.

Another much heralded new theatre, the 750-seat Quarry Theatre of the West Yorkshire Playhouse in Leeds, whose Olivier-like Greek form had been specified by theatre director John Harrison, also has no stage riser.

There are fifteen rows of seats, each 18 inches (450mm) above the row in front. This means that all but the front three rows are above the horizontal plus 5 degrees. Simple mathematics shows that 600 of the 750 members of the audience are above, looking down. In *Why not Theatres Made for People?* Swedish architect Per Edstrom detected another sightline problem to the downstage performer when describing a Swedish theatre which also lacked any stage riser and which had a shallower rake to the seating than Leeds: 'Besides all this, the whole stage is too low in relationship to the audience. The majority of the audience is forced to look down from above and if a naked ballet came on the stage most of the audience would be able to see that the dancers had hair only on their heads!'. It will be interesting to see whether raised stage platforms become the norm at the Quarry or whether a permanent increase in stage height is introduced as it was at the Olivier. It will also be interesting to see if the entrances to this steeply banked auditorium, all of which are through doors behind the back row, are modified to reduce vertigo.

In North America William Condee is studying this problem of vertical relationship in scholarly detail. At the same Calgary conference of 1989 he said: 'The vertical relationship of audience and performance is a critical aspect of theatrical production. Looking up at a performance is not the same as looking down. A lowered stage creates a sense of distance, aesthetic not physical, from the performance, even if the theatre is small. The audience is in the power position, critically examining the events before them. Raking the stage breathes a sense of aesthetic accessibility and intimacy to the audience.'

To support his thesis he told the story of a number of theatres in New York. The first was the Anspacher Theater at Joseph Papp Public where designer Ming Cho Lee had sought flexibility by not having a stage riser. But the entire audience looks down upon the stage. Wilfred Leech of NYSS felt the theatre should have been intimate but complained of 'remoteness from the actors being down in a hole. You might as well have a proscenium.' Another theatre Condee analysed was the Juillard Drama Theater, opened in 1970. This highly idiosyncratic theatre had been conceived by director Michel St Denis. There was originally a moat between the front row and the stage which was set almost 6 feet (1.8m) below the first row. Michel St Denis did not stay and others inherited this one-off arrangement. Liviu Ciulei gave up saying, 'The theatre is good for, oh, *Timon of Athens*, but not for every play.' More recently, Michael Langham filled in the moat and built a higher stage above the lower stage so as to bring the performance closer to the audience and, presumably, to get some of the audience below the actors' eye level.

Another aspect of vertical relationships is the provision of acting areas above and below the audience's centre of gravity. The checkered history of the central stage balcony at Stratford, Ontario, as conceived by Guthrie and Moiseiwitsch in 1953 and refined in 1956 when the permanent building was substituted for the tent, is a fine example. The multiple levels thus created were provided permanently to directors and designers charged with presenting the plays of Shakespeare and his contemporaries. These levels replicated philosophically, rather than precisely in a topographical sense, those of the Elizabethan stage. They had been the product of the meeting of renaissance notions of spatial symbolism and medieval traditions of hierarchical levels on both heaven and earth or, as Brook described the Elizabethan stage in *The Empty Space*, 'a diagram of the universe as seen by the sixteenth-century audience – three levels, separate and yet inter-mingling – a stage that was a perfect philosopher's machine'. Hence the contrast of the lower level for most of the play's business where the actor, out on the thrust, is surrounded by fellow human beings, below which is hell accessible only through stage traps, and the distinctly separate and higher level, where virtue is isolated or elevated (or supposed to be). The upper level of the balcony not only works for such obvious scenes as the tomb in *Antony and Cleopatra* or Flint Castle in *Richard II*, but also presents the comic possibilities of Gloucester being 'wooed' by the Lord Mayor of London in *Richard III* or of Berowne in *Love's Labour's Lost* observing judgementally the amorous indiscretion of his colleagues.

In 1974 Robin Phillips, successor at Stratford to Guthrie and Langham, instructed that the stage balcony should be removable. But once an audi-ence had seen the stage so curiously bare, the balcony when used again ceased to be structure and became scenery. The experiment of instant emasculation was short-lived. The balcony was reinstated as permanent structure.

The idea that you can reintroduce a piece of structure when you need it when the piece in question was the essence of the theatrical concept is always misguided (perhaps Lasdun's concept of 'a stage in the corner of the room' would have worked if the corner had not been removed in order to create endless scenic opportunities). Scenery rarely looks like structure. It can also be argued that the requirement for permanent levels in Eliza-bethan theatre is absolute, firstly because the plays always require the variation in vertical displacement and secondly because different levels themselves are necessary parts of the world inhabited by the characters in the play just as heaven, earth and hell were for all Elizabethans inevitable elements in the pattern of their lives.

Levels become something quite other if added as part of a pictorial treatment of the mise en scene. That an open or thrust stage should be flat and empty so that a new picture can be created for every production is as intellectually and theatrically impoverished as the notion that all the audience should sit comfortably in a single featureless tier. Both drain theatre space of tension. And to create adaptable theatres that play endless permutations in the horizontal plane only, ignoring vertical displacement altogether, produces the dullest results of all. Hierarchy is the antithesis of uniformity. In theatre architecture, as in all architecture, uniformity is dispiriting.

It is sad that the purifiers of the new movement, with their zeal for greater comfort and better sightlines, laid the foundations of an aesthetic which resulted in so many flat dull theatres that fail to connect actor to audience. Hiram Moderwell, author of *The Theater Today* published in New York in 1914, had invoked democracy: 'To build theatres in which cheap seats are acoustically, optically or hygienically bad is an insolence in a democratic age.... Democracy says ... that if possible nobody should have a bad seat in the theatre no matter how few pennies he has paid for admission.' Rarely have such good intentions had such sad results.

Peter Brook represents the reverse to Moderwell in his zeal to take theatre out of the conventional modern theatre into the village square or into 'found space', in the form of Paris and New York theatres of just the sort Moderwell disliked. In an undated essay in the collection entitled *The Shifting Point* Brook finds himself in Caracas, Venezuela, in just such a theatre/lecture hall that might have been created by an architect who had scrupulously followed the principles of the purifiers. 'I don't like this space. This time yesterday we were at Caracas University, performing under a tree; at night we are playing *Ubu* in a dilapidated abandoned movie house, and the space feels fine. Today you've invited me to join a conference on theatre spaces in your glamourous ultra-modern hall and I am ill at ease. I am asking myself: why?' Having identified the distance, i.e. the spacing row to row, as one of the first problems, he fastened on the second. 'Nothing is so unimportant as comfort; comfort in fact often devitalises the experience. For example, you are all comfortably seated; if at this moment I want to say something in the hope of getting immediate reaction out of you, I'll have to speak very loudly and try to send a charge of energy through the person nearest to me and so on, all the way to the back of the room. Even if I were to succeed your reaction would be very slow, retarded by the gaps in between people imposed by the architects, no doubt to conform with regulations.' Next came the form of auditorium. 'The arrangement for your seats, which is the usual one of course, the most logical way of accommodating the maximum number of people, results in each of us staring at the back of the neck of the person just in front. And I think you will agree that the back of the neck is the least interesting part of our neighbour's anatomy.'

He concluded: 'There are no strict rules to tell us whether a space is good or bad. In fact, all this relates to a kind of rigorous and precise science which we can only develop by continuous development and empiricism based on fact. That's it! Theorising over!' This is heady stuff and sounds good on the barricades. It is only when one wonders how there can be a 'rigorous and precise science' without 'strict rules' that one realises, as always, that Brook prefers an enigmatic paradox to a precise prescription.

For this author it was Brook's questioning of comfort and sightlines following personal experience of so many theatres, old and new, which suggested what might be the mystery that is the key to a successful theatre space. But before attempting to unfold the mystery a brief excursion is needed into the worlds of opera and dance.

Chapter 11

Opera and dance

Playhouse architecture over the past fifty years has certainly not been stuck in any one mode. The forms of new theatres have differed widely. Previous chapters have dealt with some aspects of the confusion surrounding the commissioning of a new theatre. In the world of opera and dance the process is different.

In opera 90 per cent of the current repertoire, measured in terms of performances given and seats sold, was composed between the middle of the eighteenth and the middle of the twentieth centuries and almost all performances take place in conventional opera houses with proscenium arch, richly decorated house curtain and, in front, the ubiquitous orchestra pit. In all but a few experimental opera studios the style of the productions which are to be staged are predictable enough to make it relatively easy to write a detailed design brief for a new opera house. The one area which may be fought over by architects, consultants, musicians, managements, designers and directors is the proscenium and orchestra pit zone; it is the resolution of this battle which provides the connection between opera house and playhouse design today. Backstage in the main theatre of an opera house the planning will be determined by the demands of repertoire. This means the staging on different days of the week of productions of a scale which in the commercial theatre are fitted up to run for years rather than a single night. The Nationaltheater at Munich which houses the Bayerisches Staatsoper has, for example, over ninety productions in store which are produced in revolving repertoire.

The current, 1992, price tag for a fully resourced smaller opera house (1,000 to 1,250 seats) is between £30 million and £40 million (in America between $40 and $75 million) and for a large international house (2,000 to 3,000 seats) between £120 and £300 million ($220 to $570 million). Their sheer cost makes their creation a national event. Small wonder that their design attracts great interest.

Theatres for dance companies of international status have traditionally been thought of alongside opera houses. Indeed opera and ballet companies often share the same home. How the demands of dance differ from those of opera will be examined at the end of this chapter. First it is necessary to trace the evolution of the opera house and review the current debate on what constitutes an opera house for the twenty-first century, not only for its own sake but also for the light it throws on theatre architecture in general.

The opera house and the playhouse share common antecedents. The earlier open stages of the Italian renaissance, including the still surviving Teatro Olimpico of Vicenza (1580–4) and of Sabbioneta (1588), provide antecedents both to the English-speaking playhouse, whose continuity of character from the mid seventeenth century has already been asserted, and to the opera house. But by 1639 the characteristic Italian opera house with its multi-tier 'U'-shaped auditorium embracing orchestra pit and acting forestage, beyond which was a scenic stage replete with the technology of spectacle, had already evolved in Venice with the opening of the Theatro SS Giovanni e Paolo. In time the horseshoe-shaped Italian opera house was to become as strong and enduring a cultural symbol as the Gothic cathedral, a celebration of a society united in its love for a style of opera which moved, with amazing rapidity, from formal presentations of the emotions in the mid eighteenth century to the operatic comedies of manners of Mozart that held up a mirror to nature. It was only in the mid nineteenth century, as the Romantic movement flowered, that a picture frame was interposed between auditorium and stage. Then the forestage, which as in the Georgian playhouse had projected into the auditorium, was cut back until by the beginning of the twentieth century its existence, even in theatres as late as E. M. Barry's Royal Opera House, Covent Garden, of 1856, had been forgotten. Barry's vestigial apron stage, which brought the singers out from behind the proscenium to where their voices would be assisted by the auditorium architecture, was removed in 1901 when the stage was also flattened. Even the eighteenth-century theatres that survived had their acting forestages removed; in Bavaria both the Markgrafliches Opernhaus at Bayreuth (1748) and the Cuvilliés Theater in Munich (1753) have been restored wrongly, orchestra pit or platform where once was the acting stage, the singer now standing behind the proscenium within the scenery, set on an inappropriately flat stage, all of which is severely detrimental to the sightlines from the side seats.

Just as churches have continued to be built in the Gothic style long after the end of the fifteenth century, so Italian eighteenth century opera houses have been built in every age and in almost all countries of the civilised world. Today the few opera houses at present contemplated are likely to follow this form in the broadest sense. Certainly since the opening of Wagner's Festspielhaus in Bayreuth in 1876 the debate has continued whether to substitute for the horseshoe auditorium some new form. But, despite all argument, the classical Italian opera house has survived and remains the pre-eminent form of what has come to be regarded as a 'real'

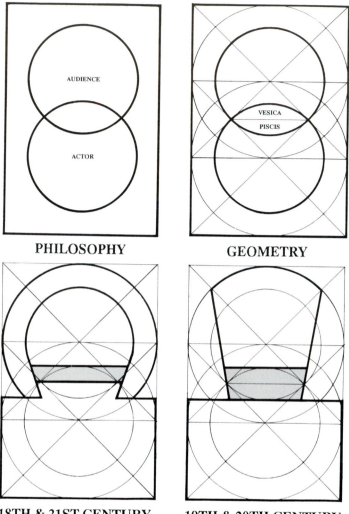

PHILOSOPHY
      GEOMETRY

18TH & 21ST CENTURY
      19TH & 20TH CENTURY

19 Ad quadratum geometry illustrates that the traditional opera house is focused on the magical area, called in sacred geometry the 'vesica piscis', where the worlds of audience and actor interconnect. In the eighteenth century this space was occupied by the musicians, tightly packed in a narrow orchestra pit, together with the actor or singer on the acting stage within the architectural volume of the house and in front of the scenic stage. The romantics, led by the scenic artists and the musicians, abolished the acting stage and enlarged the orchestra pit until it separated the audience from the performers who were pushed up stage and entrapped within a naturalistic scenic picture. Today, opera directors want to escape from the proscenium and into the house, thereby turning the wheel full circle to recapture the space lost in the first half of the nineteenth century. Architects and designers of theatre space follow cautiously.

opera house, even if today the Romantic picture frame has been grafted on to the audience-involving horseshoe.

In Italy so many first-class opera houses survive from the eighteenth and nineteenth centuries that there has been little demand for new opera houses and hence little debate on their nature. Indeed only the Turin opera house of 1973 (Carlo Mollino and Marcello Zavelani-Rossi) and the 1991 Genoa opera house designed by Aldo Rossi, have departed from tradition. In both cases this has been a disaster. In Turin art director's futurism rules while at Genoa post-modernism and a cinema-like auditorium, decorated in a style that can only be described as 'post-Eberson atmospheric', will pall only too soon.

In France too, many eighteenth- and nineteenth-century theatres and opera houses have survived. Nevertheless one great opera house has been built in this century, the monumental 3,000 million franc (£300 million, $570 million) Bastille opera house, Paris. This otherwise unimaginable extravagance commemorated the bicentenary of the French revolution in 1989. Behind an uninspiring exterior, which looks like an architectural model of itself, there is on the one hand technical perfection backstage and on the other a pedestrian 2,700-seat main auditorium which provides the perfect argument why no opera house with modern standards of comfort should hold more than 2,000. The fact that all the seats face the proscenium, in very long, almost straight rows, coupled with the sheer size, results in a house where anything other than the big production and the big voice are going to be lost. The technical facilities, which purportedly exist to create change and store sets for huge productions, will of themselves generate ever more expensive settings. Whether the budget exists to pay either for such scenic excess beyond the dreams of the most ambitious German technical director or for a roster of great singers to 'fill' the house in both senses of the word is doubtful. The bigger the house the bigger the excess of expenditure over income has ever been the rule in twentieth-century opera, a reminder that the dollar equation is never resolved by increases in size.

In Britain one can point to only three purpose-built opera houses. These are the Royal Opera House, Covent Garden, the tiny Britten Music Theatre at the Royal College of Music of 1986, designed by Casson Conder and Partners, which holds 418, and the 1,250-seat new Glyndebourne Opera House, designed by Michael Hopkins & Partners with Theatre Projects Consultants as auditorium design and technical consultants, opening in 1994. All three are horseshoe-shaped with tier upon tier and are therefore 'real' opera houses which differ substantially from all other theatres played by Britain's major opera companies.

At the Aldeburgh and the Glyndebourne festivals opera had been presented in elegant sheds. At Aldeburgh architects Arup Associates created a chamber concert hall out of an old maltings building. The acoustics are

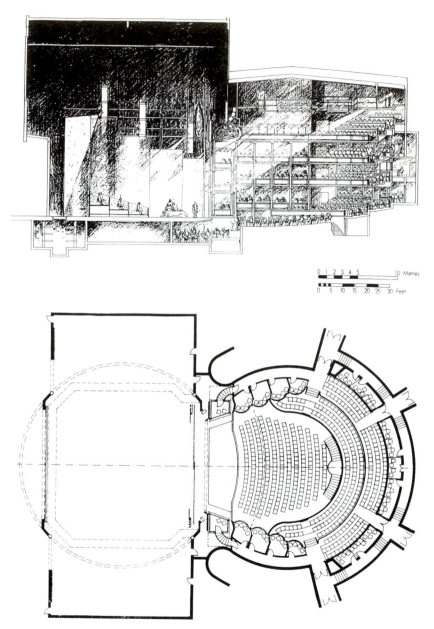

20 The 1990 concept design by Theatre Projects Consultants for the auditorium
of the new Glyndebourne Festival Opera, opening in 1994. As developed by the
architects, Michael Hopkins & Partners, in consultation with John Bury for
Glyndebourne, this design lost a gallery and had its flexible proscenium zone
replaced with a fixed arch of concrete. Nevertheless, the horseshoe form chosen in
preference to the Wagner/cinema fan re-establishes self-awareness of an audience
'assisting at' the celebration of opera.

superb. Here opera is regularly and elegantly improvised for two or three performances each year – improvised because composer Benjamin Britten ascetically insisted that the hall be kept free of necessary technical equipment so that there would be no compromise in its acoustical performance as a concert hall. The old theatre at Glyndebourne, dismantled after the 1992 festival, was a stretched version of the pitched-roof hall which sixty years ago held hardly 400 but was repeatedly adapted and extended to squeeze in 830. Both Aldeburgh and old Glyndebourne are agreeably eccentric in an English way. But the theatres which the Scottish and Welsh Opera Companies, Opera North and the Buxton Festival Opera regularly use are types of theatre peculiar to Britain: medium-scale 'lyric' theatres erected at the end of the nineteenth century and, even if they were originally called opera houses as at Buxton, built for a wide range of activities.

The Theatre Royal, Glasgow (1895), the Grand Theatre, Leeds (1878), and the Opera House, Buxton (1903), were typical of those multi-purpose theatres built by commercial interests at the end of the nineteenth century which simply requested of their architects that they accommodate the greatest possible number of spectators on a given site. The architect was instructed that the auditorium should look as grand as possible and the stage be economically equipped for the full spectrum of entertainment then available: drama, musical theatre and, very occasionally, opera or dance. The steel cantilevers, by which deep shelves of humanity were packed in one on top of each other, may have produced excellent sightlines by reason of the absence of columns but made for bad acoustics for a third of the audience. This was because at least this proportion was seated beyond the central architectural and acoustical volume of the room and instead were tucked under low ceilings produced by the gallery immediately overhead. In these houses the acoustic quality varies enormously just as it did for the drama in similar but smaller London theatres such as the Garrick Theatre, the visit by Max Beerbohm to the rear pit of which was described in Chapter 4.

British opera companies have been aware of the acoustical shortcomings of these theatres for opera but generally the public has loved them. The dramatic intensity of these relatively small theatres, the facing balcony at Glasgow being less than half the distance from the stage than that of the facing balcony in the Royal Opera House, Covent Garden, has encouraged directors and designers to give the classics a new dramatic force. It may have been the best thing for the development of opera as an art form that Edinburgh and Cardiff did not get their promised purpose-built and 'modern' opera houses in the 1960s.

There is one 'opera house' in Britain which does not belong to any of the above categories, Italian horseshoe, English shed or turn-of-the-century general purpose theatre. This is the London Coliseum into which English National Opera, then Sadler's Wells Opera, moved in 1968 from the

characterless and unloved Sadler's Wells Theatre of 1931. The London
Coliseum was built in 1904 by Britain's most prolific theatre architect,
Frank Matcham, but it was then and is now totally unlike any other of
his theatres. From the start it had a unique policy: variety, which was
what music hall had evolved into just as burlesque metamorphosed into
vaudeville in North America. This was an expensive celebration of all the
theatre arts. At the lowest level variety included low comedians, soubrettes,
jugglers and fan dancers. At the highest level at the Coliseum, with its
two royal boxes, one at the side and one, unusually for Britain, at the
centre, and, exceptionally for anywhere, reached by a railway running to
the royal entrance, the same variety bill would include drama from such
as Sarah Bernhardt, dancing by Pavlova or members of the Ballet Russe
and comics such as George Robey or Harry Lauder. A principal ingredient
was music; there was a large orchestra in the pit, often a choir or chorus
on the stage and the leading tenor of the day singing a popular repertoire.
So when Sadler's Wells Opera rediscovered the Coliseum in 1968, after it
had been languishing as a cinerama cinema, they were in effect carrying
out the intention of the theatre's creator, Oswald Stoll, in providing the
finest of the musical and other theatre arts to a fashionable audience seated
in an auditorium of the greatest possible splendour.

The Coliseum is Roman in name and in style. The side walls are richly
decorated and include boxes from which a view of the stage is possible.
The present audience of 2,350 (originally 3,389 plus standing) is accommodated in stalls and lowest circle, between which are a row of central boxes
unique in Britain, plus three large uninterrupted circles over. The latter
are not too close together and thus do not present acoustical traps as at
other theatres of the same period. At the London Coliseum 2,350 people
are accommodated closer to the performer, as well as more comfortably,
than are 2,180 at Covent Garden. The Coliseum also has fewer 'restricted
view' seats. Tyrone Guthrie, whose forays into opera were never as successful as his work in drama, would have much preferred the saloon bar
cosiness of the Coliseum to the faded grandeur of Covent Garden which
he described at a conference held in Manchester in 1962 as 'a beast of a
building'. In 1962 Guthrie argued from the general to the particular: 'it
is axiomatic in my philosophy of the theatre that the audience has got to
be packed into the place. The rapport between the stage and the audience
is tremendously conditioned by the amount of cubic space that is empty.
The Royal Opera House at Covent Garden is considered very distinguished. So I am sure it is on gala nights when the Queen is there in
jewels like stop and go lights and there are Field Marshals a mile a minute
in their feathers. On nights like that it is great. But when you or I are
there with mackintoshes on, and a bag of brussels sprouts on the floor you
are conscious that there is a great sahara of red velvet. The amount of
empty air is tremendous; it is fighting the performance all the time.' It is

a criticism which also applies to modern theatres with too much space in the middle – the equally horseshoe-shaped Toronto Opera Ballet House, had it been built as designed in 1990, was to be nearly 20 feet (6m) longer in the centre than Covent Garden simply because it was to have better sightlines and more legroom.

In using all-purpose late nineteenth-century theatres for opera Britain has fared slightly better than has North America. Very few 'real' opera houses were built in America in the nineteenth century. Many were called 'opera houses' but that was simply because the playhouse and the player were considered as fundamentally immoral as the bar and the dancing girl. However, a respectable young lady could be seen at an 'opera house' even if a single performance of Gounod's *Faust* every three years might have been the sum total of opera presented in these small town 'opera houses'.

Between 1883 and 1966 New York did have its own real opera house, the Metropolitan Opera House, which originally occupied a whole city block on Broadway between 39th and 40th Street. The old 'Met' competed in costliness and splendour with the great European opera houses and for a time New York had its own opera company plus international stars who visited from Europe on the great ocean liners. Distinguished performances took place in what, with 3,600 tightly packed seats, was billed as being 'the greatest opera house in the world' – in seating capacity it may have been the biggest but in site area it was very low down on the list compared with the national opera houses of Europe. Nevertheless great stars were needed to conquer the vast distances of the Met. Opera was still thought of as a larger-than-life and decidedly un-American activity, so brilliantly guyed by the Marx Brothers in 1936 in *A Night at the Opera*. Outside an educated elite America would not take opera seriously until after the Second World War.

The 'Met' moved to the Lincoln Center in 1966. The new house was bigger because it held over 3,600 in uniformly greater comfort. It was quickly criticised as 'reactionary' in its 'status-seeking' aping of the old theatre's 'golden horseshoe'. Architecturally it is a hybrid with a flattened horseshoe of boxes at the lower levels and above a huge stadium-like fan of gallery seats, unrelated in form to the remainder of the house.

The Met soon had a second opera house alongside, the much less lavishly equipped New York State Theater which is home both to the City Opera and to the New York City Ballet. The building of theatres designed exclusively for opera and ballet then stopped until the recent creation of opera houses in Houston, Texas, and Minneapolis, Minnesota, in the late 1980s. Meanwhile there have been two inadequate sorts of substitute. The first has been the building of new adaptable all-purpose auditoriums, the extravagant claims for which were examined in Chapter 8. The second has been the recycling of the huge ornate movie palaces which have found new life as music theatres presenting opera, dance, touring Broadway musicals and, under acoustic shells, symphony orchestras. Both have been too big for the scale and quality of the opera and ballet companies that perform in them. The ostentatious regilded glamour of the recycled movie palaces may have given donor and patron a superior sense of metropolitan sophistication but generally they have condemned the art form of opera in America to the circumscribed life of episodic part-time companies, whose reputations are built almost entirely round their being able to book the few big names able to fill these huge theatres both vocally and commercially. As always the form of the spaces available for opera has determined the character of the opera which is produced. No wonder almost all the excellent young American singers have left for Germany to practise their craft in much more appropriately sized theatres.

In Germany there has been more debate this century about opera house architecture than anywhere else. The Second World War destroyed the opera houses of most of the great cities. Rebuilding was an early priority and how the individual cities approached the problem of auditorium architecture provides a revealing change in attitudes between the 1950s, 1960s and early 1970s.

But before exploring the differences between the auditoriums of succeeding generations of German opera house what is common to all must be noted: huge stages, massive stage machinery – large gridirons with power flying, massive proscenium bridges, huge revolves and wagons moving in pre-destined grooves – which has trapped the performer in a technical straitjacket. In Germany the stage engineer has always been king. He assumed all acting, singing and dancing took place behind a picture-frame proscenium (there were never any open or thrust stages in Germany, only mechanised studios) and so his efficient technology, plus the fire marshal's strict regulations, ensured the performer stayed upstage, beyond the safety curtain, water drencher, house curtain and moving proscenium bridge and towers, bristling with lights and wide enough for technicians to walk to and fro as in a scene from Fritz Lang's *Metropolis*.

In the auditoriums which confronted these miraculous but separately defined stages, the taste at first was for fusing the two traditions of Italian horseshoe and Wagnerian fan. Frankfurt (1,387 seats – 1951), Cologne (1,346 seats – 1951), Hamburg (1,675 seats – 1955) and West Berlin (1,903 seats – 1961) may have had side boxes but with seats fixed and facing the stage. The boxes were steeply raked and had high sides like omnibus versions of a modern racing car. These were christened 'ski slope boxes'. The pattern of fan plus stepped side boxes was repeated in the smaller theatres of the smaller cities where 1,000- to 1,200-seat opera houses often had also to do service as playhouses and as dance theatres. Some new German theatres such as the Hamburgische Staatsoper were built as new auditoriums within the shell of an older theatre. In Munich they wavered, having long contemplated the bombed shell of the 1818 neo-classical National Theater (opera house) by Karl Von Fischer. In contrast to Hamburg they decided not to build a new auditorium but to rebuild the old one much as it once was, plus the obligatory fully engineered new stage.

Munich's re-creation of the past, which reopened in 1963, influenced others. In Dresden they agonised for a quarter of a century. Inside the burnt-out shell of Semper's magnificent opera house of 1878 they had prepared the foundations for a totally new auditorium. But in the 1970s they changed their minds and decided to rebuild Semper's original auditorium, albeit stretched at the sides to fit the foundations for the now abandoned 'new' auditorium – something few notice today. (Many also fail to notice that the gallery has been reduced from twelve rows to four in the name of better sightlines: 'on a commis au paradis si déterminant de Semper un vrai barbarisme' wrote Jean Vermeil in *Opéras d'Europe*. The seating capacity of this major theatre on the international circuit was thereby reduced to only 1,103.)

War-damaged opera houses were also meticulously reconstituted in central and eastern Europe. Subsidised workers sat in the plush seats to taste the same operatic and balletic sweetmeats that had been offered to their aristocratic predecessors. Some auditoriums were modernised such as the Teatr Wielki, Warsaw, in 1965 within an 1830 shell, and the Vienna Staatsoper in 1955 within an otherwise completely restored 1869 building. Warsaw and, to a lesser extent, Vienna were glitzed in a style familiar to opera goers at New York's 'Met' and subsequently to be known as 'American hotel lobby'. The reborn Warsaw and Vienna opera houses were impressive as examples of communities putting opera before what others would call the necessities of life in post-war reconstruction, but, as pieces of modern theatre architecture, they served to strengthen the hand of those who would restore in an old style rather than build afresh in a new style.

After twenty-five years of restoration new forms and fresh solutions had a brief vogue. But the tide has turned; for example the new opera house at Glyndebourne is of traditional horseshoe form. Architects and theatre design consultants as well as performers and opera goers, who have made a tour of opera houses old and new, reacted against the vast impersonality of the new Bastille opera house in Paris (2,700 seats, 1989) and the endlessly wide Musiektheater in Amsterdam (1,600 seats, 1986) which, with its three arcs of scarlet seating centred on a single radius point, is a sort of operatic Olivier Theatre. Nevertheless both are more congenial than the later German opera houses of the late 1970s such as the streamlined 950-seat house at Darmstadt and the brutalist concrete asymmetric 1,000-seat Karlsruhe Grosses Haus of 1975. Only the elegant 1,125-seat Essen opera house, which was completed in 1988 from a winning design by the late Alvar Aalto for a competition held in 1959, has shown theatre and opera goers that a modern medium-scale opera house, also used for dance music theatre and some drama, can both be a thing of beauty and maintain some of the human scale which is the hallmark of all but the biggest of the surviving eighteenth- and nineteenth-century 'Italian' opera houses.

But the success of any new opera house, great or small, as the flexibility of the stage for theatrical innovation, relies largely to the extent to which the proscenium zone allows different transitions between the world of the spectator and the world of the performer. This takes place in the all-important downstage area which, in an opera house, has to be shared with the conductor and the orchestra. Today's directors and designers are not content to be trapped within the picture frame of illusion. They want to bring the performer out into the audience chamber and in this respect are turning the clock back to the theatres of the eighteenth century where the scenic stage behind the proscenium was just that and the performer came out beyond it on to the acting stage to meet the spectator. In their attitude to this all-important zone directors and designers are now diametrically opposed to the arch-romantic Richard Wagner who spoke of the orchestra pit and of this area as follows: 'We called this the "mystic chasm" because its task was to separate the real world from the ideal. . . . The spectator has the feeling of being at a distance from the events on stage, yet perceives them with the clarity of near proximity; in consequence, the stage figures give the illusion of being enlarged and superhuman.' Thus Wagner, who is generally thought of as the forerunner of the new movement, freeing theatre from the tyranny of the decorated proscenium arch frame and from the social irrelevancies of the side boxes, is revealed in his true colours as one of the last to be enslaved by romantic illusion in the theatre. Today the director and some managements of opera are anxious to reconnect opera with society; this involves the literal connection of audience and performers in the proscenium zone, something to which some tidy-minded modern architects are resistant possibly so as to preserve the architectural integrity of their auditorium. Yet it is in this profound matter of reaching out to the audience that opera and playhouse architecture come together again and it is thus right and proper both to explore their common architectural antecedents and also to parallel recent movements.

Ballet or dance is different from opera and drama in respect of pulling the performer out from behind the proscenium arch. Choreographers rarely want to blur that division between spectator and performer. This is not just because the repertoire is based on the nineteenth-century classics which belong behind the arch but because dance is spatially more formal than either opera or drama. Innovative choreographers such as Martha Graham, Maurice Bejart and Pina Bausch have worked with the audience on three or four sides. But these events are rare; ballet and modern dance almost invariably demand a dance area of some 41 feet (12.5m) square, on only one side of which sit first the orchestra and then the audience. From this it might be assumed that the perfect auditorium for a proscenium dance theatre has its seating in rows 41 feet (12.5m) wide, so that all see into the whole of the square dancing area, and with the rows raised one behind the other, so the occupants of each row see over the heads of the rows in front to the dancers' feet or, as so often in modern dance, to the prone dancer on the floor. It might be thought that to the dancer anything other than such perfect sightlines would be considered just one more of the impositions which dance, the Cinderella of the performing arts, must endure. In fact the reasons why many dance theatres have some seats with bad sightlines are twofold: first the interaction of the needs for human scale and for economic capacity and second something more mysterious.

It is easy to demonstrate that there is a physical limit to such a dance theatre with perfect sightlines. In rows 41 feet (12.5m) wide one can fit twenty-five seats. Although perhaps the rows could widen slightly towards the back in a slight fan to thirty or even thirty-five seats the rigidity of most choreographic expression seems to demand good sightlines for all into the upstage corners. If then the seats are about 3 feet (0.9m) apart back to back such an auditorium is going to hold a maximum of 1,000 people in a single rake if the furthest spectator is to be within 80 feet (31m) of the dancer, the distance at which it might be possible to see the expression on a dancer's face (beyond this distance, said one German choreographer, you cannot fall in love with a dancer). The Nederlands Danstheater in The Hague of 1987 is exactly this size and is probably the finest modern dance theatre in the world. However, for economic reasons ballet is usually presented in theatres having many more than 1,000 seats. And since in dance, as in the other performing arts, it is the scale of the place that determines much of the character of the work, the repertoire of the major companies is weighted in favour of the big classics, in which only spectacular solos, pas-de-deux or the massed ranks of the corps de ballet can register to the distant spectator, as opposed to works which explore more complex dramatic relationships between a number of characters, more than a pair and less than a corps, and which consequently must be viewed closer to.

Major ballet companies are always complaining of the difficulty of introducing new choreographers into the repertoire. Only a very few companies such as those run by Diaghilev in the first half of the century have succeeded in presenting a constant stream of new work. This may have been because his company regularly appeared at the smaller houses, like the exquisite 600-seat Opéra of Monte Carlo built by Charles Garnier in 1879. In the larger theatres Diaghilev's company, just like any other, presented the classics in the grandest manner to provide the big effect.

The ideal world, a small theatre for that part of the repertoire, whether classical or modern, which gains from intimacy plus a large house for the money makers, whether Pavarotti in Puccini or the Kirov in *Swan Lake*, is not easily attainable. The promised second house at Covent Garden disappeared from the plans in the late 1970s. Later the proposed tenancy by New York's Met of the Majestic in Brooklyn never materialised. But the financial justification for making international opera houses smaller may be just round the corner: hi-fi flat-screen television. A close-up of a star soloist 'projecting' in a huge house can be absurd; video the same performer in a smaller house where he or she is more relaxed and hence appears more truthful, both to the small audience in a small theatre and to the viewer watching on the screen at home, and the result may be a video tape of greater quality. The resulting sales may well more than offset the loss of box office in a smaller theatre compared to that attainable from those attending 2,000/3,500-seat monsters. A corollary may be an increase in exhibition hall opera, exemplified by the *Aida*, *Carmen* and *Tosca*, staged successively in 1989, 1990 and 1991 in a 10,000-seat temporary auditorium in London's Earls Court, and elsewhere in the world by the Mark Macormack organisation. The latter brought ten years' experience in presenting international tennis to the somewhat different world of opera. However, opera as spectacle is by no means new, seasons in monumental Roman settings at the Baths of Caracalla, in Verona and in Orange, France, being regular events while in 1885 Adler and Sullivan created a 6,200-seat opera festival hall in Chicago.

To the constant battle of scale must be added another feature of the dancers' relationship to the place in which their art is performed. While dancers and choreographers always call for a theatre with perfect sightlines they are then strangely inconsistent in their preferences. Dancers, when asked which theatres they like to perform in, usually nominate traditional theatres such as Garnier's Paris Opéra, the Royal Opera House, Covent Garden, and the Royal Theatre in Copenhagen. All these theatres have a large proportion of seats at the side with bad sightlines in the horizontal plane as well as steep galleries from which the spectator may see the patterns created by the choreographer but cannot easily gauge the emotional power of the individual performance. There would seem to be two reasons why the dancers enjoy these theatres despite the sightlines. The first is the rich sense of occasion which these grand theatres impart – Guthrie hated it but a lot of people enjoy the way a theatrical experience in such a theatre differs from that found either in a modern auditorium or at a typical Broadway or West End theatre. But more profound is the dancers' need to sense the physical presence of the audience and vice versa. The dancer performing in his own cube of air is projecting energy through the fourth wall set on the edge of the stage into the auditorium. Ballet audiences react vividly to the achievement of the difficult in the dance. This energy supports the dancer. The interdependence of energies is greatly enhanced in those theatres where the audience curves round to the proscenium and which provide points at which performer and audience can connect. Once again the dancer's experience is echoed by the actor: Albert Finney described this first sensation to Peter Lewis when expressing dissatisfaction with the Olivier: 'If you stand on the stage of a "proper" theatre, there is a circuit of energy flowing out to the audience and back to the performer again. Here the circuit wasn't completed. The energy going out of me did not come back. Instead of being recharged, like a dynamo, I felt like a battery running down.'

Thus, while in opera it would seem more a question of tradition and of the sense of community of the audience with the performer that leads both to prefer houses with a proportion of side seats with bad sightlines, the reason in the dance and the drama why the architecture of the audience should enfold the performer arises from an ancient need to balance physical forces.

The complexity of this balance is illustrated by the arguments for and against a raked stage for dance. The Imperial theatres of Russia were all raked and even the rehearsal rooms at the Bolshoi still are. Russian dancers have been equivocal about flat stages: when Nijinsky first met a flat stage in Paris, for *Le Spectre de la Rose* he found he had insufficient momentum for the famous leap through the window. At the Edinburgh Festival from 1947 to 1966 the world's greatest dancers danced without much complaint at the Empire Theatre with its 1:24 rake. But this has changed and for the last twenty years, the majority vote is for a flat stage, not least because the Royal Ballet has always enjoyed the flat stage introduced at the Royal Opera House, Covent Garden, in 1901. It is also nearly a century since dancers met a raked stage in America.

The magic and the balance of raked stage to tiered auditorium is best appreciated by walking downstage on the centre line in just such a house: as one moves closer to the yielding curves of a fine horseshoe-shaped auditorium one is instantly made aware of the potential for the performer to fly forward, to penetrate the awaiting audience. The acrobat makes his move, the trapeze swings and the catcher awaits.

Contemplation of the formality of dance and of the dancers' dependence on audience reaction has led us to dig back further in the quest for the fundamentals of the mystery of theatre. Are there any rules to guide us?

Part III

Tomorrow

Chapter 12

Unfolding a mystery

Before exploring how the energy of actors and audience can be channelled, exchanged and heightened through effective theatre architecture, it is necessary to consign to the bonfire those false gods whose feet of clay have been revealed in previous chapters.

First there is the question of size and the idea that bigger is better for either commercial or social reasons. Almost all the theatres, both playhouses and opera houses, in which successful drama, opera and dance have been created, have been small. Fine work has certainly been successfully transferred to larger houses (American director and playwright George Abbott was asked on the occasion of his 100th birthday when this modern taste for playing in over large theatres started; he replied it was probably when Burbage suggested to Shakespeare that they get themselves a bigger house so that they could make more money). But great theatre is rarely originated in large houses. To those who ask 'what about the Greeks?' having in their minds the vast terraces of the well-preserved theatre at Epidaurus, one has to reply that the theatre in which the plays of Aeschylus, Sophocles, Aristophanes and Euripides were first performed in the golden age of Greek drama, from 485 (*The Oresteia*) to 405 BC (*The Bacchae*), was probably much smaller than either huge Epidaurus, built circa 330 BC and later extended in Hellenistic times, or the Theatre of Dionysus on the southern slope of the Acropolis, which dates from no earlier than 343 BC. Such a misunderstanding is rather like imagining that Handel's Covent Garden of the eighteenth century was the size of the present theatre built by Barry in 1858, when Handel's pre-Holland Covent Garden was in fact no bigger than one of the smaller West End or Broadway playhouses. Large capacities may have been achieved for fifth-century BC Greek drama performances but only with densities greater even than those of the Elizabethan theatres and certainly much more than is suggested by the generously spaced 'cavea' of the later Hellenistic amphitheatres.

The greed of today's client who wants ever bigger seating capacities, plus comfort of course, is often compounded by the architect or consultant, who claim they can make a big theatre or opera house intimate by some architectural device. Such overconfident stretching of space over which performers must communicate condemns the resulting enormous theatres to a rollercoaster of success and failure. Success is then determined not by the talent of writers, musicians and performers but by the availability of big names, either of stars or of shows which are already 'hits', which not unreasonably command big fees, and by the capacity of the producer to pay for the big effect, whether it be the 100 plus crowds of Henry Irving, ever larger flocks of cygnets in the ballet or the helicopters of the mega-musical. Out, then, with any economic argument that leads to the monster house awaiting the rare mega-show. If success is to be attained for the live performance and the audience lured away from their hi-fi home video more than lip service must be paid to intimacy.

Second there is the imperative of perfect sightlines. The paradox that good theatres have a proportion of seats with bad sightlines, while theatres with uniformly excellent sight lines are invariably bad theatres, disliked by both actor and audience, is an uncomfortable but empirically demonstrable truth. Out then with the rationalist who talks of theatre architecture as rational seating geometry, and, ironically invoking Wagner's Bayreuth, suggests that theatre architecture is no more than an outer covering for banks of well-raked easy chairs.

Third there is 'adaptability' or the overselling of 'flexibility'. The theatre that can metamorphose itself into any actor-audience relationship is likely, if it holds more than 400/450, to turn out to be no theatre but either a hangar full of costly machinery like Peter Stein's Schaubuhne or else an empty void in which you can create a theatre provided you have a lot of time and a lot of money. Out with the engineer who has a new panacea, a mechanical device enabling the customer to do anything with the space – a different position from that of the more thoughtful theatre designer who offers limited flexibility at a manageable scale.

Fourth is the star scenic designer, who, fresh from the staging of masques at the Carolean court of the seventeenth century, of beplumed follies for Ziegfeld in between-the-wars New York or of a new mechanical musical at the end of the twentieth century, demands the stage on which anything is possible. Such designers will, like their many predecessors, be almost certain to demote human values in the service of 'a shilling's worth of show'. Out then with any designer or director whose technical demands are exorbitant and who cannot make magic on a near empty stage within a well-shaped space.

Fifth there is the generalist architect, whose skills may have been demonstrated in buildings less complex than theatres, buildings where the central activity is not concerned with the magical and often illusionistic manipulation of space. Many such architects often believe that the theatrical arts require modernisation. Out therefore must go the architect who has had a vision which will revolutionise the worn, old conventional wisdom of mere theatre craftsman. True, Hans Scharoun with his in-the-round Berlin Philharmonie of 1963 succeeded in providing a sensationally successful concert hall unlike any other at the time (there have, inevitably, been second-rate derivatives since), but such a revolutionary approach to theatre architecture as opposed to concert hall architecture has invariably failed. The architect who prefers modern untested solutions to the everlasting problems of theatre architecture ought to be designing television studios, pop arenas or other temples of the twenty-first century, where the need for 'state of the art' technological solutions is unquestioned, rather than theatres or opera houses where the requirements of live and reciprocal communication have changed little over the centuries.

If the stage can be thus cleared the seeker of wisdom will discover that there are only three doors. The first is labelled 'the best of the past'. If the town has a good old theatre, then keep it. Improve the dressing rooms, the bar, the foyer, the 'load in', but do not tamper with the obviously successful chamber where performer meets audience. And if no such tried and tested old theatre exists reproduce one like the best elsewhere. This is the safe-sounding reassurance to be found inside the first door.

The second door is labelled 'instant found space'. Found space excites the theatrical director or entrepreneur if it has character and the potential for inexpensive conversion. Gurus remind the seeker that in this uncertain age we should not, even if we had the money which we usually do not, build for posterity. These are the masters of the theatrical moment. They believe that the conversion of found space for this or that style of theatre will stimulate both performer and audience in a way no conventional theatre architecture ever can. Such arguments appear convincing and their own achievements would seem to justify this approach. But is this philosophy exportable or inheritable? Can found space work as well for those other than the finder and if it does, does it not cease to be found space and become simply another theatre with its inconvenience increasingly apparent as the shock of the new wears off?

The third door has three simple words written on it: 'a new theatre'. Note the absence of a capital 'N' or 'T'. This is the door through which one passes to create any new theatre, not necessarily a new form of theatre as had been envisaged by the purifiers of the first half of the century. By choosing this door the seeker has rejected both found space and a restoration or reproduction of the best of the past.

This does not mean that the past is to be rejected. On the contrary the easiest way to understand the mystery of theatre architecture is to study the past and those channels for energy which run under attractive architectural forms and far from purposeless decoration and which director, designer and performer know how to tap through theatrical craft and working knowledge.

This will reveal that a high proportion of successful theatres are set out according to the principles of what has become known as 'sacred geometry'. The word 'sacred' should not suggest that a faith must first be embraced if one is to understand its power. Nor should 'geometry' suggest the rigid straitjacket of a grid which forces form into inflexible patterns. Rather should one think of it as a system of dynamic spatial harmony, dynamic because theatre space is to be arranged not for repose but to encourage the movement of energy, spatial for obvious reasons and harmony because it is concerned with proportions analogous to the harmonies in music.

Two examples from the last two centuries will illustrate the point, both expositions of simple *ad quadratum* geometry (there are more complex systems of geometry including *ad triangulum* which is the product of manipulating isosceles triangles within a circle, and the golden section, expressed mathematically as

$$\frac{\sqrt{5} + 1}{2} = 1.618 \text{ approx.}$$

and which is related to the so called Fibonacci series, the universal principle inherent in all growing things, where the next term is the sum of the two previous terms, i.e. 1, 2, 3, 5, 8, 13, 21, 34, 55, 89, 144, etc.).

The first is the Theatre Royal, Bury St Edmunds, built by William Wilkins in 1819. Wilkins, who was the architect of the National Gallery in Trafalgar Square, of Downing College, Cambridge, and of University College, London, had inherited the East Anglian circuit of theatres from his father. As both client and architect he had already built or remodelled the theatres in Ipswich and Cambridge before starting on Bury St Edmunds. As well as being manager of the circuit he was also, occasionally, a scenic designer and was well known for his Gothic scenes. He was a fellow of Caius College, studied mathematics, had visited Greece and had translated Vitruvius. He had been runner up to Wyatt in the 1809 competition for the new Theatre Royal, Drury Lane.

In September 1988 Axel Burrough, partner of Levitt Bernstein who were the architects responsible for the Royal Exchange, Manchester, and also, with this author, for the Wilde Theatre, Bracknell, published in the *Architectural Review* his analysis of Wilkins' geometrical plan for the Bury St Edmunds theatre. By studying this plan it became possible to establish the precise details of the original building which had been obscured first by modernisation in 1906 by Edwardian architect Bertie Crewe, second by forty years of use as a barrel store for a brewery and third by overhasty 'restoration' in 1965. The extent of the forestage, the height of the original raked stage and the box divisions, all of which had been the subject of speculation for twenty-five years, suddenly fell into place. The drawings made by Axel Burrough, which reconstruct the details of the original design (no drawings other than a site plan having survived), and its inherent geometry are reproduced opposite.

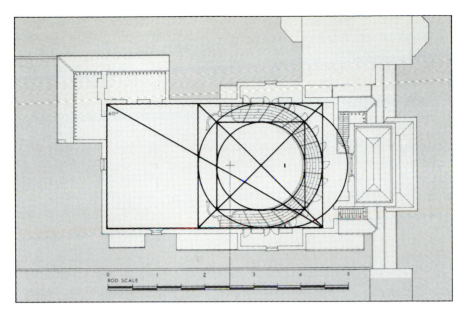

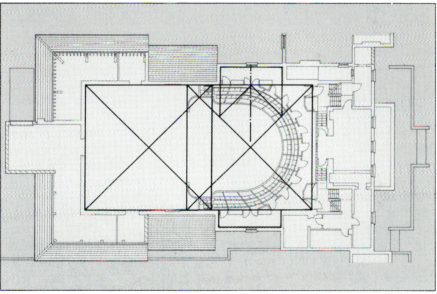

21 The Theatre Royal, Bury St Edmunds of 1819, architect William Wilkins, and still in active use today under the ownership of the National Trust. In 1988 architect Axel Burrough rediscovered the geometric basis to this universally admired theatre, the auditorium of which had been incorrectly restored in 1965 due to ignorance about the true nature of the Georgian playhouse.

The second example is the Tricycle Theatre, Kilburn. This was conceived by architect Tim Foster and this author in 1980. In 1987 it burnt, and the auditorium and stage were rebuilt unchanged except in certain minor details. It was only when the restored theatre was about to reopen in 1989 that the success of the theatre was analysed by applying simple *ad quadratum* geometry to the design. Post-rationalisation can be grounded on coincidence; but in this case it seems more likely that, by emulating the form and scale of the Georgian Theatre, Richmond, Yorkshire of 1788, the designers of the Tricycle had stumbled on an ancient mystery.

Mystery and the theatre are intertwined in the oldest treatise on theatre architecture in the world, the ancient Sanskrit text of *Natya Shastra* by Bharata. In Chapter One Bharata recounts the origins of the sacred art of theatre: 'For the eunuchs the theatre offers vulgarity, for tale tellers boastfulness, it arouses the unconscious and increases clear sightedness in the learned. Theatre is a past-time for lords and an entire meal for the poor. It is a treasure for those who live in wealth and a comfort to thirsting souls.' In the second chapter he explains how a theatre hall in which this is all possible is to be built. There are three sizes – large, medium and small – and three forms which are rectangular for end stage, square for thrust stage and triangular for theatre-in-the-round. For each the ground plan is measured ceremoniously with complex ritual. The ritual includes a precise description of the measuring string the length of which is divisible by 2, 3 and 4. This means that there must be 24 sections, a number out of which all the regular bodies can be created in a manner similar to, but different from, the 13 sections of the 'Druid's cord' favoured in the Middle Ages by the master masons. The unit of measurement is the *hasta*, which is the distance from the elbow to the outstretched fingertip or one-quarter of the full span of a man, that is 6 foot (1.8m) for an average western man today. The longest external dimension of the middle size of theatre is strictly controlled at 64 *hasta* or 96 feet (29.3m). The larger size of theatres are reserved for gods and titans only, both as performers and spectators. The medium size are to be the largest permitted to man, 'that which is built for man to walk in should be built according to man's measurements'.

Swedish architect Per Edstrom has provided convincing reconstructions of each form in his *Why not Theatres Made for People?* published in English in Sweden in 1990. Nobody is further than approximately 48 feet (14.6m) from the edge of the stage. The sacred geometry is complex but familiar. The rules were set out in picturesque language that could be remembered since they were rarely written down. What stands out clearly in the text is the constant reminder of why the magical dimensions of the three forms should never be exceeded. 'If it is made larger, it will be impossible to see the movements in the performance. In such a hall, the tale the writer has given birth to will be ruined by the echo of loud voices and lovely facial

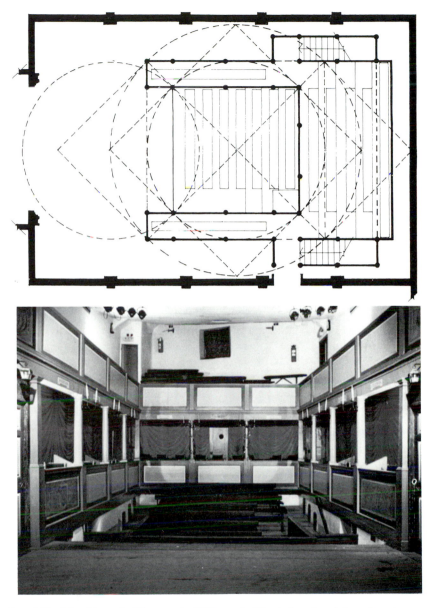

22 and 23 The Tricycle Theatre, in Kilburn in North London (plan above), was
built in 1980 out of builders scaffolding, a structure within an earlier flat floor
hall with small raised stage at one end. It burnt in 1987 and was rebuilt in 1989
to the same basic design by the same design team including architect Tim Foster
and theatre consultants Theatre Projects Consultants. Its design was consciously
modelled on the similarly scaled Georgian Theatre, Richmond, Yorkshire of 1788
(photo below), and unconsciously set out according to ad quadratum geometry.
This maps out both the structure itself and, by implication, the positions of power
for the actor in this successful theatre.

expressions that close up could be enchanting will become terribly twisted there. In such a hall a natural singing and speaking voice becomes so muted that its message is lost as it leaves the mouth and is merely a source of confusion. It is therefore desirable that the largest theatre halls are built no larger so that whatever is sung or spoken in them will be tasteful.'

The mystical element in architecture, as arrangement of human space, still endures today. In southern China, especially in materialistic Hong Kong, no office building can be contemplated or indeed furniture set out in a critical space without sending for the 'feng-shui' man, the practitioner of an ancient art allied to geomancy. Feng-shui and the geomancy which positioned and oriented the Gothic cathedrals are difficult for modern Western man to understand and tend to be ridiculed as hocus pocus. Similarly it may be difficult for some to believe that the mystery of harmonious space is at the centre of theatre architecture.

Many European architects have perceived the power of harmony. Erich Mendelsohn (1887–1953), the German architect of the Bauhaus who created the building in Berlin which Peter Stein transformed into the Schaubuhne in 1981, wrote: 'The necessity of the architect is to create the unison of parts and details which in the best buildings of any time miraculously trace back the imaginative process to mathematical quantities and geometric contexts.' Christopher Wren, architect of St Paul's Cathedral and probably of the first Drury Lane theatre, based his architecture on 'the impregnable foundations of geometry and arithmetic' which he thought to be 'the only truth void of uncertainty'.

Readers may now be searching for a pinch of salt. But if they are sitting in a room of a late nineteenth-century building or earlier they should look up and, say, compare the width of the room to its height. This author did in his own 1872 drawing room and discovered that the room's width was precisely the height multiplied by the square root of two (*ad quadratum* at its simplest). This was in a house which was clearly not designed by an architect but was measured out and built by craftsmen accustomed to apply traditional proportions to their work.

Harmonious proportions are the product either of the craftsman, who has received from his predecessors simple rules and simple tools, or of the trained mind of one who has studied beauty. Andrea Palladio (1518–80), the creator of a series of villas and public buildings that have been universally admired through the ages as well as of the Teatro Olimpico at Vicenza, wrote 'although variety and things new may please everyone, yet they ought not to be done contrary to what reason dictates; whence one sees that although the ancients did vary, yet they never departed from some universal and necessary rule of art.' For the shape of rooms in plan, as an example, he offered a choice of seven forms: circular; square; the diagonal of the square for the room's length; the square and a third; the square and a half; the square and two-thirds; and the double square.

What connects the modern movement to classical architecture is the understanding by the better architects of progressive harmonies. For instance Corbusier's 'modular' system, which was the discipline that determined the proportions of all elements in his later domestic buildings, was the product of studying the human body in standing, sitting and leaning positions and then plotting the points on a rigorously precise Fibonacci series. Such an approach is needed today for theatre architecture whose end must be to produce harmonious space in which the human spirit can express itself through the body and the voice.

If an inherently harmonious form is chosen for theatre space, then the material functionalism of acceptable sightlines and of acoustical shaping, along with the mechanics of staging and lighting, can be attended to more easily within the secure context of a proven geometrical system. As master of this mystery the theatre architect will be much more than a couturier adding an elegant style to the technically humdrum, as he was when he listened over much to the functionalist engineers. The architect is also less likely to become a design dictator requiring the art of theatre to adapt itself to an idiosyncratic architectural vision; the rules of geometry will not permit this to happen.

Theatre people have never responded well to the imposition of architectural dogma. Piscator lost interest in Gropius' unbuilt Totaltheatre of 1927, when the latter announced that he had created 'an instrument endowed with such a flexibility that its artistic direction might, thanks to a few simple but ingenious mechanisms, transform the stage in order to get all the necessary or desirable changes'. Here, as in so much of German theatre design, both problem and solution were drained of interest by being over precisely defined. Flexibility should not be thought of simply as the provision of predetermined arrangements. In architecture the concepts of flexibility and of a framework are correlative, hence the beneficial result in providing a frame for freedom, or at least something which can be 'played against' without the loss of its inherent and all-pervading sense of harmony and of mystery.

Peter Brook in his *Empty Space* of 1968 reported that 'I have had many abortive discussions with architects building new theatres – trying vainly to find words with which to communicate my own conviction that it is not a question of good buildings and bad; a beautiful place may never bring about explosion of life, while a haphazard hall may be a tremendous meeting place; this is the mystery of the theatre, but in the understanding of this mystery lies the only possibility of ordering it into a science. In other forms of architecture there is a relationship between conscious articulate design and good functioning: a well designed hospital may be more efficacious than a higgledy piggledy one; but as for theatres the problem of design cannot start logically. It is not a matter of saying analytically what are the requirements, how best they can be organised – this will usually bring into existence a tame, conventional, often cold hall. The science of theatre building must come from studying what it is that brings about the most vivid relationship between people and is this best served by asymmetry, even by disorder? If so, what can be the rule of this disorder?'

An examination of ancient theatres, whether Indian or Greek, of English theatres from Shakespeare's Globe to the end of the Greek revival in the early nineteenth century, and of successful modern theatres, suggests that there is a science which supports the mystery of theatre architecture and that this science contains the geometric rules for the creation of harmonious space. This was reinforced by the discovery in 1984 by Joy Hancox of the Byrom collection of curiously shaped 'parametric' drawings from the early eighteenth century. In 1992 she published *The Byrom Collection: Renaissance Thought, The Royal Society and the Building of the Globe Theatre* which shows how the plans of the Globe, Rose, Hope and Swan theatres, plus King's College Chapel and Westminster Abbey, can be inferred from circular and triangular cards inscribed according to the principles of sacred geometry as understood by magi such as John Dee, Robert Fludd, Michel le Blon and the cabalist society of which John Byrom (1691–1763) was a member.

Attractive though this global and rigid theory of form may be, sacred geometry seems to fail when it comes to what Brook might categorise as the haphazard, the commercially successful theatres of Frank Matcham in Britain and of J. B. McElfatrick in America, who created before the First World War a generation of theatres including the Majestic in Brooklyn. It may be relatively easy to detect an underlying geometry in both classical and modern buildings, but how on earth are we going to discover any pattern in more architecturally haphazard but equally successful turn-of-the-century theatres?

A clue is presented by the experience of Dutch architect Onno Greiner, who restored the 1865/1908 auditorium of the Leidse Schouwburg in 1976. When the restoration was nearing completion Greiner discovered the oval forms in plan, section and elevation, i.e. in all three planes, which he claimed 'create an egg shape not discernible by visitors to the theatre but which suggests a magnetic field in space which exerts a positive influence on them'. If Greiner's observations are correct, then the power of harmonious space is not only dependent on either sacred Sanskrit geometry or Palladian precision but also can exist in the less regular and more Romantic theatrical forms of the end of the nineteenth century.

That almost all successful theatres might be analysable in terms of fields of energy has not yet been proved but seems plausible. It is possible that the majority of theatres built between 1870 and 1915, which actors, directors and designers instantly recognised as marvellous tools for their trade despite being unable to say precisely why, can be resolved into geometric patterns of a recurrent 'sacred' sort involving *ad quadratum* and *ad triangulum*.

The recent practice of reanimating some of these later old theatres in a new way rather than simply restoring them as they once were, has illustrated perfectly another important feature of these spaces. It is that they seem to work just as well as 'found space', in which the original line between stage and auditorium is dissolved and the action advanced along the central axis into what was once the territory of the audience, as they do when reconstructed to contain the production authentically within the proscenium.

Such escapes from the proscenium may not have been envisaged by the original architect but turn out to be successful, as at the Bouffes du Nord and the Majestic, because the theatre's form had itself evolved from earlier more courtyard-like spaces of the seventeenth and eighteenth centuries where shifts of focus along the central axis had always been possible. This was especially so in the circus theatres of the late eighteenth century which had both a proscenium end stage and, out in the middle of the auditorium, a circus ring, between 41 feet (12.5m) and 42 foot (12.8m) in diameter, an unchanging dimension determined by the tightest radius on which a horse can gallop. In addition almost all theatres until the middle of the nineteenth century had a second life as ballrooms with the central area of seating floored over level with the stage. It is this feature which today provides opportunities for experiments in promenade or environmental theatre, both in old theatres and in new theatres designed with this in mind which share a geometry that supports movement along the central axis.

Who will be more successful in their attempt to revive a fine old theatre: the building committee who instruct the architect to carry out a 'period' restoration emphasising a sanitised view of 'heritage' or the director who handles an old theatre in a more workmanlike and simple fashion, ignoring the gilding of the plasterwork but recognising its potential for the channelling of theatre energy? The answer must be that it is the latter who is more likely successfully to tap the original source of energy that once animated an old theatre while the polychromatic re-creation of the past by the former runs the risk of being deadly dull though decoratively correct.

The recognition of the potential of a fine old theatre is easier for today's leaders in drama, opera and dance than the creation of a new one. But if the drama, dance and opera are to flourish in communities that lack either an old theatre or appropriate 'found space' the problems of creating a new theatre have to be addressed. In conclusion, therefore, and as a résumé of the author's own approach, here are a dozen notes for the guidance for all who would create new theatre spaces, whether director, owner, patron, architect or consultant.

1 The argument that the architecture of auditorium and stage are of marginal importance is often supported by memories of great performances in second-rate theatres. This is false: the exception of a great *King Lear* seen to good effect and against all odds in some converted swimming baths does not alter the fact that generally good theatre architecture supports the actor and assists the audience.

2 A theatre space of whatever form must have the quality of both rest and movement. It cannot be assessed without audience and actors. Every architectural journal which prints photographs of empty auditoriums misleads. A visit to a theatre without seeing it clothed with audience and actors generally confuses.

3 Since research suggests that most successful theatre spaces have been set out according to some geometric sets of rules, the wise theatre architect or designer will not reject established geometry in favour of a new untested vision. The geometry of harmonious space is compatible with a variety of architectural styles: classicism, modernism, postmodernism, even deconstructivism.

4 An over slavish provision for current technology can result in a building that dates quickly. Thus a good auditorium design will simply organise the placing of the lighting and other equipment specified by technicians of the day rather than attempting to build in the ephemeral which is what 'state of the art' technology usually turns out to be.

5 The platitude that all must see and hear is just that, a platitude. Perfect sightlines result always in 'the tame, conventional, often cold hall' which Brook feared. Seats need not all face the playing area which may itself alter its position. Nor is it necessary for all the spectators to see equally and perfectly the full scenic picture. The architect or designer's prior duty is to arrange people into 'the most vivid relationship one with another' to quote Brook in 1968 or so as to 'appear to form part of the spectacle one to the other, ranged as books are in a library' to quote Algarotti in 1767.

6 While the components of a good theatre are sometimes vividly expressed – Fred Bentham once suggested that an effective forestage or thrust stage succeeded by reason of its angular straight male form penetrating the yielding female curves of the auditorium – it must be remembered that both architects and actors may have received a narrow education and consequently find it difficult to exchange ideas with each other about the metaphysical aspects of design. Although Brook baulked at the task, it continues to be the job of the literate theatre person to explain to the architect the metaphysical functionalism of a good theatre. Otherwise the theatrical briefing becomes no more than the provision of a technical shopping list.

7 The desire for adaptability or flexibility is much more complex than a requirement for different actor-audience relationships in plan form

(Greek, Roman, proscenium, thrust, in the round, etc.). However, the endlessly adaptable theatre space is a mirage. Without an architectural framework a 'free' space is not a theatre space but rather a hangar or film studio awaiting the construction within it of an entire theatrical environment, that is to say a theatre.

8　A fixed form theatre in one of the established theatrical forms, be it thrust or proscenium, which provides modest opportunities for altering the transition between the worlds of actor and audience, offers one sort of flexibility. For example, a traditional proscenium theatre capable of use either with the technology of illusion mysteriously concealed or with the lights full up, with no scenic decoration and with no pretence at illusion, is flexible in the different attitudes to the theatrical event it allows to both actors and audience. The courtyard, which provides an architectural framework for theatrical freedom is even more flexible.

9　Since smaller theatre spaces, which have the continuity of character observed in these pages, have always proved more successful for creative theatre than larger auditoriums and since the performer's success is largely measured by the response of the audience, it follows that the density of audience as well as the size of the auditorium is central to theatre architecture. Less densely packed auditoriums dilute the response received by the performer. A single-tier auditorium is less space efficient than a multi-tier auditorium and hence more difficult for the actor to animate. In addition a more comfortable audience is generally less alert.

10　Seating capacity is a misleading yardstick for comparing sizes of theatres. New theatres are larger than old theatres of the same seating capacity even when that of the latter has been already reduced from the original even denser capacity of the nineteenth century. The Royal Opera House, Covent Garden, with a quoted capacity of 2,158, would seat only 1,700 if the audience were given the legroom and seat width of a modern auditorium and the ratio of seats with restricted view was reduced. Conversely New York's Metropolitan Opera would seat well over 4,000 if occupied at Covent Garden density. The Theatre Royal, Glasgow, would hold only 1,000 rather than the present 1,560 if the seats with 'unacceptable' acoustics were removed. With galleries inserted a reconstructed Olivier Theatre might hold 500 more without increasing the internal volume, etc., etc.

11　Hard benches for all, Brook fashion, rather than comfort will provide for a more concentrated response and hence heightened theatricality but may deter the attendance of 'the tired business man', or 'carriage trade' of previous generations, who cannot be ignored by any theatre management anxious to balance the books. The answer may be a return to heterogeneity in seating provision: comfort and perfect sightlines for some who pay for the higher-priced seats, more densely packed areas for the young who pay less. This is very different from designing for homogeneous subscribers. A wide seating price policy, which reflects the worth of each position, will attract the greatest possible spread of age, wealth and education into the theatre.

12 A theatre architect or design consultant, who manipulates audience density, comfort and sightlines, will find it easier to design a dynamic space animated by cross-currents of energy. In a fan-shaped auditorium where all are comfortably equal the show on offer is less likely to ignite the conflagration of communication and more likely simply to seep from the stage like a slowly radiating stain.

To summarise: the chief purpose of theatre architecture is to provide a channel for energy. Although this energy flows chiefly from performer to audience the performer is rendered impotent unless he or she receives in return a charge from the audience. This can be laughter in a farce, a shared sense of awe in tragedy and even a physical reciprocity to the achievement of dancer or actor. The energy must flow both ways so that the two forces fuse together to create an ecstasy which is comparable only to that experienced in a religious or sexual encounter.

The audience's role in this is rarely spelt out. Wrote Adolphe Appia in 1912: 'Up until now, all we have asked of the audience has been to sit still and pay attention. In order to encourage it in this direction, we have offered it a comfortable seat and have plunged it into a semi-darkness that favours the state of complete passivity. . . . If the playwright and those who perform his work are to bring about a change of direction – a conversion – then the spectator must, in his turn, submit to it (the awakening of art in oneself) too. His starting point is himself, his own body. From that body, living art must radiate and spread out into space, upon which it will confer life.'

There are many mysteries in the theatrical experience. Architectural space that provides the channel for the energy flowing back and forth between actor and audience is as much a mystery as is the matter of the play or the art of the player. This book has attempted to show how some theatre spaces are better than others and to suggest what are the factors of size, scale and shape that contribute to their success. The mysterious and harmonious elements that determine theatrical character have been identified as worthy of study by all involved in creating a new theatre or reanimating an old one.

The English-speaking peoples have generally tended to play down 'place' and prefer the measurable to the mystical. However, Shakespeare, who had a hand in the creation of both the first and second Globes, regarded place and its very limitations as a springboard for the imagination. In conclusion the reader is invited to look again at the opening speech of *Henry V*, and think both of how it might once have been performed in the theatre which Shakespeare helped create and also what theatrical and architectural arrangements of actor and audience from the past and present are likely to drag the actor down, reducing this of all speeches to a tedious prologue. Think, therefore, of what sort of place, what sort of theatre architecture, can, in the control of a sensitive actor 'working the house', create that prickle on the back of the audience's neck before the speech is half way spoken:

Oh for a Muse of fire, that would ascend
The brightest heaven of invention!
A kingdom for a stage, princes to act,
And monarchs to behold the swelling scene!
Then should the warlike Harry, like himself,
Assume the port of Mars; and at his heels,
Leash'd in like hounds, should famine, sword, and fire,
Crouch for employment. But pardon, gentles all,
The flat unraised spirit that hath dar'd
On this unworthy scaffold to bring forth
So great an object: can this cockpit hold
The vasty fields of France? or may we cram
Within this wooden O the very casques
That did affright the air at Agincourt?
O, pardon! since a crooked figure may
Attest in little place a million;
And let us, ciphers to this great accompt,
On your imaginary forces work.
Suppose within the girdle of these walls
Are now confin'd two mighty monarchies,
Whose high upreared and abutting fronts
The perilous narrow ocean parts asunder:
Piece out our imperfections with your thoughts:
Into a thousand parts divide one man,
And make imaginary puissance;
Think, when we talk of horses, that you see them
Printing their proud hoofs i'the receiving earth;
For 'tis your thoughts that now must deck our kings,
Carry them here and there; jumping o'er times,
Turning the accomplishment of many years
Into an hour-glass: for the which supply,
Admit me Chorus to this history;
Who, prologue-like, your humble patience pray,
Gently to hear, kindly to judge, our play.

Select bibliography

Count Francesco Algarotti *An Essay on the Opera* (English translation) 1767 (London).

Leslie Armstrong and Roger Morgan *Space for Dance, an Architectural Design Guide* 1984 (Washington).

Dennis and Marie-Louise Bablet *Adolphe Appia 1862–1928 actor–space–light* 1982 (London and New York).

Christopher Brereton, John Earl, Iain Mackintosh and others *CURTAINS!!! or A New Life for Old Theatres* 1982 (Eastbourne).

Gaelle Breton *Theatres, Theaters* 1989 (Paris).

Peter Brook *The Empty Space* 1968 (London).

Peter Brook *The Shifting Point* 1987 (New York).

Clement Contant and Joseph de Filippi *Le Parallèle des principaux théâtres modernes d'Europe* 1860 (Paris); 1968 (New York).

Gordon Craig *The Art of the Theatre* 1911.

Gabrielle Dumont *Parallèle de plans des plus belles salles de spectacle d'Italie et de France* 1774 (Paris).

Per Edstrom *Why not Theatres Made for People?* 1990 (Varmdo).

Harley Granville Barker *The Exemplary Theatre* 1922 (London).

Andrew Gurr with John Orrell *Rebuilding Shakespeare's Globe* 1989 (London).

Tyrone Guthrie *A Life in the Theatre* 1960 (London).

Ben M. Hall *The Best Remaining Seats* 1961 (New York).

Roderick Ham *Theatre Planning* 1972 and 1987 (London).

Joy Hancox *The Byrom Collection: Renaissance Thought, The Royal Society and the Building of the Globe Theatre* 1992 (London).

Franklin J. Hildy *New Issues in the Reconstruction of Shakespear's Theatre* 1990 (New York).

George Izenour *Theatre Design* 1977 (New York).

Stephen Joseph (editor) *Actor and Architect* 1964 (Manchester).

Stephen Joseph *New Theatre Forms* 1968 (London).

Richard Leacroft *The Development of the English Playhouse* 1973 (London).

Richard and Helen Leacroft *Theatres and Playhouses: an Illustrated Survey of Theatre Building from Ancient Greece to the Present Day* 1985 (London).

Peter Lewis *The National: a Dream made Concrete* 1990 (London).

Jo Mielziner *The Shapes of Our Theatre* 1970 (New York).

Fabrizio Carini Motta *Trattato sopra la struttura de' theatri e scene* 1676 (Mantua) translated and edited by Orville K. Larson 1987 (Southern Illinois).

Donald C. Mullin *The Development of the Playhouse* 1970 (California).

David Naylor *American Picture Palaces: The Architecture of Fantasy* 1981 (New York).

Pierre Patte *Essai sur l'Architecture Théâtrale* 1772 (Paris).

Nigel Pennick *Sacred Geometry* 1980 (Wellingborough).

Edwin O. Sachs and Ernest Woodrow *Modern Opera Houses and Theatres* 1896–8 (London); 1968 (New York).

George Saunders *A Treatise on Theatres* 1790 (London).

Richard Southern *The Seven Ages of the Theatre* 1964 (London).

Judith Strong *The Arts Council Guide to Building for the Arts* 1990 (London).

Jean Vermeil *Opéras d'Europe* 1989 (Paris).

Frances Yates *Theatre of the World* 1969 (London).

Apologia and acknowledgements

My three lives are interwoven in this book, as theatre producer from 1961 to 1973 and again in 1985, as designer of theatre space from 1973 to the present and as historian of theatre architecture and painting from the 1970s onwards.

'You've read the book, now see the theatres' introduces expressions of deep gratitude to all clients and design collaborators – architects, colleagues at Theatre Projects Consultants and others – on those new or remodelled theatres to the design of which I contributed. These include, with dates of completion: Eden Court, Inverness 1976; the Cottesloe at the National Theatre of Great Britain 1977; Loretto School, Musselburgh, Scotland 1979; Dulwich College Theatre, London 1983; the remodelled Bluma Appel Theater in the St Lawrence Center, Toronto 1983; Wilde Theatre, Bracknell, England 1984; Martha Cohen Theater, Calgary, Canada 1985; the remodelled Twentse Schouwburg, the Netherlands 1985; Westminster School Theater, Connecticut 1989; De Maagd, a church reconstituted as a theatre in Bergen-op-Zoom, the Netherlands 1990; the new Orange Tree Theatre, Richmond 1991; and the Milton Academy Theater, near Boston, Massachusetts 1991. In addition there were deeply fascinating restorations of old theatres: Theatre Royal, Nottingham 1865, 1897 and then 1978; the Opera House, Buxton, England 1903 and 1979; the Lyric Theatre, Hammersmith, London 1895, dismantled 1969 and reconstituted on a new site 1979; and the Opera House, Dunfermline 1900, 1920, dismantled 1982 and then sold to Florida and reopened as the main stage of the Asolo Center for Performing Arts, Sarasota 1989.

At the time of my writing this book there were four major projects current, all to open in 1994: the new Glyndebourne Festival Opera House, the restored and partially rebuilt Edinburgh Empire of 1928, the Norwich Playhouse and the Lawrence Batley Theatre, Huddersfield, within the shell of a vast 1819 chapel.

Out of all the collaborators on these projects I would like to mention a few of those who, in addition to their own achievements, contributed, perhaps unwittingly, to the ideas that emerge in this book: Rodney Atkinson, Stuart Barger, Joel Barrett, Axel Burrough, John Bury, James Dunbar-Nasmith, Tim Foster, Jerry Godden, Onno Greiner, Graham Gund, Gerhard Kallman, Graham Law, Anne Minors, Richard Pilbrow, John Prokos, Colin Ross, Alan Russell, Jennifer Scobie, David Staples, Derek Sugden, David Taylor and the late Ron Thom.

Producing plays, with some stage management and scene design thrown in, was also an essential background to the writing of this book. Central to this experience were co-founders of the Prospect Theatre Company to whom I am ever grateful, Richard Cottrell and Elizabeth Sweeting, joined later by chairman Laurence Harbottle and artistic director Toby Robertson. Together with leading actors such as Ian McKellen and Timothy West and designers such as Robin Archer and Kenneth

Rowell we took seventy productions to 125 theatres in twenty-one countries between 1961 and 1973. For a later return to production in 1985 I secured the derelict Lyceum Theatre for a twelve-week run of *The Mysteries*. This taught me so much about 'found space' in what was once a theatre. For this I must thank director Bill Bryden, designer William Dudley and the cast of the National's Cottesloe Company as well as co-producers Anthony Field and Richard Pilbrow. When talking of producing I must also mention those clients for new theatres who have been so stimulating: Sir George Christie and John Bury at Glyndebourne, Eddie Gilbert at the St Lawrence Center, Toronto, Gavin Henderson at Bracknell, Michael Dobbin at Calgary, Ken Chubb and Nicolas Kent at the Tricycle, Sam Walters at the Orange Tree and many others.

The third strand is theatre history. I was fortunate to be involved in two major exhibitions, *The Georgian Playhouse 1730–1830* at the Hayward Gallery, London in 1975 and *The Royal Opera House Retrospective 1732–1982* at the Royal Academy, London in 1982–3. For the success of these, and of *Thirty Different Likenesses, David Garrick in Portrait and Performance* in 1981 at the Buxton Festival, I owe a great debt of gratitude to my late collaborator, art historian Geoffrey Ashton. So many attitudes to theatre history expressed in this book emerged when we were working closely together. Other scholars I thank are William Appleton, Babs Craven, the late Robert Eddison, Celina Fox, the late Richard Leacroft, Brooks McNamara, the late Joe Mitchenson, John Orrell and all the professors of universities and architectural schools who, by inviting me to teach or lecture, made me sort out some ideas.

Part history, part building, part exhibition was the project entitled *CURTAINS!!! or A New Life for Old Theatres*. This was the first gazetteer of all theatres built in Britain prior to 1914 and an associated exhibition launched in 1982, having been worked up over five years by a group including the late Christopher Brereton, David Cheshire, John Earl, Victor Glasstone, Michael Sell and David Wilmore. This led to being invited to join the Theatres Trust: from chairmen Lord Goodman and Sir David Crouch and from fellow trustees over six years I learnt how the cause of conservation can be furthered by quiet political manoeuvring and, from the sudden Rose confrontation of 1989, how a rapid injection of practical engineering could save from penetration by piling powerful pieces of our English-speaking heritage.

Another forum that has provided a continuous critique, in this instance of contemporary theatre architecture, is the Theatre Planning Committee of the Association of British Theatre Technicians which has reviewed the plans of over 250 theatres and arts centres since I joined in 1967. The committee membership has included, in addition to many I have acknowledged elsewhere, architects Rod Ham, Eric Jordan, Peter Moro and Nick Thompson, consultants Peter Angier, Martin Carr and John Wyckham, acoustician Richard Cowell, director Michael Elliott, stage designer Patrick Robertson, technicians James Sergeant and Ken Smalley and two who have always been much more than 'lighting men', Fred Bentham and Francis Reid. In this context another key influence has been Jason Barnes, production manager of the Cottesloe since its opening in 1977, who has provided continuous feedback on how directors and designers use that space.

Lastly, I would like to thank all those who have helped over the preparation of this book, among them Gregory Mosher and Richard Pilbrow who read the typescript, John Russell Brown, the editor of the series and its onlie true begetter, a succession of editors at Routledge culminating in Talia Rodgers assisted by Rosamund Howe, Julia Hall and Penny Wheeler, all those who assisted with the illustrations, those who typed, primarily Vanessa Gray and Elizabeth Lomas, and most of all my eternally patient wife, actress Jan Carey.

Index